The Child as a Cartesian Thinker

The Child as a Cartesian Thinker

Children's Reasonings about Metaphysical Aspects of Reality

Eugene V. Subbotsky
University of Lancaster, UK

Psychology Press
An imprint of Erlbaum (UK) Taylor & Francis

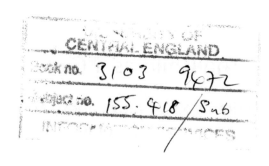
© 1996 by Psychology Press, an imprint of
Erlbaum (UK) Taylor & Francis Ltd

Psychology Press
27 Church Road
Hove
East Sussex, BN3 2FA
UK

British Library Cataloguing in Publication Data

A catalogue record for this book is available from the British Library

   ISBN 0–86377–419–9

Cover design by Peter Richards
Typeset by DP Photosetting, Aylesbury, Bucks.
Printed and bound by TJ Press (Padstow) Ltd.

Contents

Introduction

The idea of this book stems from my long and strong interest in Descartes' philosophy and yet it came to me quite accidentally. In late September 1980, my 4-year-old son Aliosha and I got stranded at the seaside in the Crimea. The weather was nasty, it was raining day and night, but the time for our departure had not yet come. Contrary to my rule not to work during vacations, I started to reread selected works by Descartes. Suddenly, it occurred to me that it might be interesting to ask my son a few questions that Descartes asked himself and which I felt were almost irrelevant to the age of the person to whom they were addressed.

"Do you think that you exist in the world?", I began my conversation with my son. "Yes, I do" he said. "And do you have dreams sometimes?" I wondered. "Yes, I do" he replied. "Do you sometimes see in your dreams an object or a person which does not really exist?" I enquired. "Yes, I did. Once I saw a monster." "But could it be the case that it is now that you are dreaming and imagining that you exist, but in reality you don't exist, like that monster of yours?" For a moment my son was puzzled. He looked around, apparently in search of a suitable answer, before replying: "Well, I know that I am not sleeping now."

This was not a particularly profound answer, but it was a start. I began to get interested and kept asking him questions. These questions concerned the relationships between body and mind, between sensory images and physical objects, about the definition of truth, about the existence of a Supreme Being, and so on. What struck me was that my son didn't find any of these questions unusual or odd, and he had answers for most of them.

So, as soon as I arrived back in Moscow, I commenced my "Cartesian conversations" with children, at first in a nearby kindergarten, then in a local school. I soon found that although the children's answers varied widely, there was some "inner logic" behind them. Surprisingly, most of the children discussed these metaphysical problems as if they had been thinking about them for a long time, although I knew that they had not. What was it, then?

It occurred to me that the problems were fundamental and therefore to a large extent irrelevant to a subject's age. Of course, the ways these problems are presented to children of different ages can vary, as well as the answers that the children give to the problems, which will depend on the level of each child's intellectual and linguistic development. Yet, as soon as children emerge from infancy, they are confronted with these problems and have to resolve them in one way or another, even if at a subconscious level and without being aware of it. It appeared that the children's solutions did change with age, though not all of them and the changes were slow. The older the children were, the more "rationalistic" were their views on many metaphysical problems and the closer they were to those suggested by Descartes. However, some of the problems seemed to follow a reverse order: young preschoolers reasoned very close to the way Descartes did, but schoolchildren did not. There were also some Cartesian ideas that were totally alien to the children, both to the younger and the older ones. It became clear that steady intellectual progress as a "growth of mental functions in structural complexity" was not the best way to account for the development of metaphysical judgements in children.

In the field of developmental psychology, I was well acquainted with Piaget's early studies, in particular with "The child's conception of the world". Although metaphysical problems had been touched upon by Piaget, he increasingly focused on the sciences and the development of scientific thinking, as well as on children's acquisition of those specific notions (e.g. number, logic, necessity, and causality) that form the foundation of scientific thinking and yet are entirely within the scope of "physics" (or in the scope of science to be exact) and are not "truly metaphysical". Many recent studies of children's judgements on metaphysical problems have been inspiring and intriguing; however, they have lacked coherence and have been aimed at isolated problems (such as children's judgements on the relationships between body and mind, on death and dying, on the distinction between animated and non-animated objects, etc.). A certain unified and systematic study of the development of metaphysical judgements in children appeared warranted.

I decided to extend my study to include children's judgements on metaphysical problems of a human being. While creating a new set of dialogues, I used the rationalistic models of human beings found in many contemporary psychological developmental theories, for instance Vygotsky's theory of mental development. I also applied a model developed by another distinguished French rationalistic philosopher, Condillac, who invented an amazingly simple way of talking about the human senses and their relationships with physical objects. Conducting these dialogues with children was especially interesting for me because I have long been puzzled by the lack of psychological education in the kindergarten and school curriculums, to say nothing about discussing problems that go beyond psychology in its own right, such as relationships between personal freedom and moral feelings and actions, the fundamental drives of a human being for development and expansion of his or her needs and passions, for eternal life, for a "dreamlike world" of accomplished wishes, and so on. When studying the psychological development of children, there is often little interest in what the children themselves might think about it. However, even a superficial observation shows that children as young as 5 are interested in and do have theories about human development, and not only about human birth. And again, I found certain trends in children's judgements about human sensations, the role of language, relationships between moral knowledge and moral behaviour, between human feelings and human behaviours, and so on, which in some respects were very much in line with general laws of children's intellectual development, and in other respects substantially deviated from them.

While conducting this study, I was completely aware that there were no other ways of learning about children's metaphysical notions than talking with them—non-verbal methods, which are highly effective in studies of various aspects of child development,[1] would be unsuitable here. It was also clear to me that much would depend on the children's language and their capacity to express what they think, and so qualitative, rather than quantitative, analysis of the children's answers would be necessary. Finally, I realised the study would have to be primarily phenomenological: the characteristics of the development of children's metaphysical thinking are too multiple and complex for me to determine but a few of them. So I decided to follow Teilhard de Chardin's maxim, "Rien que le Phénomene. Mais aussi tout le Phénomene."[2]

Of course, I do not think that what children say is a good indicator of what they do; in fact, two of my previous titles concentrated on the discrepancies which often occur between people's words and their deeds (Subbotsky, 1993a, 1993b). But I do believe that what children say reflects what they think—provided that the questions they are asked are clear, their language is proficient enough, and there is no reason for them to conceal their thoughts. As a result, I found that in certain respects children indeed reason like little rationalists. Even so, it appeared that their rationalistic views had to be developed, mainly through the independent work of their minds. It seemed also that this development is highly important for the children's later achievements, both intellectually and socially. Indeed, whether we like it or not, in Europe the sciences, the law, the arts and even religious beliefs have been heavily influenced by dominant rationalistic views; in order to succeed in learning and in life, children have first to learn this "language of metaphysics" which will later enable them to cope with scientific education and social laws. Therefore, children have to acquire a certain metaphysical proficiency very early in life. This was another reason why I found this study interesting and inspiring.

To a large extent, this was an individual and solitary work. However, it may never have appeared if but for a lecture I attended on Descartes given by the brilliant philosopher Mirab Mamardashvili. I also thank Margaret Chalmers and Les Smith for their careful reading of the manuscript and constructive comments. I am indebted to the children who shared with me the labour and pleasure of talking about metaphysics, and to my students who joined me in this. Finally, thanks to the children's teachers who, although puzzled, allowed me to keep asking the children a lot of strange questions.

NOTES

1. In my previous studies of children's cognitive and personality development (Subbotsky, 1993a, 1993b), I employed mostly non-verbal methods.
2. Translates as "Nothing but a phenomenon. But the whole phenomenon as well" (Teilhard de Chardin, 1955, p. 21).

1

The Child as a Philosopher

STUDIES OF CHILDREN'S METAPHYSICAL THINKING IN DEVELOPMENTAL PSYCHOLOGY

Physics and Metaphysics: Conceptual Relationships

The subject of this book is children's judgements about some metaphysical notions which, according to many philosophers (e.g. Husserl, 1977), laid the foundation for the contemporary European outlook on the world. In contrast to most general physical concepts (such as space, time, causality, physical objects, etc.), metaphysical concepts (in the original Aristotelian meaning of the word) belong to the realm that extends "beyond physics", a realm which is rather difficult to capture using rigorous definitions. Although it intersects with many sciences (e.g. psychology, logic, biology, theology), it nevertheless transcends their traditional limits.

Thus, for instance, such a notion as "the criterion of truth" is a traditional subject of logic; however, at its deepest roots it goes beyond logic to the realm of primary intuitions regarding what can be called "true" and "false". The concept "a living cell" is a subject matter of biology, but the quality that distinguishes a living cell from a dead one (and any living creature from an inanimate object)—life in its own right—escapes definition in rigorous biological terms. Psychology, in a sense, stands closer to metaphysics than any other science; however, due to the dominance of the scientific mode of thinking in our culture, most psychological studies have been conducted in a traditional empiricist manner which has prevented psychology from entering the realm of metaphysics.

In other words, metaphysical concepts are those that reflect our most general beliefs about the world, which constitute a foundation for a scientific approach to nature, but which cannot be proved or disproved by means of traditional logic. Similar to religious beliefs, metaphysical beliefs are culturally and historically biased and in that respect they are myths. However, these beliefs differ from religious beliefs and other traditional mythological systems in one important respect: They appeal not to certain dogmatic structures imposed on the individual by society, but to the primordial intuitions of the individual him- or herself, to certain *a priori* given anthropological characteristics of a human individual. In other words, if religious beliefs are to be accepted by an individual before any sensible and consistent "religious truth" can be discussed, metaphysical beliefs will have had to appeal to the individual's critical thinking and to his or her primary intuitions about what is "really true" in this world and what is clear and obvious to such an extent that there are no possible doubts.

The studies presented in the book focus on one particular group of metaphysical beliefs, namely those that constitute the foundation of the European rationalistic (or, some would say, modern) way of thinking. European rationality is interpreted here as a specific spiritual orientation of European (or, speaking more broadly, Western) mentality that has its origins in ancient Greece and whose modern features were outlined most clearly and explicitly in the 17th and 18th centuries by such great European thinkers as Descartes and Kant. The main feature of this mental orientation was anti-dogmatism—the individual's claim to perceive and master the world "directly" and rely exclusively on one's own personal authentic experience. This mental orientation manifested itself in a number of special structures: conceptions about consciousness, being, truth, relationships between mind and body, image and object, and so on. It also created a particular "model" of man—a special view of the functions, capacities, and development of the human mind.

Justification for the Study

As mentioned above, for the last few hundred years Western rationality has had a significant influence on the whole body of European (and not only European) culture and has penetrated all of its components: the sciences, arts, law, education, religion itself. This means that the fundamental ideas of Western rationality (such as "body–mind parallelism", the identity between "being and thinking", between "being and truth", etc.) are no longer confined to philosophy, but are an implicit foundation of "everyday" consciousness. In other words, to be able to live in a modern European culture,[1] an ordinary person has to be able to act and think, consciously or unconsciously, in accordance with these fundamental structures. It also means that these fundamental structures (ideas, intuitions) have to be acquired by children in their early years, since most of the more advanced and sophisticated structures (such as the basic notions and laws of arts and sciences taught at school) are based upon these metaphysical ideas. Any delay or distortion to this acquisition may influence the children's performance at school and their general adaptation to the culture of which they are a part. With this in mind, there are at least two reasons to justify the study of metaphysical thinking in children.

The first is of a mainly theoretical and philosophical nature. As already stated, a system of the metaphysical structures that constitute the core of Western rationality is a system of concepts that goes beyond physics and, indeed, beyond logic. As axioms of geometry, metaphysical "axioms" are structures to "be believed in", and not "to be proved" by logical or scientific means. As such, metaphysical beliefs are similar to religious beliefs; yet, they constitute a specific world outlook which is different, if not an alternative, to the existing religious mythologies.

The relationship between the rationalistic view of the world and the traditional religious one has long been an important issue and is discussed under various names, such as the relationship between science and religion. In such discussions, the priority given to the scientific approach is often seen to be due to the empirical and logical nature of science; however, it is often overlooked that science itself is based on a system of beliefs—those that we call metaphysical beliefs. Yet it is generally assumed that there is a fundamental difference between the metaphysical and religious systems of beliefs: Whereas the latter is culturally and historically biased, the former is rooted in human anthropology and is largely culturally invariant. Another consequence of this concerns a developmental aspect: if metaphysical beliefs do indeed have natural-anthropological rather than cultural-historical origins, then they can be expected to appear in children at an early age and without the special teaching that religious education requires.

But is this really the case? Do, for instance, beliefs concerning the body–mind relationship or the distinction between subjective images and objects in their own right appear spontaneously in very young children or do they have to be taught like any other system of beliefs? And if they do appear spontaneously does the whole gamut of metaphysical beliefs appear at once or is there some developmental succession in their appearance in the child's mind? Answers to these questions will help shed additional light on the issue of the "ultimate foundation of science"; that is, whether science reflects some kind of "fundamental truth" about the world, or is culturally and developmentally determined and creates a model of the world that has no "primary" advantage over the traditional religious models.

The second consideration is of a more practical nature. Whatever the status of Western rationality regarding the traditional religious mythology, that rationality already exists and has to be acquired by children in one way or another if they are to deal with more advanced "stores of knowledge" (e.g. the sciences, arts, and languages). The system of metaphysical beliefs is itself a specific "language" which, like any other language, is acquired by children spontaneously and mainly at a subconscious level. Under normal circumstances, we do not have to consider this "language acquisition" process at all and the task of its scientific investigation seems superfluous. Yet there are times when this kind of study is important and necessary.

Thus, for instance, in ordinary life, a fundamental metaphysical distinction between the psychological and physical ways of describing an object seems to be of no major importance. Indeed, in our everyday language we normally describe a certain object as, for instance, red in colour, round in shape, and heavy, and not as one which reflects light rays of a certain wavelength and is affected by the force of gravity. More than that, in ordinary life psychological sensations quite successfully represent their physical prototypes and the "split" between the two can be largely ignored. Some professional psychologists may think that it is of no real importance whether an individual understands that the "redness" and "heaviness" of an object are not its real physical properties and, for them to be attributed to the object in its own right, they have to be translated into the language of physical theories (like the wave theory of light or the gravitational theory of matter).

However, if individuals enter the world of science without any real metaphysical intuition of psycho-physical parallelism, it may be more difficult for them to understand elementary physics. And even in ordinary life the lack of a proper understanding of this distinction can foster in individuals an egocentric confusion between their feelings and views about objects and events and the objects (the events) as they "really are". It is, therefore, important to examine the way children acquire fundamental intuitions about the double character of reality, in which almost all objects have a least two manifestations: a subjective image (a visible image of a cube, for instance) and its rational construction (the same cube as a physical body with such unchangeable characteristics as magnitude, shape, molecular structure, etc.). Despite the fact that much of psychology is devoted to the examination of how certain rational constructions develop in children (e.g. various concepts of conservation), very little is known about the onset of the general understanding of this fundamental rationalistic distinction. The same is true with regard to other basic metaphysical structures of Western rationality. However exotic this topic may seem at first glance, it is of crucial importance in understanding how our minds work.

Experimental Studies of Metaphysical Thinking in Children: The Problem of Methodology

Although investigation of children's concepts about the world has a long tradition in developmental psychology, it has focused in the main on the development of the prerequisites for scientific and physical concepts in children, such as causality, reversibility, logical and physical concepts, and so on (see Piaget, 1930, 1952, 1962; White, 1995). In recent years, a number of problems closely associated with metaphysical concepts have attracted the attention of developmentalists. These include children's developing conceptions of mind and mental processes (Baron-Cohen, Leslie, & Frith, 1985; Flavell, Everett, Croft, & Flavell, 1981; Harris, 1990; Lewis & Osborne, 1990; Pillow & Flavell, 1986), the origins of illness (Kister & Patterson, 1980), procreation and child development (Goldman & Goldman, 1982; Russell & Russell, 1982) and death (Weininger, 1979; White, Elsom, & Prawat, 1978). These studies, however intriguing and important in their own right, touched upon metaphysical problems only indirectly; most of them were still devoted to matters conceivable within the scope of modern science.

A number of studies, however, are relevant within the context of this book, studies which dealt directly with the development of metaphysical concepts, such as children's concept of God (Nye & Carson, 1984), relationships between mind and brain (Johnson, 1990; Johnson & Wellman, 1982), mind and body (Inagaki & Hatano, 1993), real and apparent (Flavell, 1986; Harris, 1990), and children's insights into the nature of consciousness (Flavell, Green, & Farell, 1993). Matthews (1980) collected and analysed cases of children's philosophical judgements and he showed that even young children were able to produce pieces of genuine philosophical reasoning regarding such fundamental metaphysical problems as the distinction between dream and reality, animated versus non-animated objects, the problem of personal identity, relationships between sensory images and real physical objects, and so on. There are several aspects of Matthews' book that seem to be especially relevant to the study of children's metaphysical judgements. First, it clearly showed that in certain circumstances children as young as 4 years can come up with questions about and be puzzled by problems that have traditionally been seen to belong to the realm of metaphysics. Second, it cast new light on the difficult question of interpretation of children's metaphysical judgements. In his criticism of Piaget's stage-structured approach, Matthews argued that many fundamental philosophical problems have no privileged "correct" solution and that many of the answers that Piaget interpreted as reflecting the most primitive lower stage (e.g. answers suggesting that people think with their "mouths" or "voices"), have as much theoretical merit as those answers considered by

Piaget to be the most "progressive". Obviously, this undermines Piaget's stage theory approach and what might be called the "replacement model" in understanding children's intellectual development (see Subbotsky, 1993a). Third, the book contains many interesting intuitive observations, including the fact that young children are more likely to produce genuine philosophical judgements than older children, partly because of their unrestricted naivety and partly because they have no experience of pressure from institutionalised education.

So should philosophy and logic deal with the development of children's metaphysical judgements? The fact is that children's metaphysical judgements no more belong to philosophy than children's judgements about physical causality belong to physics or children's naive theories of language belong to linguistics. However interesting and genuine, these judgements are occasional and sporadic experiences. In order for them to be incorporated into philosophy they have to be interpreted, and it is the interpretation of the children's judgements by a philosopher together with the judgements themselves that makes the judgements "a piece of philosophy". In a sense, the early philosophical maturity of children is similar to the early "cognitive maturity" of infants: when an infant of a few months can make "inferences" about an object's physical properties, it is often forgotten that the child's striking capacities are merely behavioural patterns which, in order to be viewed as "inferences", have to be interpreted by an experimenter. So who should the interpreter be with respect to children's metaphysical judgements? In my view, it does not matter whether it is a psychology-educated philosopher or a psychologist with some background in philosophy. What is important is a framework or a scale that can be employed as the basis for interpretation.

Regarding children's judgements about various scientific concepts, the framework employed is normally of existing scientific concepts and theories. Since in science the concepts "true" and "false" are used in their rigorous sense, children's judgements can be classified along a scale as corresponding or not corresponding to the theories that are viewed as "true" in contemporary science. With respect to metaphysical judgements, the solution is not that simple. As has already been mentioned, most metaphysical problems have no definite "true" solutions; instead, they allow for various, often conflicting, interpretations.

This fact has two important implications, which could account for the differences between traditional studies of children's cognitive development and studies concerning the growth of children's "metaphysical proficiency". First, to obtain a relatively stable scale for use in our work with children, we need to consider which of the many existing (and conflicting) metaphysical systems should be part of the framework for our analysis. Because various systems provide different solutions to similar metaphysical problems, such a task is rather difficult. Second, the traditional way of viewing cognitive development as a succession of stages which progressively lead the child to the top of the "pyramid of cognition"[2] can hardly be applied to the development of metaphysical knowledge. The reason is not that a system of successful stages is a wrong way of accounting for cognitive development, but rather that this model works better in those areas for which it was originally created, namely the acquisition of scientific or social knowledge. In contrast to this kind of knowledge, metaphysical beliefs do not possess a certain definite structure (in contrast to, for example, visual perception or logical thinking) and their development cannot, therefore, be portrayed as a teleological progression.

However, this does not mean that the concept of "development" cannot be applied to the growth of metaphysical concepts. There is no doubt, for example, that certain differences (which can even be viewed as some sort of "stages") can be expected to exist between metaphysical proficiency in children of varying ages and, possibly, varying cultures. Such development, however, takes the form of "growth of awareness", rather the traditional "growth in complexity": the steadiness that can be expected from this kind of development manifests itself in the ease and mastery with which children of various ages can realise and express metaphysical problems, rather than in the "presence versus absence" of these problems in the child's life and mind. In other words, the development of metaphysical understanding can be seen as the continuously widening "foundation" upon which the "pyramid of cognitive growth" is being built.

Also, this kind of development is rather spontaneous; that is, it is triggered by the spontaneous activities of a child's mind and personality. Of course, it does not exclude certain social and cultural influences on children's answers to questions about metaphysical problems. However, because of the very nature of metaphysical problems, which are rooted in the foundation of an individual mind and represent the "anthropological essences" of a human individual rather than his or her social and cultural belonging, cultural influences could be expected to be much less important than, for instance, they are in the traditional learning of various disciplines—scientific, social, or religious.

Returning to the fact that solutions to metaphysical problems are inherently "open to interpretation", it is clear that in order to obtain a relatively stable scale in our work with children, one of these interpretations has to be chosen. In the first study in this book, Rene Descartes' "Meditations on First Philosophy" and his "Discourse on the Method" have been chosen as the basis for such a scale.

Although Cartesian philosophy cannot be identified exclusively with the Western rationalistic tradition and reflects only one, though major, trend within this tradition, several reasons prompted me to select these particular writings. First, they are classical masterpieces of philosophy which draw upon such interesting metaphysical problems as finding the truth criterion, relationships between body and mind, between true knowledge and personal existence, between physical objects and their sensory images, and so on. Second, all these fundamental problems have certain clear solutions which, although they are not "absolute", nevertheless laid the foundations for the modern rationalistic world outlook (Husserl, 1977). Third, in contrast to other existing interpretations of the rationalistic philosophy (such as those of Kant and Hegel), which employ a lot of special terminology and sophisticated philosophical techniques, these works by Descartes have some kind of intellectual freshness and naivety about them, features that do not undermine their profound philosophical nature but at the same time make them perfectly suitable to adaptation if dialogue with children is the aim. Last but not least, these works present a series of metaphysical questions that have a certain philosophical and logical unity, but nevertheless several successive and consistent steps can be distinguished.

Clearly, employing this kind of "frame of reference" gives us the opportunity to classify children's answers according to their proximity to the solutions given by Descartes—the kind of subordination which does not necessarily imply the concepts of "philosophical progress" and of any ultimately "right" solutions but which, nevertheless, is not an arbitrary classification either, since the subjects under investigation belong to the culture whose metaphysical foundations are supposed to have been laid by philosophers like Descartes.

A second problem that arises if children's metaphysical judgements are to be studied is the problem of finding an adequate methodology. In previous studies, three basic methodologies can be distinguished. The first is a case study based on the collection of children's spontaneous metaphysical questions and judgements (this methodology was most consistently applied by Matthews, 1980, 1984). Together with its obvious merits, this methodology has serious drawbacks: it depends on children's sporadic reasoning given under various, mostly uncontrolled, circumstances. Children's judgements like these do have metaphysical authenticity in them, but they are difficult to interpret using a unified scale and touch upon occasional and mostly unconnected metaphysical problems. Developmental psychology deals with mass samples of children and not all of them are capable of asking interesting metaphysical questions, although metaphysical problems do challenge every child.

In contrast to this first methodology, the second is strictly oriented towards following a classic model of scientific experimentation (see, for example, Johnson, 1990; Johnson & Wellman, 1982). According to this second methodology, children are asked metaphysical questions in a certain standardised way and their answers are reduced to "yes" and "no". Such a methodology makes the coding and application of traditional statistical analysis (such as analysis of variance) easier, but it lacks the flexibility of the case-study methodology. Clearly, the reasons why children answer "yes" to the same question vary, and what this method misses is, perhaps, the most important and interesting part of metaphysical judgements—the very process of "metaphysical meditation". The problems of whether children's judgements about certain cognitive tasks (i.e. conservation) should be completed with justifications, and about the status of the justifications as reliable indices of children's cognitive capacities, have recently been debated (Flavell, Miller, & Miller, 1993; Light, 1986). Some authors argue that relying exclusively on children's judgements (by which brief answers of the type "yes" or "no" are meant here) without justifications can be misleading in the assessment of children's operational skills (Neilson, Dockrell, & McKechnie, 1983); others view justifications themselves as a possible source for a misjudgement about children's capacity to understand (Brainerd, 1973; Donaldson, 1983). It is argued, for instance, that justifications are strictly required in the case of studying children's understanding of necessity (Smith, 1993).

In this study, in the case of metaphysical problems, justifications were also seen to be necessary, as nearly all metaphysical problems are ambiguous and cannot be shaped in the form of a clear experimental test of the type used to test conservation. It is essential, therefore, when asking children questions like whether they really exist in the world or just have an illusion (a dream) about their personal existence, to supplement the question with requests for justifications; otherwise, the child's positive answer could be indeterminate with regard to the very point of the question, namely, whether the child understands the need for a link between conscious awareness of a subjective state (like a dream or a hallucination) and personal existence, or he/she simply states it as an empirical fact ("I know that I exist", "My mum told me that I exist").

The third type of methodology is the one used by Piaget in most of his studies. It is a sort of "directive clinical interview" in which children are asked a set of standard questions (to be exact, Piaget himself never strictly observed the procedure, varying the questions slightly from child to child) and encouraged to justify their answers. It is the justifications (or reasoning) given by the children and not their "yes" or "no" answers that are the subject for analysis and classification within this methodological approach. This approach, if applied, produces a rather diverse spectrum of answers which are more difficult to analyse statistically than dichotomous answers, but it reflects a real richness and diversity of possible solutions for metaphysical problems.

This third type of methodology was applied in the studies presented in this book (Subbotsky, 1986a,b,c, 1989a,b). In contrast to Piaget's original procedure, however, all the children reported here were asked identical questions and their answers, together with their justifications, were classified on the basis of a standard "frame of reference". Nevertheless, in a number of cases I did not stop at registering the children's answers and justifications, but continued with the interrogation in the form of a discussion. My aim was to determine how firmly children's answers reflect their real convictions and whether children are able to withstand objections to their views. These deviations from the standard procedure are analysed separately.

Two studies were also conducted in compliance with the traditional analytical tradition of experimentation in psychology (see Dialogues 6 and 7). Their objective was to create a link between phenomenological and analytical types of studies and to show that phenomenological analysis can be viewed as the first step in a more extended analysis and can later be developed in a traditional analytical investigation targeting theoretical (Dialogue 6) or applicational (Dialogue 7) questions. Lastly, a replication of the most important dialogues in Britain was undertaken to understand the role of cultural and contextual factors in the development of metaphysical judgements in children.

DESCARTES' "MEDITATIONS ON FIRST PHILOSOPHY" AS A FRAMEWORK FOR THE STUDY OF CHILDREN'S METAPHYSICAL JUDGEMENTS

In Descartes' discourse, seven main steps can be distinguished (which can also be traced in other works by Descartes, such as "Discourse on the Method", "Principles of Philosophy", etc.). The first step is a brief introduction in which Descartes states that his knowledge and his views up until the present time are highly contradictory and unreliable and can be placed in doubt. Therefore, he says "it was necessary, once in the course of my life, to demolish everything completely and to start again right from the foundations, if I wanted to establish anything at all in the sciences that was stable and likely to last" (Descartes, 1988, p. 76).

The second step consists in outlining the limits of this doubt. Not only are the facts one learns at school doubtful, but also some of the knowledge that earlier seemed to be absolutely obvious and true. The latter include the belief that images of objects (including the image of our own body) which our sensations provide us with represent the objects "as they are in their own right", the belief in the existence of the external world, and even the belief in our personal existence. One reason for such profound doubt Descartes sees as our susceptibility to perceptual illusions: everything, he says, that "I have now accepted as most true I have acquired through the senses. But from time to time I have found that the senses deceive, and it is prudent never to trust completely those who have deceived us even once" (ibid., p. 76).

Another reason is the fact that it is impossible to draw an absolute borderline between dreams and reality. Since in dreams things can appear different from what they are in reality and can include images of objects that do not even exist, such doubt has to be radical, reasons Descartes. It is possible that at this very moment you are dreaming and, therefore, not only are the shapes of objects different in reality but the objects themselves may not exist and the whole world may be nothing more than mere illusion. "I shall consider myself as not having hands or eyes, or flesh, or blood or senses, but as falsely believing that I have all these things" (ibid., p. 79).

Having performed this crucial doubt, Descartes makes the third step. If one can go as far as to have doubts about the very existence of the world, he reasoned, then is there anything at all one can consider to be the truth? In answering this rhetorical question, Descartes formulated his cardinal metaphysical discovery, "cogito ergo sum":

> But immediately I noticed that while I was endeavouring in this way to think that everything was false, it was necessary that I, who was thinking this, was something. And observing that this truth "I am thinking, therefore I exist" was so firm and sure that all the most extravagant suppositions of the sceptics were incapable of shaking it, I decided that I could accept it without scruple as the first principle of the philosophy I was seeking (ibid., p. 36).

The next three steps of Descartes' discourse consist of the explication of the content that is already incorporated in "cogito" implicitly. They are (step 4) the idea of the fundamental distinction between body and mind, (step 5) the definition of the truth criterion, and (step 6) the so-called "ontological proof" of the existence of the "perfect subject". He states that such attributes as "shape", "spatial location", "movement", "weight", "nourishment", "divisibility", "accessibility to our senses", and so on, belong to our physical body but not to our mind. The essential feature of the mind is thinking, which Descartes subdivides into several kinds: thinking in the form of doubt, in the form of imagination, in the form of feeling, and so on. If I can see light and feel warmth, Descartes said, all this can be a mistake, but "I certainly *seem* to see, to hear, and to be warmed. This cannot be false; what is called 'having a sensory perception' is strictly just this, and in this restricted sense of the term it is simply thinking" (ibid., p. 83).

Descartes then speaks of the independence of the human mind from the body and about the possibility of the mind's posthumous existence:

> on the one hand I have a clear and distinct idea of myself, in so far as I am simply a thinking, non-extended thing; and on the other hand I have a distinct idea of body, in so far as this is simply an extended, non-thinking thing. And accordingly, it is certain that I am really distinct from my body, and can exist without it (ibid., pp. 114–115).

At the same time, the inseparable link between mind and body is evident: "I am not merely present in my body as a sailor is present in a ship, but ... I am very closely joined and, as it were, intermingled with it, so that I and the body form a unit" (ibid., p. 116).

Extension of the "cogito"-based meditation brings Descartes to the problem of determining the truth criterion: he comes to the conclusion that the necessary and sufficient criterion of true knowledge is in its clarity and distinctiveness. This means that true knowledge "can speak for itself":

> I observed that there is nothing at all in the proposition "I am thinking, therefore I exist" to assure me that I am speaking of the truth, except that I see very clearly that in order to think it is necessary to exist. So I decided that I could take it as a general rule that the things we conceive very clearly and very distinctly are all true; only there is some difficulty in recognizing which are the things that we distinctly conceive (ibid., p. 36).

Proceeding with the analysis of "cogito", Descartes discovers that there is, together with the ideas about thinking, body, truth, etc., also the idea of the "perfect subject". Indeed, the essential feature of "cogito" is doubt; that is, all subjects have some uncertainty and imperfection (insufficiency) in them. Therefore, a subject who is fulfilling "cogito" can be conceived only in contrast to the subject who is perfect and possesses all the attributions of "perfection": omnipotence, omnipresence, and so on. In Descartes' terms, the subject is God. An important feature of this conclusion (which for most people is notoriously difficult to understand) is that having a single idea of God is a sufficient proof of God's actual existence. This is the case because the denial of God's actual existence is contradictory to the idea of God's perfection:

> ... from the fact that I cannot think of God except as existing, it follows that existence is inseparable from God, and hence that he really exists. It is not that my thought makes it so, or imposes any necessity on any thing; on the contrary, it is the necessity of the thing itself, namely the existence of God, which determines my thinking in this respect. For I am not free to think of God without existence (that is, a supremely perfect being without a supreme perfection) as I am free to imagine a horse with or without wings (ibid., p. 107).

In the concluding part of his discourse (the seventh step), Descartes returned to the problem of the external world's existence. If one has images of things, he reasoned, then there must be something in the outer world that initiated those images. But in no case are these images identical to the external objects that caused them, as they are in their own right. Colour, warmth, pain, and so on, belong to the subject and not to external objects. If I can feel heat and pain from a fire, Descartes said, there is no convincing argument for supposing that there is something in the fire which resembles the heat, any more than for supposing that there is something that resembles the pain. There is simply reason to suppose that there is something in the fire, whatever it may eventually turn out to be, which produces in us feelings of heat or pain (ibid., p. 118).

Having denied his initial doubts about the reality of the external objects, Descartes also ruled out his assumptions about the impossibility of distinguishing between dreams and reality. Although images that we have in our dreams can have the same degree of clarity and distinctiveness that the images we have in our vigilant state, our thoughts and reasoning in our dreams can never catch up with what they are in our vigilant state; besides, dream images are casual and unconnected both among themselves and with the rest of our personal experience, in contrast to images as they are in reality.

Since Descartes' major philosophical works were published, his views have been subjected to serious criticism as well as acclaim. Well-known critical reviews include those by Kant (1965) and Husserl (1977); for more recent works, see Versfeld (1940), Smith (1966), Kenny (1968), Rée (1974), Wilson (1978), and Voss (1993). A number of studies have questioned nearly all aspects of Descartes' metaphysics. Although some of the objections will be discussed later in the appropriate dialogues, it is not the aim of this book to make a philosophical assessment of Descartes' views in the light of these studies, especially from the perspective of right and wrong. As already mentioned, in metaphysical problems the criteria "right" and "wrong" in their strict logical sense are irrelevant, as the very idea of true knowledge has its roots in metaphysical notions and judging these notions on the basis of their "true" or "false" nature would create a vicious circle.

Instead, metaphysical problems (such as the dualism between body and mind, the ontological proof of the existence of the Supreme Being, the relationships between external objects and their mental images, the metaphysical criterion of truth) are open to various, even alternative, interpretations, and it is this very "openness" of the metaphysical problems to interpretations that allows for the pluralism of philosophical views and, in the end, for the diversity of conscious life on this planet. The aim of this book is to assess how and when European children of various ages come to appreciate one particular way of solving fundamental metaphysical puzzles—that is, Descartes' way, selected on the grounds discussed above. In no way should this prevent or stop others from investigating the developing child's views on the basis of other metaphysical systems, like those offered by Plato, Hume, or Kant, for example.

NOTES

1. The term "European culture" is not linked here to a particular geographical or national region, but includes all those countries that have absorbed the fundamental elements of the culture that has its origins in Europe.
2. The view traditionally (and with good reason) ascribed to Piaget (see Piaget, 1936, 1986b; see also Bremner, 1994; Johnson-Laird, 1990; Matthews, 1980; White, 1995), although there have been some unorthodox interpretations of Piaget's views on development (Smith, 1993).

2

Children and Cartesian Metaphysics: An Experimental Study of Children's Metaphysical Reasonings

According to the steps in Descartes' discourse, seven dialogues were created in which problems raised by Descartes were put to children aged 4 to 14 years in a form accessible to them (see Fig. 1). Together with key questions about the problems under consideration, additional questions were also asked whose function was to "warm the children up" and to "keep the interrogation going". If a child's answer was not clear, he or she was asked additional auxiliary questions after which the key question was repeated. The dialogues were tape-recorded.

A general aim of the study was to determine to what extent children of various ages are able to produce answers similar to (or deviating from) answers given by Descartes. Based on an analysis of the children's answers and justifications, I intended to establish at what age and in what form children begin to realise the classical metaphysical problems and what kinds of solutions for these problems they are able to offer.

Altogether, 95 children participated in the original study conducted in Moscow: 4-year-olds [$n = 15$, mean age 4 years 6 months (4:6 years)], 5-year-olds ($n = 15$, $\bar{x} = 5:4$ years), and 6-year-olds ($n = 15$, $\bar{x} = 6:8$ years) were recruited from kindergartens in Moscow; 7-year-olds ($n = 15$, $\bar{x} = 7:4$ years), 9-year-olds ($n = 15$, $\bar{x} = 9:2$ years), 11-year-olds ($n = 10$, $\bar{x} = 11:5$ years), and 13- and 14-year-olds ($n = 10$, $\bar{x} = 13:10$ years) were recruited from the first, third, fifth, and seventh grades of Moscow schools respectively. There were approximately equal numbers of males and females in each age group.

DESCARTES

Dialogue 1. Introduction	Step 1. Introduction
Dialogue 2. Objects' shapes and the existence of the external world	Step 2. Everything I know can be doubted
Dialogue 3. Personal existence of the child	Step 3. The only true knowledge is "cogito ergo sum"
Dialogue 4. The distinction between body and mind	Step 4. Body and mind are totally different one from the other yet linked to each other
Dialogue 5. The criterion of truth	Step 5. Truth is everything, which is as clear as "cogito ergo sum"
Dialogue 6. The existence of the almighty wizard	Step 6. If I have an idea of the Supreme Subject, then the Subject must really exist
Dialogue 7. The relationships between sensations and physical objects. The distinction between dreams and reality	Step 7. Sensations and images of objects belong to the subject's mind and not to the objects that produced them

FIG. 1.   The stages of Descartes' meditation and dialogues with children.

After a brief warm-up session during which the experimenter visited a kindergarten group or a classroom and talked with the teacher and the children for a while, the children were asked the questions individually in a separate room. All seven dialogues were conducted in one session, always working from Dialogue 1 through to Dialogue 7.[1]

To provide a cross-cultural comparison of the judgements of Russian and British children, Dialogues 1–4, 6 and 7 in this chapter were replicated in Lancaster in the UK. For the comparative study in Britain, most children were taken from suburban primary and secondary schools. Comparisons were made of Russian and British children of the same ages, although due to differences between the Russian and British educational systems, the children from both samples would have had different experiences. For instance, in Russia most children attend a kindergarten before the age of 7, an institution where they spend most of the day and are systematically engaged in play and learning activities. In Britain, children of 4 and 5 visit playgroups and primary schools where, according to my own observations, there is less stress on scientific teaching than in Russian kindergartens.

However, starting from the age of 7 years, these differences begin to disappear and children from both cultural groups are involved in compulsory teaching to an approximately equal extent, with most disciplines (e.g. maths, physics, history, language, literature) being part of both school curriculums (at least as far as comprehensive schools in Britain are concerned), although there is more emphasis on "exploration" in British schools and a greater emphasis on "instruction" in Russian schools. Also the differentiation between various scientific disciplines (e.g. physics, chemistry, biology, geography) is adhered to more strongly in Russia than in Britain, where various subjects are grouped under the same heading, "science".

Yet, as stated in the Introduction, metaphysical problems are of such a general nature that the differences in education mentioned above are unlikely to have affected the children's answers to a significant extent; rather, it is the children's age (that is, the amount of time each child has had to accumulate metaphysical experience and develop his or her metaphysical intuitions) that is of importance here. It was on this basis that groups of children of similar age (and not groups of children selected on the basis of their IQs or other cognitive tests) were chosen for the cross-cultural comparisons.

In the replication study, which involved Dialogues 1–3, 6 and 7, 95 children participated as subjects: 4-year-olds ($n = 15$, mean age 4:5 years), 5-year-olds ($n = 15$, $\bar{x} = 5:5$ years), 6-year-olds ($n = 15$, $\bar{x} = 6:6$ years), 9-year-olds ($n = 15$, $\bar{x} = 9:3$ years), 11-year-olds ($n = 15$, $\bar{x} = 11:9$ years), and 13- and 14-year-olds ($n = 15$, $\bar{x} = 13:11$) years. There were approximately equal numbers of males and females in each age group.[2] Parts of Dialogue 4 were reproduced with ten 4- to 5-year-olds, twenty 7- to 9-year-olds, twenty 11- to 13-year-olds, and twelve adults, all groups having equal numbers of males and females.[3]

There were also two analytical studies conducted on the basis of Dialogues 6 and 7. The study based on Dialogue 6 involved 28 males (mean age 21:1 years) and 34 females ($\bar{x}$ = 20:1 years), and the study based on Dialogue 7 involved thirty-two 6-year-olds ($\bar{x}$ = 6:5 years), thirty-two 9-year-olds ($\bar{x}$ = 9.5 years), thirty-one males with a mean age of 23:0 years, and thirty-one females with a mean age of 21:4 years.

DIALOGUE 1: THE INTRODUCTION

The major objectives of this dialogue were to introduce the children to the discussion, to hint that knowledge they get from adults can be doubted and to determine whether they could understand the word "existence" and relate it correctly to various objects, some of which are available in their immediate perceptual field (the table), others which are real but not available in the immediate perceptual field (an elephant, a hippopotamus) and others which are not real (an elepotamus, a centaur). The last objective of the questions was to draw the children's attention to the fact of their own existence. The questions were as follows:

1. Tell me please, do you know much about the world? Do you know the names of the objects that surround us? Can you tell me what "the world" is? Can you tell me what "man" is?
2. And whom did you learn all this from? Did you learn this from adults? Do you always agree with what adults say? In what cases do you disagree?
3. Do you agree that this table exists or do you think that it doesn't exist? Why do you think so?
4. And an elephant—does it exist or not? And a hippopotamus—does it exist or not?
5. And an elepotamus—does it exist or not? And this creature [the child is shown a picture of a centaur]—does it exist or not?
6. And yourself—do you exist or not? Why do you think so?

The results (see Fig. 2)[4] showed that about half of the preschoolers (the 4-, 5- and 6-year-olds) had difficulty providing a definition of "man" and "the world".[5] Some of them responded with a tautological answer ("man is man", "man is people", etc.); however, the number of sensible answers increased significantly among the 7-year-olds when compared with the 6-year-olds (χ^2 = 6.80, P < 0.01 regarding the definition of "man"; χ^2 = 8.35, P < 0.003 regarding the definition of what "the world" is).[6] For most

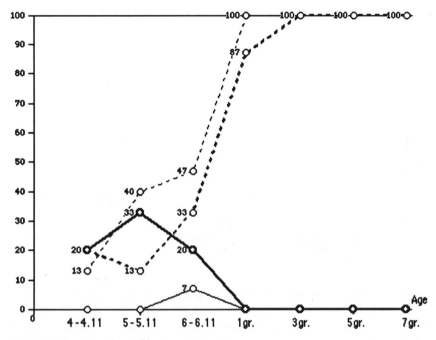

Tautological answer: the world —o—, man —o—
Sensible answer: the world - -o- -, man - -o- -

FIG. 2. Percentages of children producing answers in response to Question 1 regarding the concepts "the world" and "man". (gr. = grade).

6-year-olds, "the world" was the synonym of a certain "container" ("the world is Earth", "a country", "a street..."). Some of the children defined "man" in a transductive way, pointing out certain attributes of a human individual ("man is who walks along the streets", "who can breathe with air", "who has hands and legs", "it is a kind of living creature"); they were unable, however, to identify essential features of "man". The older children described "the world" in less "spatial" terms ("this is nature", "this is plants, houses, people", "this is what surrounds us", etc.), and many of them were capable of identifying essential characteristics of "man" ("man is an intelligent animal"; "this is a creature who can do almost everything, and the cleverest in the world"). Other typical features that distinguished "man" from other living beings included labour, language, intelligence, and voluntary behaviour ("man is a sort of an automat who can control its own actions").

In response to the questions about the source of their knowledge (Fig. 3), 20–40% of the children stated that they had learned everything on their own

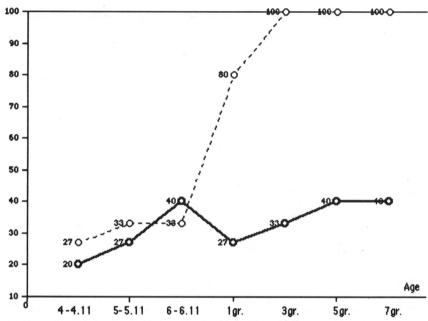

A source of knowledge: learned independently —o— or learned from other people (the rest of the subjects).
Reliability of knowledge learned from adults: children who said that they (1) sometimes disagree with adults - -o- - (2) always agree with adults (the rest of the subjects).

FIG. 3. Percentages of children producing answers in response to Question 2 regarding the source of personal knowledge and the possibility of doubting such knowledge.

without help (i.e. from books); others acknowledged that adults (peers) had contributed to their knowledge. Among preschoolers, almost 70% said that they always agreed with adults; when they didn't, the disagreements were evoked not by the children's doubts in adults' competence but rather by the children's caprices and whims ("I disagree when they don't do what I want"). The overwhelming majority of the schoolchildren acknowledged that they disagree with adults and the reasons given were mostly objective ("I disagree when they think differently from what I think", "when they deceive me", "when they make fun of me"). Many children pointed out that in some cases adults' judgements contradict each other and are incoherent ("I read something in the book, and they say this isn't true"; "they write one thing in one book and other things in a different book about the same subject"; "a teacher says a certain thing about something and my parents say it's not true", etc.). The number of children doubting the opinions of adults (e.g. their parents, teachers, authors of books) increased significantly with age (e.g. increase 6 years to 7 years: $\chi^2 = 4.88$, $P < 0.02$).

The children's answers to questions regarding objects' existence (Fig. 4) were the least varied. Naturally, all the children expressed their firm belief in the existence of objects present in their perceptual field; however, 4- and 5-year-olds could not produce any grounds for this, whereas 6-year-olds and the older schoolchildren grounded their positive answers by pointing out the clarity and distinctiveness of their sensations ("I can see it clearly", "here it is", "the recorder is standing on it", "I can touch it", "if I punch it with my wrist it'll crack", etc.). To confirm the table's existence, some children kicked it, shook it, and so on. Other children pointed out the table's functions as a proof of its existence ("it exists because it always is in the classroom"; "if tables didn't exist, there would not be anywhere to put something on"). Only one 13-year-old boy allowed for the possibility of the table's non-existence: "There can be everything. Here I can touch it, it exists, but maybe it doesn't, maybe there is no table and even we are not sitting here now".

The children were equally unanimous in their acknowledgement of the existence of objects that were real but absent from their perceptual field (e.g. an elephant, a hippopotamus). By contrast, all but four of the children

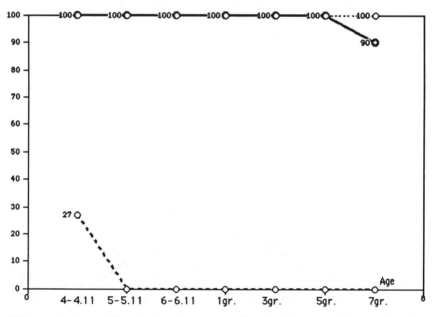

Children who were confident in the existence of an object that (1) was actually present in their perceptual field (q.3, —o—), (2) was real but absent in their perceptual field (q.4, - -o- -), (3) was an unreal (fantastic) object (q.5, - -o- -).

FIG. 4. Percentages of children producing answers in response to Questions 3, 4, and 5 regarding objects' existence.

denied that the centaur existed ("there can be no such creatures"), with the older children making their negative answers more precise by adding that the centaur didn't exist in reality but did exist "in legends", "in myths", "in fairy tales", "in pictures", etc. ("it is from Greek mythology"; "it is a fairy tale character"; "this all was created by Greeks, they had myths, they believed in all this"). Lastly, some of the children stated that at present there are no such creatures but they did exist a long time ago ("it existed in other centuries", "it is from ancient times").

Quite naturally, none of the children put their own personal existence in doubt. The youngest children (4-year-olds) merely confirmed their own personal existence ("I am", "I exist"); the older children tried to support their judgements by providing some sort of justifications (Fig. 5). Some simply pointed to the fact that they could perceive themselves ("I am, because look—I am here", "because I can see myself", "because I can walk", "because I can feel and touch myself") (increase 6 years to 11 years: $\chi^2 = 6.80$, $P < 0.01$); others saw the proof of their personal existence in the

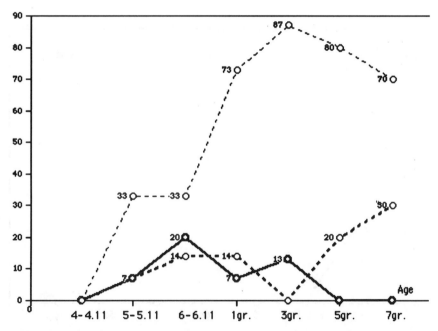

Children who (1) referred to the clear and obvious character of their perceptions of themselves (- -o- -), (2) pointed out the fact that other people exist in the world (—o—), (3) produced tautological justifications (- -o- -), (4) gave no justifications (the rest of the children).

FIG. 5.   Percentages of children producing answers in response to Question 6, which confirmed their belief in their own personal existence.

fact of other people's existence ("everybody can see me, and if I didn't exist, nobody would be able to see me and hear me"; "I always talk with my mum"; "I am called, I am addressed to"; "If I didn't exist there would be nobody for you to talk to now"); others provided tautological reasons ("I exist because I am living", "because I was born"). Notably, the over-whelming majority of the children produced grounds of the first type, seeing the proof of their personal existence in the clarity of their self-perceptions ("I am because I can move, jump, run, learn, do something, touch myself, see myself, feel myself, hear myself", etc.).

In the comparative study in Britain, the British children produced defi-nitions of the terms "the world" and "man" similar to those given by Russian children, the only difference being that some of the British children (but none of the Russian children) provided a Christian definition of man ("man is a person created by God from his own image"). As can be seen from Fig. 6, there were no significant differences between the numbers of logically sensible answers given by the Russian and British children, apart from Russian 9-year-olds giving a grounded definition of "man" more often

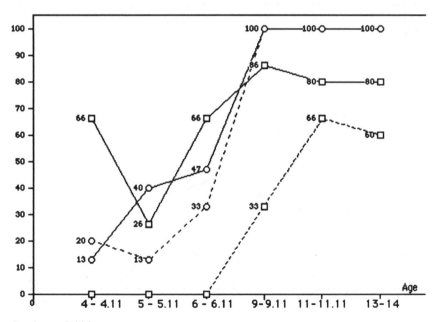

Russian ○, British □
The world —, man - -

FIG. 6. Percentages of Russian and British children producing sensible answers in response to Question 1 regarding the concepts "the world" and "man".

than British 9-year-olds ($\chi^2 = 8.5$, $P < 0.004$), whereas British 4-year-olds performed better when defining "the world" ($\chi^2 = 6.8$, $P < 0.01$).

With regard to sources of knowledge, there were large differences found between the judgements of Russian and British children; namely, British 6-, 11-, and 13- to 14-year-olds were less inclined to attribute their knowledge exclusively to themselves than were their Russian peers ($\chi^2 = 6.54$, $P < 0.02$), whereas British 6-year-olds more often acknowledged that they sometimes disagreed with adults than did Russian 6-year-olds ($\chi^2 = 9.2$, $P < 0.003$) (Fig. 7). There was a major shift observed among British 6-year-olds in the realisation of the external origins of their knowledge (66% of 5-year-olds denied that their knowledge was acquired from other people; none of the 6-year-olds felt this way).

Combined with the growing realisation of their occasional disagreements with adults, this shift among British 6-year-olds can be attributed to the beginning of intensive schooling, an assumption that finds support in the fact that a similar divergence occurs among Russian children 1 year later (i.e. at age 7), the age at which Russian children normally start school (see

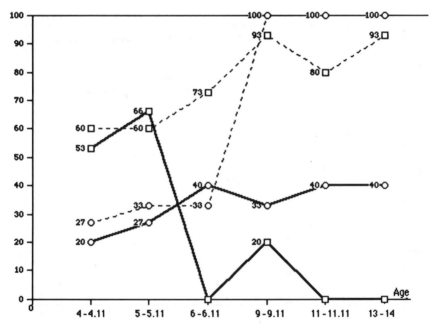

Russian ○, British □
(1) —, (2) - -

FIG. 7.   Percentages of Russian and British children who (1) believed they learned knowledge independently from other people and (2) sometimes disagree with adults.

Fig. 2). However, a significant (although moderate) number of Russian senior schoolchildren retained the illusion of "independently acquired knowledge", whereas this all but disappeared among the British children older than 6 years, a result that challenges further and more detailed comparative analysis of the characteristics of the British and Russian educational systems.

Questions about the existential nature of objects actually present in the perceptual field, real objects absent from the immediate perceptual field, and fantastic objects yielded similar answers among the British and Russian children (see Fig. 4). With regard to their justifications for their belief in their own personal existence, the British children produced the same kinds of judgements as the Russian children, the only age difference being related to the argument "clearness of subjective manifestations". As can be seen from Fig. 8, British 4-year-olds produced significantly more ($\chi^2 = 8.4$, $P < 0.004$) and British 9-year-olds significantly less ($\chi^2 = 4.3$, p < 0.04) of this type of justification than their Russian peers. Basically, the British children revealed no age dynamics in their reliance on the clearness of their subjective manifestations, whereas the Russian children's tendency to produce this kind of justification increased significantly with age.

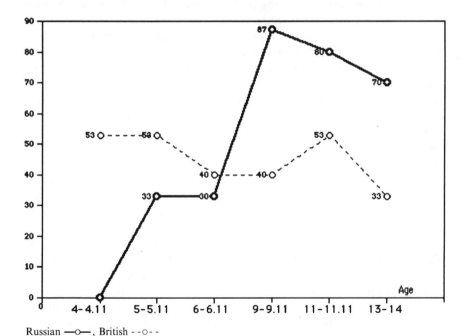

Russian —o—, British - -o- -

FIG. 8.   Percentages of Russian and British children who justified their existence by referring to the clear and obvious nature of their subjective experiences.

A few points need to be explained about the data. First, the results show that major shifts in children's judgements occur at the border between preschool and school. It was the primary schoolchildren who began to give sensible and essential characteristics to the notions of "man" and "the world". It is at this age that most children stress their capacity to assess critically the knowledge that they have received from other people. Second, although by school age most children are quick to admit that other people's opinions could be wrong, they nevertheless do not question their own personal existence, which most of them try to prove in the same way that they use to prove the existence of a table—by merely referring to the fact of perceiving themselves.

The results allow one to suggest that older preschoolers and primary schoolchildren are at a stage which is very similar to that from which Descartes started his journey in "the deep of doubt". On the one hand, the children lose their original naivety and begin to question some kinds of knowledge. On the other hand, quite naturally, this critical capacity does not extend beyond a certain body of knowledge, leaving vast areas of knowledge (such as knowledge of the existence of external objects, of personal existence, etc.) in the realm of facts that it would be odd to question. This creates a reason for moving on to the second dialogue, in which some of these apparently reliable truths begin to be questioned.

Although asking questions about the reliability of our fundamental beliefs (such as our belief in the existence of the external world or our personal existence) might seem an artificial and unnatural enterprise, this procedure is necessary to (1) separate the fundamental beliefs that are really true (such as the belief in our personal existence) from those that only appear to be true (i.e. the belief that external objects in their own right are identical to their perceptual images), and (2) highlight the fact that the fundamental beliefs that are really true can withstand any possible doubt and therefore are not the sort of beliefs that are accepted dogmatically or because of sheer suggestion and pressure from the social environment. Indeed, the fundamental task of Descartes' metaphysical method was not the construction of a certain new knowledge, but the reconstruction of existing knowledge on the basis of clear and necessary foundations.

At first glance, it would seem an odd task to reconstruct knowledge that is already there, without adding new facts and data. However, it soon became clear that this kind of reconstruction (which was based by Descartes on his idea of "cogito") was necessary, as it was the only way to bring unity and consistency to the scientific picture of the world, which otherwise presented a bizarre mixture of unrelated theories and studies. The fact was that scientists in various fields of science used scientific method without being aware of its fundamental principles and foundations, and it was exactly these principles and foundations that Descartes was after in his metaphysical studies.

An example from everyday life may be helpful here. Most educated people in contemporary industrial societies are users of sophisticated hi-tech equipment (e.g. computers, CD players), but have no idea about the construction and the essential "mechanics" of the hardware they use; it simply works until it breaks down. At this point, the user has to contact a specialist who is in possession of knowledge of how the hardware works. It was finding out what makes all rationally constructed theories (like those of cosmology or physics) seem to be true, that Descartes' metaphysical reconstruction succeeded at.

DIALOGUE 2: DISCUSSING THE POSSIBILITY OF QUESTIONING THE ADEQUACY OF THE PERCEPTIVE IMAGES OF OBJECTS AND THE EXISTENCE OF THE EXTERNAL WORLD

In accordance with Descartes' argumentation, this dialogue tested to what extent the children were able to (1) acknowledge the absence of an absolute borderline between the two states of mind (vigilant state and dreaming), (2) question the adequacy of their perceptual images of physical objects (including shapes of their own bodies), and (3) question the fact of the real existence of the external world. The questions were as follows:

1. Do you have dreams sometimes? Do you see yourself in your dreams?
2. And can it happen in your dream that you are fully dressed, you go somewhere and do something, whereas in reality you are in your bed and asleep?
3. And can the following happen: in your dream you see a certain creature and think that it exists, but when you wake up you realise that it doesn't really exist?
4. Are you asleep at the moment?
5. Can it be the case that it only seems to you that you have two hands, two legs and a head, that you are sitting here in front of me but in reality you are asleep and see all this in your dream, and if you wake up you will find that your body has a different shape, for instance it looks like an octopus and you live on another planet (for the youngest children the wording was slightly different: Your body looks like a fish and you are living in the ocean)?
6. Does this table exist? Is it hard or soft?
7. Can it be the case that in your dreams objects are as you see them at the moment, but that when you wake up you will see that, in reality, they are different: tables are made of soft cotton, the sun has a square shape and this room is a big bubble of glass?

8. And can the following occur: in your dream you see a certain object which in reality doesn't exist; for instance, you have a dream about a dragon, and dragons don't exist in reality?
9. And is it the case that all these objects—the table, the sun and the whole world—only exist in your dreams, like the dragon, that in reality none of them really exist?
10. I'd like to propose an interesting game. Its name is "Unusual dream". In this game we agree that we are in a dream and all this—the sun, the table and the world—they are part of the dream, but in reality they don't exist. Can we play such a game or not?

The above questions were designed to put in doubt certain beliefs which children had viewed as absolutely indisputable, namely that external objects (including their own bodies) are as they seem to be and that the outer world exists. To achieve this, Descartes' tactic of "shifting" the spheres of reality was used: according to this tactic, as everything we see in reality can look different in dreams and there is no absolute borderline between the two, it is therefore possible that all objects have different shapes from those we think they have. Although the possibility that the external world does not exist does not follow from this, the questions related to this possibility (Questions 9 and 10) were asked to make sure that the children understood that it is not possible to discuss the total absence of the outer world.

A deviation from the standard procedure occurred here, in that after asking Question 5 and Question 10 and registering the child's answers, the experimenter produced one or two objections in order to examine how stable the child's beliefs in the invariability of the objects' shapes and external world's unconditional existence were.

All the children acknowledged that they do sometimes have dreams. They also acknowledged that occasionally they see themselves in the dreams as well as the creatures that don't exist in reality and confirmed that at the moment of conversation they were in a vigilant state.

Having been asked Question 5 (suggesting that their body may, perhaps, have a different shape to that they think it has), the children were puzzled. As a result, most of the preschoolers and first graders refuted the possibility (Fig. 9). Some stopped at that, others provided tautological answers ("This can't be the case because I am not an octopus"; "This can't be true because I am not in a dream at the moment") or produced transductive justifications ("A fish can swim and I cannot, therefore I am not a fish"). Many children, however, offered various sensible justifications in favour of their negative answers (increase 4 years to 6 years, $\chi^2 = 4.26$, $P < 0.03$): some of them suggested that alien creatures (a fish, an extraterrestrial creature) cannot see human beings in their dreams because they do not know anything about humans ("A fish can only see fish in its dreams", "Inhabitants of other

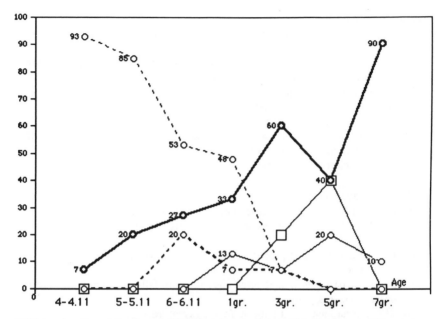

Children who allowed for the possibility that their bodies could in fact have a different shape
(—o—).
Children who denied that this was possible and (1) gave no grounds or produced tautological
and transductive justifications (- -o- -), (2) reasoned that an alien creature cannot see a human
being in its dreams (- -o- -), (3) said that what they were seeing was not a dream because
dreams could not last for so long (—□—), (4) said that what they were seeing could not
possibly be a dream because of the clarity and obviousness of their experiences (—o—).

FIG. 9.   Percentages of children producing answers in response to Question 5 regarding the
possibility of their bodies having a shape different from that which it appeared to have.

planets cannot live on Earth, how can they know that there are living
creatures here?"); others grounded their negations by claiming that such a
long and strange dream was impossible ("There can't be something like that,
I would have woken up a long time ago"); still others referred to the clear
and distinct character of their perceptions, which they saw as an indication
that the perceptions were real ("I wouldn't be able to see everything so
clearly in a dream"). The experimenter's counterarguments seemed to have
no impact on the children's opinions. In contrast, about 30% of 6- and 7-
year-olds and the majority of 9- to 13-year-olds acknowledged that the
shapes of their bodies could in fact be different (increase 5 years to 13 years:
$\chi^2 = 12.34$, $P < 0.001$). At the beginning these children also responded in
the negative; however, unlike the younger children, they changed their
minds after the experimenter put forward his considerations in favour of the
hypothesis. Here are two examples:

Nikita (boy aged 9 years)

N: No, I am not a creature from another planet because they cannot be asleep for so long—9 years, and see such a long dream that me is me.

E (Experimenter):   How do you know? Maybe they live for 100,000 years and have nights that last for 60 years each.

N: Well, I don't know, perhaps this may happen, but I still slightly disagree. Because if I were an extraterrestrial creature, how would I be able to have a dream about this planet and not about some other one?

E: Well, it's difficult to say why people see exactly this in their dreams and not something else. So, can this happen or not?

N: This can happen, of course.

Andrei (boy aged 11 years)

A: No, this cannot be the case, because our scientists do not yet know whether alien creatures exist or not; therefore, I cannot be an alien creature.

E: But is there a certain probability that they exist, or is there not?

A: Yes, there is.

E: So can it be the case that some alien creature falls asleep and sees in its dream that it is you?

A: This can happen, but I am not an alien creature.

E: So, there is no probability whatsoever that your body has a different shape in reality, is there?

A: Well, there is some probability.

The children responded to Questions 6 and 7 in a similar fashion (Fig. 10). Most of the preschoolers and schoolchildren emphatically denied that external objects could have shapes other than those they seem to have. Some of the children provided tautological answers ("A table cannot be soft because it is hard"); others referred to the impossibility of having such a long dream; still others referred to the clarity and distinctiveness of their perceptions ("I could not see and feel everything so clearly in a dream, this is all real"). Lastly, a few children noted that each object has its own particular functions and this determines the object's shape ("This cannot be the case, you can't eat on the table if it is made of down"). And yet some 9-year-olds and most 11- and 13-year-olds finally agreed that objects could indeed have different shapes (increase 7 years to 11 years: $\chi^2 = 6.02$, $P < 0.02$). Here are two examples:

Sasha (boy aged 9 years)

S: I think objects cannot be different. What kind of a table would it be if it were made from down? It would be soft, you can't write on it, and this recorder could not rest on it.

E: But maybe in the real world there is no need to write and there are no recorders?

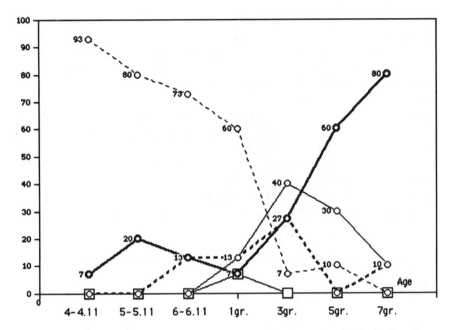

Children who acknowledged that physical objects could in fact have shapes different from those they appear to have (—o—).
Children who denied that this was possible and (1) gave no grounds or produced tautological and transductive justifications (- -o- -), (2) said that what they were perceiving could not possibly be a dream because of the clarity and obviousness of their experiences (- -o- -), (3) said that what they were perceiving could not be a dream because dreams could not last for so long (—□—), (4) named various functions of objects as the determinants of the objects' shapes (—o—).

FIG. 10.   Percentages of children producing answers in response to Question 7 regarding the possibility of physical objects having a shape different from that which they appear to have.

S: And what are tables for then?
E: I don't know. So, is it possible, or is there no possibility of it at all?
S: Well, it is possible, but only slightly.

Dima (boy aged 11 years)
D: No, this cannot be true, because if tables were made of down you won't be able to put anything on them, they would collapse.
E: But in the real world even gravity may be absent and nothing would collapse?
D: Well, there is some small probability of all this, but it is not very likely.

The children were, however, less lenient when asked if there was any doubt about the existence of the external world (Questions 9 and 10). Only a few preschoolers and one 7-year-old acknowledged that there was any possibility of this, with the overwhelming majority firmly denying it (Fig. 11). Most preschoolers were unable to provide grounds for their negative answers; among the arguments given by the rest of the children, four types can be distinguished. The first three types of argument were given by small numbers of subjects: they were tautological arguments ("the world exists because all this is real and really exists"), appellations to the clear and distinct character of perceptions ("The world exists because I can feel all this clearly"; "Here cars are passing by, and birds are flying, I could not see all this in a dream that clearly"; "I can see that the table is hard, it is made of timber and the walls are made from bricks"), and stating the impossibility of having such a long dream. Most of the subjects chose a fourth type of argument in which they declared the impossibility of their own existence in a non-existent world

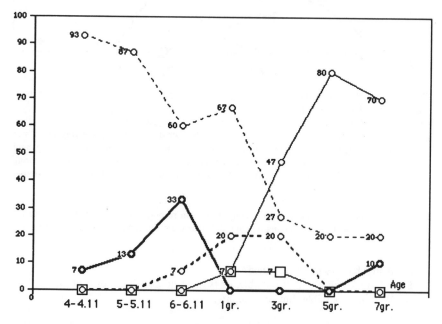

Children who acknowledged that it was possible to doubt the existence of the external world (—o—).

Children who denied that this was possible and (1) gave no grounds or produced tautological and transductive justifications (- -o- -), (2) said that what they were perceiving could not possibly be a dream because of the clarity and obviousness of their experiences (- -o- -), (3) said that what they were perceiving was not a dream because dreams could not last for so long (— □—), (4) pointed out that there would be no people if the world did not exist (—o—).

FIG. 11.   Percentages of children producing answers in response to Question 9 regarding the possibility of doubting the existence of the external world.

("The world exists because we have to live somewhere"; "If there were no galaxies there would be no planets and I would not exist either"; "This can't be the case, otherwise where would I be situated?"; "I do exist, and how would I be able to exist without this world?"; "If it were the case, where would I wake up then?") (increase 6 years to 11 years: $\chi^2 = 6.70$, $P < 0.01$).

Characteristically, the "proof" provided by the experimenter in support of the world's non-existence hypothesis had no effect on the children. Here are two examples:

Lena S. (girl aged 11 years)
In the course of the dialogue, Lena acknowledged that it was possible for objects to have shapes different from what they normally are, but when asked that the external world might not exist, she replied in the negative. The experimenter went on:

E: Well, if objects can be different from what they seem to be, why can't it be the case that there are no objects at all?

L: And where I would be asleep then? No, it can't be the case that there are no objects at all.

E: But can you acknowledge that there is at least a small probability of this being possible?

L: No, I cannot. Where would I be sleeping then?

Roma (boy aged 13 years)
During the conversations, Roma agreed that it was possible for objects and his own body to have different shapes, but he firmly denied that the world did not exist:

R: I don't think this is possible because if there were nothing, then I would have no dreams at all and there would be no me either.

E: Do you think that there is a slight possibility of this being true?

R: No, because ... in order for me to exist without the world ... no. There is not the slightest possibility of that.

Interestingly, a significant number of subjects (about 30% of the total sample) denied that it was possible for the outer world not to exist even in play. Most argued along the lines that it would be impossible to play the game "without the world" because there would be no place to play the game. Others agreed that such a game can be played, but it would be "only fantasy" and not the real thing.

The study of the British children showed that, starting at the age of 9 years, they are significantly more reluctant to acknowledge that their bodies could in fact have different shapes than are their Russian peers (see Fig. 12). When trying to justify this, the British children gave the same answers as the

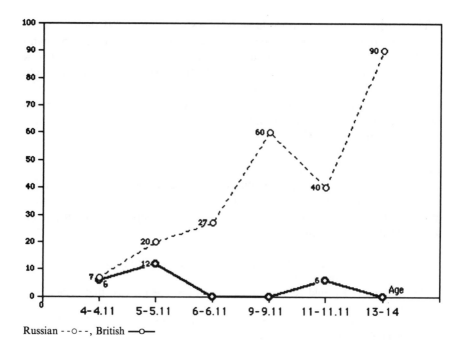

Russian - -o- -, British —o—

FIG. 12. Percentages of Russian and British children who acknowledged that their bodies may have a shape different from that which they appear to have.

Russian children; however, tautological "explanations" dominated. A similar pattern of answers was received in response to the question about the possibility of doubting the shape of physical objects (see Fig. 13). The differences in the answers of the British and Russian senior schoolchildren, however, are likely to be due to differences in questioning technique, as in the Russian study the experimenter employed some arguments against the rejection of the possibility of doubt that was almost universal among the Russian children when they were asked the question for the first time, whereas in the British study the experimenter simply asked the children the question without any subsequent discussion.

Interestingly, the same differences in questioning technique did not affect the children's answers to the question about the possibility of the external world not existing—an option that was denied by the overwhelming majority of subjects in both cultural samples, no matter whether the denial was or was not challenged by the experimenter (Fig. 14). This stresses once again the fundamental difference that exists between beliefs about the appearance of external objects and belief in their actual existence; whereas the appearance of physical objects—however convincing they may seem—

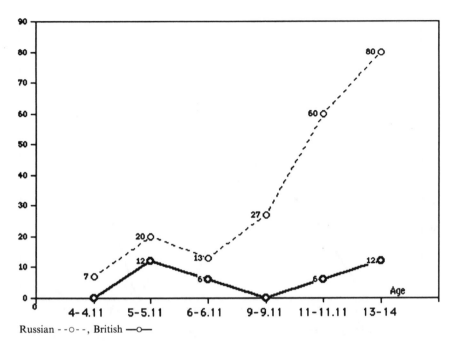

FIG. 13.   Percentages of Russian and British children who acknowledged that physical objects could in fact have a shape different from that which they appear to have.

can be doubted, the existence of external objects (i.e. the existence of the external world) is something that resists all scepticism.

Overall, at the beginning of the dialogue, the vast majority of subjects refused to accept that there was any possibility of doubting the relevancy of the perceptual images that they had about their bodies; however, some of them changed their minds in the course of the discussion with the experimenter and agreed that even such an extravagant hypothesis had some likelihood of being true. There were significantly more 11-year-olds who conceded this than preschoolers. A similar pattern was found for the answers to the question about the possibility of doubting the adequacy of objects' shapes. In contrast, the majority of the children of all age groups emphatically denied that there was any possibility that the external world did not exist. The reasons given by most children showed that their strong belief in the impossibility of the world not to exist rested on their belief in their own personal existence ("If there were no world, I would not exist either"). Essentially, answers like this suggested that the children had an intuitive belief in the inseparable unity between subject and object (the external world); that is, they viewed a subject and the world as two mutually

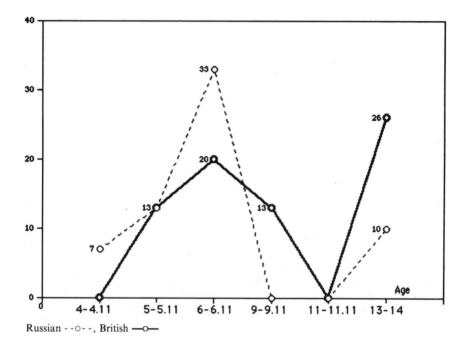

Russian - -o- - , British —o—

FIG. 14. Percentages of Russian and British children who acknowledged the possibility of doubting the existence of the external world.

dependent notions, each of which is a necessary condition for the existence of the other.

So far, the answers of the 9- to 13-year-old children seem to show their sensitivity to the first step of Descartes' "sceptical revolution" (by doubting the shapes of objects and the human body), but they did not go so far as to doubt the existence of the external world—the second step of Descartes, which indeed does not seem to follow logically from the fact that everything can be distorted in dreams or illusions.

This refusal to doubt the existence of the external world, however plain and tautological it may look, nevertheless brings with it something new and useful in the children's minds, as it clearly shows that there exists an important difference between the beliefs that earlier seemed to be equally true, such as the beliefs that objects really are what they look like and that objects, whatever they are, really exist outside the subject's mind; it turns out that only the latter is undeniably true and the former is not.

Since the children's belief in the outer world's existence proved to be rooted in the necessity for them "to be somewhere" (that is, for them to exist as subjects), the time has come to shift the emphasis from the existence of objects to the subject's own individual existence.

DIALOGUE 3: EXAMINING CHILDREN'S CAPACITY TO DOUBT THEIR OWN INDIVIDUAL EXISTENCE

In accordance with the development of Descartes' discourse, the children were asked questions that intended to determine whether they could doubt their own personal existence. The dialogue also aimed to double check the reliability of the children's answers given in response to the experimenter's objections in the previous dialogue: if those children who could doubt the adequacy of their perceptual images of objects (including images of their own bodies) did this because of their susceptibility to the experimenter's arguments, then they would be quick to agree that their personal existence is also in doubt. To examine this, Dialogue 3 took the form of a discussion between a child and the experimenter in which the experimenter repeatedly and in different ways asked the child questions about whether it was possible to doubt his or her own existence. The questions were as follows:

1. So, you claim that you exist, don't you?
2. But could it be that it only seems to you that you exist, but in reality you don't exist?
3. Let us assume that you are asleep at the moment and it seems to you in your dream that you exist, that you are sitting here and answering my questions, but in reality, if you wake up, you will find that you don't exist. Is this possible?
4. And can it seem to you in your dream that you don't exist?
5. And when you are asleep without dreaming, do you exist or not? Why do you think so?
6. You know, I invented an interesting game. In this game, we pretend that we are asleep and have a dream that we exist, but in reality when we wake up we find that we don't exist. Can we play a game like that? Why do you think so?

As in some of the other dialogues, in this dialogue the first question verified a trivial fact of the child's personal existence, which had the function of launching the conversation. Questions 2 and 3 examined the children's capacity to provide some proof of the fact that their personal existence could not be doubted if subjected to the tactic of "shifting realities". The next three questions were variations on Questions 2 and 3 which examined whether the children were able to accept that they may not exist in the domains of reality other than everyday reality, that is in their dreams, in play, and in the condition in which they have no conscious state whatsoever (sleeping without dreams).

The first question was unanimously answered "yes", the second and the third ones almost universally "no". Only four of 95 children replied "yes" to

Questions 2 or 3, and they were unable to provide any reasons for this. All the rest strongly denied the possibility that they might not exist (Fig. 15).

Those children who could provide arguments to support their negative answers were allocated to four major groups. The most popular argument was very similar to that given by Descartes; it consisted of pointing out that it was not possible for someone to be aware of something (to have a dream for instance) and not to exist at the same time. "I am thinking, therefore I exist". Justifications for this first appeared among some 5-year-olds, although in a rather primitive form ("I exist in this world. When I was in my mum's belly I had no dreams"; "If I didn't exist then there would be no dreams, no dream can emerge, and if I do exist then there is a dream").

The older children expressed themselves in a more exact way: "Yes, I exist, otherwise how could I be able to feel myself?"; "If I didn't exist, then I

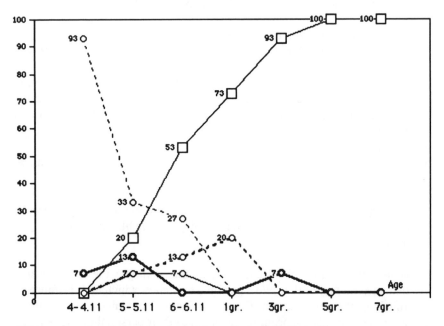

Children who acknowledged that they might not in fact exist (—o—).
Children who denied that this was possible and (1) gave no grounds or produced tautological and transductive justifications (- -o- -), (2) said that it was not possible for them to have subjective experiences of any sort and not to exist at the moment of having the experiences (—□—), (3) said that their experiences were so clear and obvious that it was not possible for them not to exist (—o—), (4) produced other types of justifications (- -o- -).

FIG. 15. Percentages of children producing answers in response to Question 3 regarding the possibility of a child not existing in the domain of everyday reality at the moment of being asked.

wouldn't be able to think or sleep"; "If I didn't exist, how would I be able to have the dream that I don't exist?"; "If I didn't exist, then nothing would seem to me, nobody cannot have dreams"; "If there were no myself I would not be able to feel that I am"; "I would not be able to imagine that I exist"; "If there is something that appears to be, then there must be somebody to whom this appears". Grounds like these were provided by most 6-year-olds and older children (increase 4 years to 6 years: $\chi^2 = 8.35$, $P < 0.004$). The rest of the subjects tried to support their opinions in various ways, all producing justifications different from those based on "cogito": some referred to the clarity of their self-perceptions ("I exist because I am sitting here right now"); others appealed to adults' opinions ("Mum told me that if a person is on Earth then it is for life"); still others pointed to the fact that such a long dream was impossible and, therefore, what they were seeing and feeling at the moment was not a dream but reality.

Questions 4–6 were similar to Question 3, but they investigated the possibility of doubting one's personal existence in the domains of reality where the limitations of everyday reality were relaxed (play) or absent (a dream). Question 5 examined the possibility of acknowledging one's non-existence when one has no conscious state at all.

So, is it possible to have a dream in which the author of the dream does not exist? At first glance the answer is obvious: anything can occur in dreams. Nevertheless, many of the children objected to this idea: "I cannot see this in my dream because if I didn't exist the world would be empty and there would be no people in this world"; "What kind of dream would it be? This would mean there will be no dreams at all if I didn't exist"; "If there is nobody, then there is nothing to dream about"; "All the dreams—they are still your dreams, even if you watch them as though from the outside, even if you have a dream without you acting in it ... otherwise you simply won't have any dreams" (increase 4 years to 6 years: $\chi^2 = 5.71$, $P < 0.01$).

In the domain of play, which is closer to everyday reality than the domain of dreams, any possibility of doubting one's personal existence was denied by most children aged 6 years and older (increase 4 years to 6 years: $\chi^2 = 11.25$, $P < 0.001$) with most of the children offering similar arguments: "You can't play such a game, because if we don't exist we cannot play"; "How can we play something if there are no ourselves?"; "When people create rules for a play, then that is it—they exist already"; "Somebody has to play the game—nobody cannot play"; "No, how can we imagine that we don't exist?"; "Look, we've got legs and hands, and if we are to play such a game, where would we hide our hands?" Other types of arguments, such as an appeal to other people's existence or self-perception, were in the minority.

Paradoxically, an even larger number of children denied the possibility of personal non-existence in their responses to Question 5 (sleeping without dreams). Here the possibility of doubting one's personal existence was rejected by the majority of children in all age groups, apart from the oldest ones (decrease 7 years to 13 years: $\chi^2 = 6.02$, $P < 0.02$). Most preschoolers provided no grounds for their answers, whereas most schoolchildren once more appealed to the argument which was closest to "cogito ergo sum", either viewing sleeping without dreams as a certain state of consciousness ("Yet I am asleep, therefore I exist"; "I still am, I exist, I am lying in my bed"; "If I can be in my bed, therefore I exist") or as a temporary break in a stream of such conscious states ("I am, I am asleep, but I don't disappear anywhere"; "I exist, I am lying in my bed seeing no dreams, but then I wake up and see something, right?"; "I exist, because sometimes I wake up during the night, and if I wake up—I am, am I not?"). In both cases, the children revealed their inability either to imagine a subject who has no conscious states or to get to grips with the idea that such an absence means termination of the "subject–object" division and, therefore, the cessation of the subject's existence. In both cases, the children's argumentation was based not on the conscious states (or the absence of such states) of the imaginative subject who is "sleeping without dreams", but on their own "here and now" conscious states. Lastly, other types of arguments given in response to this question were as follows: (1) appealing to the clear and distinctive character of self-perception ("I am, I can still feel that I exist even if I have no dreams whatsoever"; "I exist because I feel it, there is this special feeling that I am") and (2) referring to the fact of other people's existence ("I exist because you and all the people exist, and I exist too").

Yet, as is obvious from Fig. 16, a large number of subjects acknowledge the possibility of their non-existence in the domains of dreams or play. Nevertheless, while acknowledging that a person can see a dream in which he or she does not figure personally and play a game "as if it seems to us that we exist but in reality we don't", the majority of the children used accompanying statements that these assumptions were conventional ("as though"), but not real. Obviously, the children felt that answers to Questions 4–6 implicated a subjects' presence in two areas of reality at one time: in the sphere of everyday reality (i.e. at the moment when the conversation was taking place) and in the spheres of dreams and play. In those spheres of reality in which logical control is relaxed or absent altogether, there are situations where it is possible for a subject to be unaware of his or her own activity ("Yes, because I can see a dream in which I am not acting but some other people are acting there"; "Yes, you can play such a game but only … as a fantasy"; "In play everything can happen but in reality this cannot happen"; "You cannot play this game really, but you can in your imagination"; "You can play this, but when you wake up—you still exist"); while acknowledging this, the children were nevertheless sure that "really and truly" they existed.

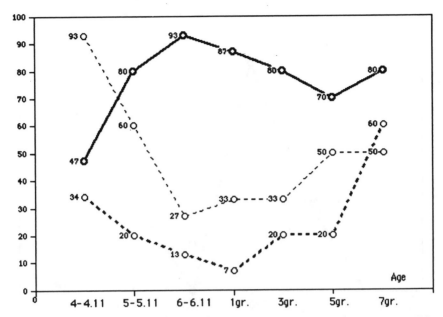

Children who acknowledged that they might not in fact exist (1) in their dreams (—o—), (2) in their play (- -o- -), and (3) when they have no experiences of any kind (- -o- -).

FIG. 16.   Percentages of children producing answers regarding the possibility of a child not existing in his or her dreams (Question 4), play (Question 6), or when he or she has no experience of any kind (Question 5).

The same was the case regarding the question of sleeping without dreams. Some of the children did acknowledge that at that moment they did not exist, but they too accompanied the acknowledgements with comments that it was not "really so" ("I don't exist but ... in reality I do"; "I do not exist during this state, but when I wake up I exist again"; "I do not exist for myself at that time, but for other people I do"; "It would seem to me that there is no myself and there is darkness only, but when I wake up I can touch my body and see that I exist"; "I do not exist for myself, I somehow ... go out of myself, but from the outside, if you have a look at me, I exist").

The results of the replication study in Britain revealed that there were no significant differences between the Russian and British children's answers with regard to questions about their own existence at the moment of interrogation. The overwhelming majority of the British children of all age groups emphatically denied that it was possible for them not to exist (see Fig. 17), and produced arguments similar to those given by their Russian peers.

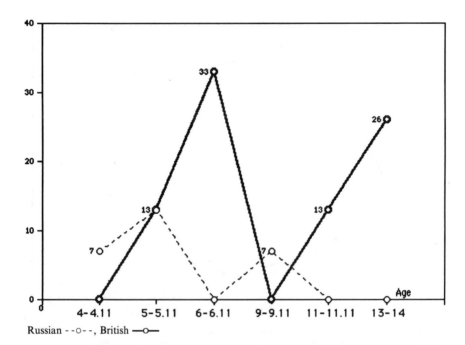

Russian - -o- -, British —o—

FIG. 17. Percentages of Russian and British children who acknowledged the possibility of doubting their own existence at the moment of being asked.

The British children's answers were, however, different from those of the Russian children regarding their personal non-existence in the domains of the mind other than everyday reality. Thus, 5-, 6-, and 9-year-old British children were significantly less inclined to acknowledge that they could not exist in their dreams than their Russian peers, as were British 13- and 14-year-olds with regard to the possibility of them not existing in states where all subjective activity was absent (see Fig. 18). However, more British than Russian 6-year-olds admitted that they might not exist during imaginative role play (Fig. 18). The fact that cultural differences only appeared with regard to unusual states of mind (play, dreams, and the absence of conscious states) and were absent as far as everyday reality was concerned, supports further the conclusion that a subject's personal existence within everyday reality is viewed as a fundamental and unquestionable truth which is independent of age or cultural differences.

The results uncovered some curious facts, however. First, they confirmed the fundamental and stable character of children's beliefs in their personal existence (see Dialogue 1): not only in response to direct questioning as to their doubt of personal existence, but also indirect suggestions that, under

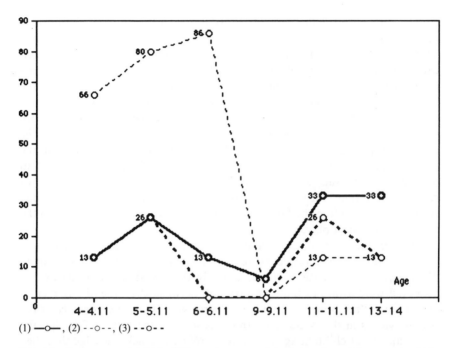

FIG. 18. Percentages of British children who acknowledged that they might not exist (1) in their dreams, (2) in their play, and (3) while having no subjective experiences of any kind.

certain circumstances (dream, play, sleeping without dreams), personal existence can be doubted. Both types of questioning were answered negatively by almost all subjects.

Second, the dialogue revealed a new type of argumentation that many children used in order to prove the fact of their personal existence. When asked to provide grounds for their positive answer to the question "Do you exist or not?" in Dialogue 1, most schoolchildren simply appealed to the clear and distinctive character of their self-perceptions, which they viewed as reliable proof of their personal existence. In contrast, in this dialogue, in which it was suggested that their perceptions can be misleading, most children introduced a new form of argument that was very close to "cogito ergo sum". Interestingly, the children invented this type of proof quite independently of the experimenter. The 5-year-olds were the youngest to point out that *thinking* (doubting, feeling, experiencing, perceiving, etc.) was identical to *being*. With advancing age, the frequency of such answers grows, and the formulations of "cogito" become more mature and free from any naturalistic flavour (for example, from the identification of being with *physical being* only).

The strength of the children's belief in the fact of their personal existence was also evident from their answers to Questions 4–6, which took the conversation into the domains of reality in which the boundaries of every-day reality were relaxed (play, dream) or absent (sleeping without dreams). Thus, most of the children allowed for the possibility of their personal non-existence in the domain of dreams (perhaps taking their personal experiences of dreaming into account); however, almost all of them stressed the illusory character of the dream reality and pointed out that "in reality" they still existed. In the domain of play, the possibility of personal non-existence was acknowledged by a significantly smaller number of subjects, and the arguments provided made it clear that the children were aware of the impossibility of eliminating reflection during play. Indeed, in contrast to dreams, play presupposes a subject's parallel acting in two domains of reality at one time—in the domain of play and in the domain of everyday reality—and therefore the fact of personal existence remains obvious to the subject involved in play.

The fact that a significant number of subjects in all age groups, though with reservations, acknowledged that they might not exist in dreams or in play, requires explanation. It was unlikely that children as young as 5–9 years old were aware of the necessary link between the state of any mental activity (e.g. "doubting", "thinking", "perceiving") and the existence of the person who is in that state. That this was so is clear from the fact that the vast majority of children aged 4–11 years refused to acknowledge that they don't exist when they have no mental state at all (see Fig. 12). How did they come to the conclusion that in dreams or in play (in which they obviously did have certain mental activities) they might not exist? A plausible explanation for this is the way the children understood the question. When saying "I may not exist in play or dream", the children may have viewed themselves not as those who played the game or had the dream, but as the characters in the play or the dream. Clearly, the children may have experienced dreams in which they didn't act as characters; they may also have played games in which they impersonated individuals other than themselves. It follows from the justifications the children used to back their judgements, that it was in this sense that they acknowledged themselves not existing.

As for the condition in which the children were supposed not to have any mental state at all (sleeping without dreams), most of the children denied that they did not exist in this condition; the number of negative answers for this condition significantly exceeded those for play ($z = 6.6$, $P < 0.05$) and dreams ($z = 4.7$, $P < 0.05$).[7] Although every child enters into this state periodically, unlike play and dreams nothing is experienced and no trace of it is left in memory; therefore, understanding that in this state a subject does not exist for him- or herself can only be based on the child's ability to clearly see the relationship between "being" and "thinking". This was exactly what most 4- to 11-year-olds lacked and only the 13-year-olds managed to get to grips with this "negative mirror image" of "cogito ergo sum" (that is, grasping the idea that "a subject having no subjective states" means that the subject does not exist for him- or herself).

There may be a misunderstanding here that Descartes' procedure aimed to make a normal person doubt his or her own existence. This is not the case; just the opposite in fact. The purpose of Descartes' procedure was to show the subject that his or her belief in his or her personal existence is not an ordinary kind of belief, but a kind of belief which is undeniably and really true—something that can only be achieved through the (unsuccessful) attempt to put this fundamental belief in doubt.

As in the previous dialogues, although the children's unanimous denial of the possibility of their personal non-existence in everyday reality may seem to add nothing to the trivial belief of a normal person in his or her own existence, it adds a new quality to this belief, as it convinces the person that this belief is undeniably true even if questioned and is not a kind of dogmatic belief acquired through pressure from outside.

DIALOGUE 4: THE ACKNOWLEDGEMENT OF THE CONCEPTUAL DIFFERENCE AND EMPIRICAL INSEPARABLE UNITY BETWEEN MIND AND BODY

In contrast to other "Cartesian structures", the fundamental difference between the human body and the human mind has received some attention in developmental psychology. The distinction between these categories is one of the most prominent fundamental structures of the European world outlook, and has been incorporated into the system of semantic meanings, concepts, fine arts, and other cultural structures. Piaget was the first to try to demonstrate empirically the fact that as a child grows older, he or she begins to differentiate between mental states (e.g. dreams) and physical objects that are often confused by younger children (Piaget, 1929/1983, 1962). In his studies, however, children's theories about mental and physical phenomena were examined separately and were not linked to the "body–mind" relationship proper.

This problem was raised directly in the study by Johnson and Wellman (1982), who found that children's concepts about the "ontological status" of certain mental and brain functions change with age. Thus, primary schoolchildren (7–11 years) assumed much more frequently than pre-schoolers that only the brain participates in acts of sensation, behavioural acts and in involuntary acts (coughing, sneezing), whereas the "mind" is only involved in "higher mental acts" (e.g. thinking, memory, feeling). The number of children who viewed the brain as something physical and the mind as non-physical was found to increase considerably with age. Although this study was a pioneering one, it suffered certain methodological limitations: first, the criterion used for distinguishing between the physical and the mental was only one of many possible (accessibility or inaccessibility of phenomena to sensations); second, the emphasis of the study was on statistical comparisons between numbers of positive answers ("yes" or "no") given to standard questions at the expense of qualitative analysis of grounds given by the children. In another study (Johnson, 1990), elementary schoolchildren (older than 7 years) were shown to acquire understanding of the brain as the locus of psychological attributes and identity. Even more optimistic results were obtained by Inagaki and Hatano (1993), who found 4- and 5-year-olds to be able to distinguish between certain bodily and mental properties and realise that bodily organs function independently of a person's conscious intentions.

Although the present dialogue was based on the criteria and logic of Descartes, in certain aspects it can be viewed as a development and extension of the above-mentioned studies. It tested the children's capacity (1) to note the inapplicability of categorical attributes of matter (form, position, movement in space, nutrition, mass, divisibility, accessibility to sense organs, etc.) to mental phenomena; (2) to ascribe to mental phenomena properties and functions that belong to them (such as knowledge, thinking, imagination, sensation); and (3) to understand the empirically obvious inseparable unity between the subject's body and the subject's mind.

As mental phenomena, the categories "I" and "thought" were used in this dialogue.[8] Since "I" is related both to the body and to the mind of a person (see, for example, Kon, 1978), the questions were posed in such a way as to determine whether the child was able to distinguish between the above-mentioned aspects and, if so, then to which of them (the mental or the physical) he or she tended to associate his or her "I". The following questions were asked in this dialogue:

Part 1. Physical attributes: Conceptual relationships between the notion of the body and the notion of "I" (thoughts)

1. Tell me please, do you exist, yes or no?
2. Can you show me what you are?
3. So, your body is you, isn't it? And your hand—is it you as well? And your finger—is it you, too?
4. And your "I"—is it you, yes or no?
5. Tell me now, your "I" and your body, are they one and the same thing or are they not? What is the difference?
6. Can you draw your body on a sheet of paper, yes or no? What shape is it? Does it have a square shape or a round shape?
7. And can you draw your "I"? What shape does it have—a round shape or a square shape?
8. Can you draw your thoughts? What colour are they?

9. Where is your body at the moment? Is it sitting in the chair?
10. And where is your "I" and your thoughts at the moment? Are they sitting in the chair as well?
11. Can your body be thrown up in the air?
12. Can your "I" and your thoughts be thrown up in the air?
13. What is the weight of your body?
14. And what is the weight of your "I" and your thoughts?
15. What does your body eat?
16. And what does your "I" eat?
17. And what do your thoughts eat?
18. Can you see your body and touch your body?
19. Can you touch your "I"?
20. Can you touch your thoughts?
21. Can you cut a small piece (nails, hairs) from your body?
22. Can you cut a small piece from your "I"? Can you cut a small piece from your thoughts?

Part 2. Mental manifestations: Conceptual relationships between the notion of the body and the notion of the "I" (thoughts)

23. Do you know some verse? Who knows this verse: your "I" or your body? Who knows this verse: your thoughts or your brain?
24. Can you think of something now? What is it you are thinking of? Who is thinking about..., your "I" or your body? Who is thinking about..., your thoughts or your brain?
25. Can you imagine an elephant now? And who is imagining the elephant, your "I" or your body? Who is imagining the elephant, your thoughts or your brain?
26. Can you see me? And who is seeing me now, your "I" or your body? Who is seeing me now, your thoughts or your brain?

Part 3. The body and "I" (thoughts): The ontological link

27. Tell me, have you ever been ill? And who was ill, your body or your "I"? Who was ill, your body or your thoughts? Can your "I" get ill? And can your thoughts get ill?
28. Tell me, if someone's body died, would the "I" of this person die as well? And what about the person's thoughts, would they die as well?
29. So, if someone's body ceases to exist, his or her "I" and thoughts cease to exist either, don't they?
30. Tell me, can a cat make a scratch on your body?
31. And can the cat make a scratch on your "I"? Can it make a scratch on your thoughts?

32. If the cat made a scratch on you, who is it who feels pain, your "I" or your body? Who feels pain, your thoughts or your body? Can your "I" feel pain? And can your thoughts feel pain?
33. When you fall asleep, does your "I" disappear or does it remain? And what about your thoughts, do they disappear or remain if you are asleep?
34. When you fall asleep, does your body disappear, or does it stay? Where is it? What does it do?
35. If you are asleep without dreaming, does your "I" exist or does it not exist? And what about your thoughts, do they exist if you are asleep without dreaming?

Let us briefly consider the results, placing emphasis on the children's comparisons between the body and the "I". Although the children treated "I" and thoughts differently (with "I" being viewed as something closer to the body than thoughts), most of the differences were insignificant, so that average numbers of answers with respect to the "I" and thoughts taken together are presented in Figs. 19 and 20.

With regard to Part 1 of the dialogue (the discrimination between the attributes of the body and mental phenomena), the key questions bearing on the distinction were Questions 5–22. Starting with the 5-year-olds, the majority said that the body and the "I" were not the same; however, not all of them were able to discriminate between the properties of mental phenomena and those of the body (see Figs. 19 and 20).

The children fell into two groups (Fig. 19) with regard to their answers to questions bearing on the categorisation of such attributes as form, position, movement in space, mass, nutrition, accessibility to sense organs (seeing and touching), and divisibility. The children in the first group attributed all these material properties exclusively to the body, denying that they could be attributed to the "I" and to thoughts, whereas the children in the second group related them both to the body and to mental phenomena.[9] Thus, most 4- to 6-year-olds said that "I" and thoughts could be drawn, and even named their shapes and colours, though without providing arguments in support of this (the "I" for these children was "round" or "square", and thoughts were "blue", "yellow", etc.). The number of such children fell sharply with age.

Children who denied that mental phenomena had shape (increase 5 years to 6 years: $\chi^2 = 7.35$, $P < 0.01$) almost always gave some reasons to support their view. Most 6-year-olds just stated that it was not possible to depict the "I" or thoughts graphically ("'I' is a letter, and you can say it but you can't draw it"; "'I' is a word, you can't see a word. Thoughts also cannot be drawn, since they are words and talking"). Others supported this assertion with the argument that the "I" did not exist ("The 'I' is all these things, not

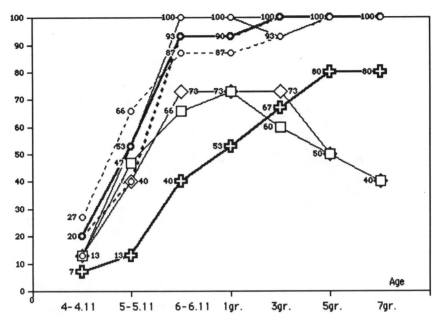

Children who attributed shape (qq. 6–8, - -o- -), spatial location (qq. 9 & 10, —□—), displacement (qq. 11 & 12, —◇—), mass (qq. 13 & 14, —✛—), nutrition (qq. 15–17, —o—), accessibility to sense organs (qq. 18–20, —o—), and divisibility (qq. 21 & 22, - -o- -) only to the body, with the rest of the children attributing these properties both to the body and to the "I" (thoughts).

FIG. 19.   Percentages of children producing answers in response to questions regarding the distinction between attributes of the body and those of the "I" (thoughts).

living things, but playthings; you can only say 'I', there are no such things"; " 'I' is nothing, you can only write down the letter 'I' "). Still others said that "I" existed, but was invisible ("No, you can't draw it, because we can not see it and imagine it"; "Well, the body is a kind of object, and the 'I' is inside of me, it isn't really something, for example you can't see it"). Finally, some of the children tried to describe the nature of this invisible reality ("No, you can't draw my 'I', because it only can show itself up in my good deeds and bad deeds"; " 'I'—it is my interests and fancies, how can I draw my fancies?"). The children reasoned about the impossibility of drawing thoughts in the same way.

In discussing the spatial location of the body, most children simply agreed with the experimenter, saying that it was "sitting on the chair". In contrast to the question about shape, not only most 5- and 6-year-olds but 30–60% of the older children said that "I" had a position in space and was either "sitting on the chair" together with the body or located "somewhere

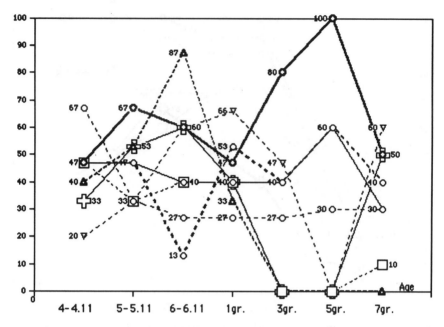

Children who attributed capacities of knowledge (q. 23, - -o- -), thinking (q. 24, —o—), imagination (q. 25, - -o- -), and perception (q. 26, —o—) only to the body (to the brain). Children who attributed capacities of knowledge (- -△- -), thinking (—✛—), imagination (- -▽- -), and perception (- -□- -) only to the "I" and thoughts. Children who attributed the above-mentioned capacities both to the body (brain) and to the mental entities (to the "I" and thoughts)—the rest of the children.

FIG. 20.   Percentages of children producing answers in response to Questions 23–26 regarding the attribution of mental functions to the body or to the mental entities "I" and thoughts.

near" the body ("My 'I' is around me ... well, it is sitting here, but not on the chair, but elsewhere; you simply can't think of it like that; it's something ... you can't grasp it, but it's in the mind"). Yet most of the children denied that "I" had a location in space (increase 4 years to 6 years: $\chi^2 = 6.80$, $P < 0.01$): some said it was because the "I" simply didn't exist ("It is nowhere, no matter how long you look for it, it is nowhere"), whereas others pointed out that the "I" was "in the word", "in the voice", "in the mind" (i.e. in those entities that had no specific location).

    The question about the capacity to move was answered in a similar fashion. All children acknowledged that the body could be tossed in the air. About half of the subjects said that their "I" could move in space and most added that their "I" would be moving together with their body (" 'I' will be together with my body, you can't take it away, the body is somehow attached to it"; "The 'I' can swing; my grandad would take my body and toss it in the air"); some identified movement of the "I" with the movement of sound ("When I say 'I', I am tossing it in the air"). Those who denied that "I" could be moved in space (increase 4 years to 6 years: $\chi^2 = 8.68$, $P < 0.004$) referred either to the fact that "I" did not exist ("It seems that it exists, but it does not") or that it is a kind of extraspatial reality (" 'I' is only a letter"; "It is something not physical, something unusual, invisible"). Finally, two of the subjects admitted only the possibility of an imaginative non-physical movement of the "I" ("If the 'I' wants this it can be tossed in the air together with the body, but if it doesn't wish that, it stays still and the body will be tossed in the air alone"; "Yes, it can move, for example, I will be sitting and thinking that I am flying").

More than half of the subjects ascribed weight to the "I"; some said that "I" weighed as much as the body, while others said that their "I" weighed "very little" (like a bit of down), but nonetheless had a definitive weight ("more than the air", "more than a match"). All these children answered an additional question: "If your 'I' is put on the scales will the scale indicator move or will it stay still?", in the sense that the indicator would move. It was mainly the older preschoolers and schoolchildren who denied that the "I" had weight (increase 4 years to 7 years: $\chi^2 = 5.7$, $P < 0.02$), some on the grounds that "I" did not exist ("It doesn't weigh anything at all, since it doesn't exist, it can only be pronounced"), whereas others pointed to its non-physical nature ("I" is a figure of speech; it doesn't weigh anything at all").

Most 5-year-olds and half the 6-year-olds thought that mental phenomena had the capacity to eat; they said that the "I" and thoughts eat the same as the body, or they simply named various foods. The other children denied that "I" and thoughts could eat (increase, 4 years to 6 years: $\chi^2 = 8.68$, $P < 0.004$); in their reasoning, they again referred either to the fact that the "I" does not exist ("It doesn't eat anything, because it is not real") or that it is not alive ("It doesn't eat anything, it is not a person—my 'I' "); others stressed the "I" had a non-physical nature ("It is a word, and a word doesn't eat anything"). They had similar things to say about thoughts: thoughts do not eat because either they do not exist, or they exist but are not alive, or they are not at all material, though they do, to some extent, depend on a person's eating ("It is the brain that needs eating, and the brain produces our thoughts. If it doesn't eat, thoughts will be stupid and there will be few of them. But thoughts cannot eat, it is the brain").

Many preschoolers believed that "I" and thoughts could be seen and touched, although most older children emphatically denied this (increase 5 years to 6 years: $\chi^2 = 6.70$, $P < 0.01$). Some of the children (mostly the younger ones) thought it impossible for the "I" to be seen and touched, stating that it was hidden under the surface of the body ("It can't be seen and touched, it is in my head"; "You can't open up a person, so how can you touch it?"); others said that "I" didn't exist, whereas others argued that it was non-physical and symbolic ("You can't touch a word, can you? You cannot see or hear how it gets through the mouth"). Finally, a group of children simply pointed out that "I" was inaccessible to sense organs ("It is only space, it's invisible", "It is something that you can't feel"; "It is my range of interests, how can I touch it?"). In discussing the inaccessibility of thoughts to vision and touch, the children used similar arguments.

A small number of children (mainly in the two younger age groups) admitted the divisibility of the "I", although they could not justify their views. Others denied that it was possible to divide the "I" in the corporeal or material sense (increase 4 years to 6 years: $\chi^2 = 8.68$, $P < 0.004$) and produced several kinds of reasons. Preschoolers often referred to the fact that the "I" was hidden under the surface of the body ("No, you can't cut it off because it is in your mouth"); others linked the indivisibility of the "I" to its non-existence ("You can't cut it off, 'I' is only a letter and not some sort of being"). A third kind of argument was that "I" was the material shell of a sign, and that it couldn't be divided ("No, this is a word, and you can't cut anything off the word"). A final group of children described "I" as some kind of ideal reality to which the concept of division is inapplicable ("No, you can't. You can cut off a piece from my 'I' in an abstract sense, perhaps, in some way destroy part of the soul—for example, humiliate a person"; "No, it's impossible. For example, if you cut off a finger, I would remain without my finger, but I will still be myself, my 'I' would remain as it was").

On the whole, the results show a sharp decrease in the number of children investing their "I's" with material attributes, beginning at about 5 or 6 (Fig. 10). From this age on, physical properties were ascribed to mental phenomena by an average 20% of subjects, and characteristically this ascription had to do almost exclusively with the "I" and very seldom with "thoughts". Thus, although some children perceived the body as a full-fledged bearer of all physical attributes and thoughts, as something relatively disconnected from these attributes, "I" in the view of most subjects had an intermediate status: on the one hand, it was something that was non-material and non-physical, whereas on the other, it still had some physical properties (mostly location, capacity for movement, weight and divisibility).

The extent to which various physical attributes were made into mental attributes also varied. The children linked such attributes as shape, nutrition, accessibility to sensations, and divisibility with "I" to a significantly lesser extent than location, displacement, and (however strange it may seem) weight (the difference between these two groups for the total sample was significant: $z = 7.2$, $P < 0.5$).

Now let us consider the children's replies to the questions bearing on the possibility of relating various manifestations and properties of mental activity to the body and to the "I" (thoughts) (Questions 23–26). As our results show (Fig. 20), one group of children related psychological functions mainly to the body, whereas another group viewed them as special characteristics of "I" (thoughts). The age-related dynamics of the children's answers was rather bizarre, with only one stable decrease in the number of children attributing the capacity of having knowledge exclusively to the "I" (thoughts) (6 years to 9 years: $\chi^2 = 19.54$, $P < 0.001$). Basically, among children of school age, the tendency to relate mental activities exclusively to the "I" and thoughts attenuated considerably: there emerged a large group of children who tended to ascribe these attributes to both the body and mental phenomena at the same time (third group). The number of children who ascribed various attributes of mental activity exclusively to the body remained quite high (about 50%).

Let us now look at the reasons given by children in the first group. The children of the two youngest age groups answered the questions in monosyllables, with reasonable justifications being given by 7-year-olds. Some of the children simply noted that thought, vision, imagination, and cognition belonged to the body ("It's the eyes that can see, and they belong to the body"; "It's the brain that can see; thoughts cannot see, because they don't have any eyes"; "It's the eyes that can imagine", etc.). Others pointed out that thoughts and "I" did not exist and were incorporeal, and hence could neither think nor imagine ("The body started to think; thoughts cannot think, they are only there"; "It's the brain which knows something, thoughts cannot have knowledge, because they are air, and air can't have knowledge of anything"; "It's the brain that can see; thoughts cannot see because they are not physical"). The third group referred to the fact that thoughts were passive and derivative of a subject, and hence could not have the attributes of mental activity; it was the subject himself or herself who has these attributes, and the children identified the subject with the head, with the brain, or with the living person in general ("It's the brain that can think; thoughts do not think, they come out when the brain thinks them"; "The brain can know something, and if thoughts lived, they could know something too").

The children in the second group provided two types of argument. Some simply noted the relationship between mental attributes and mental structures ("It is thoughts that think; the body cannot think, because after all it is the body"; "It's thoughts that think, the body cannot think, and the brain cannot think, because the brain is not thoughts"). Others viewed thoughts as an active agent and ascribed mental activities to them, while viewing the brain as a passive "place" ("It's thoughts that have knowledge; the brain has not, because the brain is a bone"; "The brain cannot think because it's a bone, because it can't feel anything"; "It is my thinking that thinks; the brain cannot think, because the brain is the same as the body"). Finally, children in the third group (mainly schoolchildren) expressed criticism about the way the question was posed; instead, they related mental activities to the category of an integral subject ("It is 'I' who knows"; "It is neither the brain nor my thoughts, but 'I' myself who knows this poem"; "Well, the entire head, thoughts and brain, think together"); some of the children simply ascribed mental activities to both thoughts and the body ("My 'I' thinks this, and my brain too"; "The brain thinks, and thoughts too are able to think").

As it can be seen from the above data, two different age-related tendencies are apparent: one towards polarisation of physical attributes and another towards depolarisation of attributes of mental activities. As children grow older, the physical attributes are concentrated increasingly around the pole of the body, while the "I" (thoughts) pole is gradually freed from them. In contrast, attributes of mental activity lose their one-sidedness and are increasingly ascribed to both the body and mental phenomena. Thus, on the one hand, the transition from preschool to school age was accompanied by a liberation of the categories "I" and thoughts from the grips of "corporeality", the children instead becoming aware of them as something different from the category of "body"; on the other hand, the mental activities became increasingly more immersed in "corporeality", since the children of this age began to realise that a close relationship exists between the body and mental phenomena, and that "pure" spiritual activity that does not involve the body is impossible. It can be assumed that these tendencies taken together reveal the formation in a child of an embryonic notion about him- or herself as an integrated subject of activity: the "I" gradually becomes for the child a symbol of a complex unity between his/her body (including his/her brain and sense organs) and his/her mental psychological functions.

Let us now look at Part 3 of the dialogue, which examined the children's concepts about the ontological relationships between the body and mental phenomena. The reader should be reminded here that, in contrast to the relationship between the concepts of "body" and "mind" ("I" thoughts), which is purely theoretical and concerned with abstract definitions rather than with "real things", the ontological relationship between the body and the mind ("I" thoughts) refers to the body and the mind of a real human individual.

With respect to Question 27 regarding the influence of body state on mental phenomena ("I" and thoughts), the children's answers fell into two major groups (Fig. 21). The children in the first group (mainly preschoolers) acknowledged that a morbid state of the body also influences the state of the "I" and thoughts, mainly by making them deteriorate.

Paradoxically, however, most children denied the relationship between illness and mental phenomena (second group; increase 4 years to 11 years: $\chi = 5.58$, $P < 0.02$). Their main argument was that "I" and thoughts are ideal non-physical realities ("It was the body that became ill. The 'I' cannot

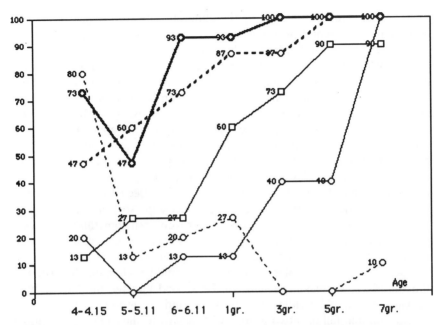

Children who thought that the illness that affects the body of an individual does not affect the individual's "I" (thoughts) (q. 27, - -o- -), with the rest of the children thinking that it does.
Children who thought that the individual's "I" and thoughts remain after the death of the individual's body (q. 29, - -o- -), with the rest of the children thinking that they do not.
Children who believed that physical pain experienced by an individual does not affect the condition of the individual's "I" and thoughts (q. 32, —o—), with the rest of the children thinking that it does.
Children who believed that the individual's body remains while his or her "I" and thoughts disappear if the individual is in a sleeping state (qq. 33 & 34, —o—), with the rest of the children thinking that both the body and the mental entities stay in the sleeping state.
Children who believed that an individual's "I" and thoughts do not exist if the individual is asleep without dreams (q. 35, —□—), with the rest of the subjects thinking that they do.

FIG. 21.   Percentages of children producing answers in response to questions regarding the link between states of the body and mind.

become ill—letters don't get sick"; "Thoughts cannot get sick because they are merely words and sounds contained in the brain; it's the brain that can get sick").

The children answered the questions concerning the influence of physical pain (bodily injury) on the state of the mind in a similar fashion (Questions 30–32). Only a few preschoolers thought that "I" could feel pain; some of the subjects said that pain was felt by the body and the "I" (thoughts) together ("The 'I' and the body feel together"; "My body and my thoughts feel together").

An overwhelming majority of the children, however, denied that pain could influence mental phenomena (increase 5 years to 6 years: $\chi^5 = 5.71$, $P < 0.02$). The grounds for this they saw mainly in the fact that mental entities belong to the symbolic sphere, are invisible, and do not exist in the physical sense ("'I' and thoughts cannot feel pain because you only think these things, they do not exist"; "The brain can feel pain if you hit it hard enough, but thoughts cannot; they are space, thinking"). Other subjects specified that thoughts do not feel pain, but can think about it as though reflecting it in their "mirror" ("Thoughts can only think about pain, they can imagine pain"; "It is the body that feels pain, thoughts cannot. They cannot feel pain, but they can think about that pain"). Finally, a third group of children denied that "I" and thoughts can be affected by physical pain, but they specified that mental entities can feel some sort of "psychological pain" ("Thoughts can feel pain a bit, when you wish something, but what you want doesn't happen. For instance, you want to become an engineer, but they don't accept you at the college"). Arguments of the first type were characteristic of preschoolers and young and middle schoolchildren (first to third grades), whereas arguments of the second and the third types were provided by the older children (fifth, sixth, and seventh grades).

The children fell into two groups with regard to their judgements about the relationships between body and mind in the state of sleeping (Questions 33 and 34). The majority of children (the first group) said that both the body and "I" (thoughts) existed during sleep, with the mental phenomena either taking the shape of dreams ("The body is in the bed and sleeps, it is lying there and breathing. The 'I' too remains, it is showing dreams"; "The body is sleeping in the bed. The 'I' stays too, because I can see dreams, and I can think without thoughts") or being in a latent potential state ("The body remains under the covers, and the 'I' remains too; it is silent because I can't say anything when I am asleep"; "The 'I' too remains, in the mouth; that's where it lies"). Other children (the second group; increase 7 years to 13 years: $\chi^2 = 14.75$, $P < 0.001$) said that the body remained during sleep but that mental entities disappeared ("The body remains in the bed, and the 'I' disappears: my 'I' are my interests, and they disappear at night").

Similar age dynamics showed up in children's replies to the same question (Question 35) posed in a more emphatic way (the existence of the "I" and thoughts during sleep without dreams). Most of the preschoolers and some of the schoolchildren said that mental entities existed in this state as well: some argued that mental entities were fixed in the brain and existed in the form of these material traces ("Thoughts depend on the brain, but the brain doesn't disappear during sleep"; "I remember these thoughts. They are not manifested, but they exist if I remember them"); others referred to the indestructibility of mental entities so long as the body was alive ("Thoughts exist, so long as I am not dead ... thoughts remain anyway"; "Thoughts must remain. If they cease to be in me, then how will I be able to think about them the next time?"; "The 'I' remains in me even if I'm sleeping; I am alive"). In contrast, some of the preschoolers and the majority of the schoolchildren (increase 6 years to 11 years: $\chi^2 = 4.80$, $P < 0.05$) confirmed the existence of the body but denied that mental entities existed during sleep without dreams ("The 'I' doesn't exist, because when I have dreams I am thinking about something, and when I am sleeping soundly, I'm not thinking about anything").

Finally, let us examine the children's replies to Questions 28 and 29 about the relationships between the existence of the body and the existence of the mental entities of a subject. The first group included children who said that the "I" and thoughts persisted even after the death of the body. Interestingly, this group included mainly preschoolers and was poorly represented among schoolchildren (decrease 4 years to 5 years: $\chi^2 = 10.84$, $P < 0.001$). Four- and 5-year-olds gave no justifications for their opinions, simply stating that the "I" remains ("The 'I' remains; I don't know where it is, may be in the stomach"; "It can remain in your mouth"), whereas the older children argued that since mental entities were non-material, they could not die ("The 'I' stays, but the body dies; the 'I' is always there". *Experimenter:* "Where?" "In my will." *Experimenter:* "And can it live without the body?" "Yes, it goes out into the air." "The 'I' remains; it can't die because it isn't anything. It goes to another person, to its neighbour, and maybe even to some unknown person." "The 'I' doesn't die, but you never hear from the person again this 'I'." "The 'I' remains in the person's head." *Experimenter:* "But what about the body and the head, do they die?" "Well, they do, but the 'I' ... if a person dies, the 'I' flies away." *Experimenter:* "But where does it go?" "It simply turns into the air, that is it, or it turns into the wind; it is nothing." *Experimenter:* "But do thoughts die?" "No, they fly away somewhere too, that is it." "The 'I' remains around the person." *Experimenter:* "But where it is then?" "The 'I' is in the air; that means that it can go where it wants", etc.).

However, the majority of the children were sure that mental entities died with the body (the second group). The preschoolers and younger schoolchildren simply noted this ("The 'I' dies with the body. You don't see a dead person saying 'I-I-I' "; "It dies with the body, because the 'I' is the person who is dying. Thoughts die too, because the person dies and his thoughts cannot think any more"). Some schoolchildren specified that it was only individual mental entities that die, although they could remain in a "converted" alienated form ("If thoughts were written down, they stay"; "Thoughts stay, like Tsiolkovsky. He invented spaceships, and died, and after him Korolev continued his work. But a person's feelings die, because the person can't feel them any longer").

Parts of this dialogue were replicated with the British subjects.[10] In this study, questions about conceptual (6 and 7 about shape; 9 and 10 about location; 11 and 12 about displacement; 13 and 14 about mass; 15 and 16 about nutrition; 18 and 19 about accessibility to senses; 20 and 21 about divisibility) and ontological (28 about what happens to an individual's "I" and thoughts when the individual's body died; 32 about whether the "I" of the individual can experience physical pain) relationships between the body and the mind were put to the groups of 4- and 5-year-old children, 7- and 9-year old children, and 11- and 13-year-old children. The first group consisted of 10 white children, and the other two groups included 10 white children and 10 Asian children. Each of the groups had equal numbers of males and females.

The method used was the same as in the original study with the Russian children; however, as already mentioned, instead of the word "I" (which in the English language orally resembles "eye"), the word "self" was used for designation of the mental entities. To avoid confusion between "self" used in this context and the common term "yourself", the word "self" was emphasised by the interviewer.

The comparisons between the data on understanding the conceptual relationships between bodily and mental phenomena by Russian (with regard to "I") and British children are shown in Fig. 22 and Fig. 23. As can be seen from these two figures, there were no significant differences between Russian and British 4- and 5-year-olds; however, all the physical qualities studied (shape, spacial location, displacement, mass, nutrition, accessibility to senses, and divisibility) were attributed solely to the body by Russian 7- and 8-year-olds significantly more often then by their British peers. The 11- and 13-year-old British children also proved to be less aware of the non-physical nature of "self" than the Russian children of the same age: shape, nutrition, accessibility to senses, and divisibility were attributed to both "self" and "body" significantly more often by the British children than the Russian children.

The stronger awareness of the body–mind relationship by the Russian children can be explained either by certain cultural factors which made it easier for the Russian children to appreciate the non-physical nature of "mental entities", or by the linguistic differences between the terms employed in the dialogues ("I" for the Russian children and "self" for the British children). To clarify this, 12 British adult subjects (6 white, 6 Asian) were asked the same questions as the British children. It was assumed that if the differences between the responses of the Russian and British children were linguistically (rather than culturally) based, then the responses given by the British adults would be closer to the responses of the British children than those of the Russian children, since linguistic peculiarities of the term "self" are likely to be felt by children and adults to the same extent. If, however, it was cultural factors that made it more difficult for the British children to appreciate the body–mind parallelism, then the adults could be

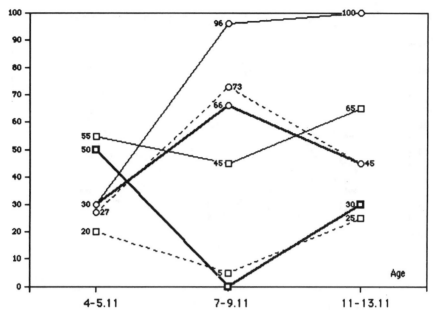

Russian -○-, British -□-
Shape —, spatial location —, displacement - -

FIG. 22.   Percentages of Russian and British children who attributed shape, spatial location, and displacement to the body alone, with the remaining children attributing these properties to the body and to the "I" (Self).

expected to produce answers similar to those given by the Russian children, as the latter reflected the rationalistic views common to all Western countries (in particular, that mental entities possess no physical characteristics). Indeed, both the Russian and British cultures have a European origin and can be expected to share fundamental metaphysical beliefs, with a strong conceptual body–mind parallelism being one of them.

The results of the comparison between the responses given by the Russian 11- and 13-year-olds and the British adults (Fig. 24) showed that the adults acknowledged even more strongly than the Russian teenagers that psychological entities ("self") have no physical characteristics. This makes the "linguistic" explanation of the relatively slow progress of British children in their awareness of the body–mind distinction unlikely; rather, the difference between the Russian and British children's answers ought to be explained by cultural factors. One possible explanation is the fact that Russian school education (and the general psychosocial background of Russian culture that has been strongly influenced by Marxist and materialistic ideas) in the early 1980s was strongly atheistically and rationalistically

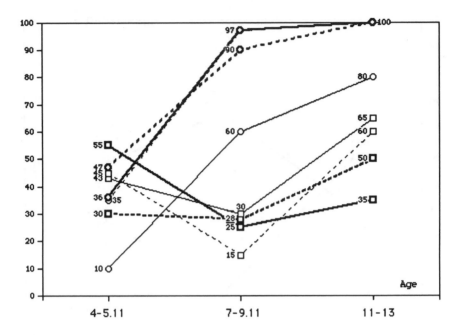

Russian -○-, British -□-
Mass —, nutrition —, accessibility to senses - -, divisibility - - -

FIG. 23. Percentages of Russian and British children who attributed mass, nutrition, accessibility to the senses, and divisibility to the body alone, with the remaining children attributing these properties to the body and to the "I" (Self).

oriented, which implies that stress was placed on the physical structure of the world, whereas all sorts of "animation" of natural forces were strongly discouraged. As concepts like "I", "soul" and "thoughts" are definitely of a non-physical nature, their disseminating to physical objects was inevitably emphasised in the minds of children who were experiencing this kind of education.

In contrast, in the British culture, which has never been ideologically biased by materialism, stress on the universal power of matter was less significant than in Soviet culture; hence, the fundamental difference between "self" and "body" didn't seem to be of major importance. This may have been reflected in school curriculums and in the general knowledge about what "self" is that children in this culture were getting from their social environment. Yet, the difference between "self" and "body" is acknowledged in British culture too; this was revealed by the fact that British adults were very particular in not allowing "self" to have any physical attributes.

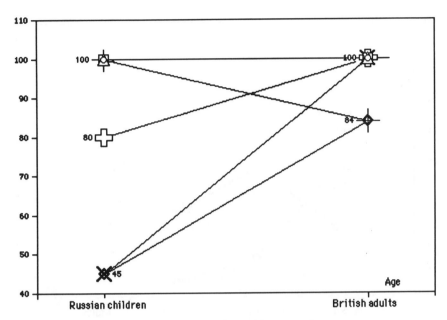

Shape —○—, spatial location —◇—, displacement ✕, mass —⊕—,
nutrition +, accessibility to senses —△—, divisibility —□—

FIG. 24. Percentages of Russian 11- to 13-year-olds and British adults who attributed shape, spatial location, displacement, mass, nutrition, accessibility to the senses, and divisibility to the body alone, with the remainder attributing these properties to the body and to the "I" (Self).

This explanation gains some support from the fact that a significantly smaller number of Russian children in both age groups attributed a posthumous existence to the "I" than did the British children (see Fig. 25). In this case, too, the answers of British adults were closer to those given by Russian schoolchildren than British schoolchildren. The fact that significantly more Russian schoolchildren than British schoolchildren thought that physical pain did not affect "I" ("self") testified in the same direction; namely, that among Russian schoolchildren the awareness of the body–mind distinction was stronger than among their British peers. In this case, however, British adults showed a pattern of answers that was closer to that of British children than to that of the Russian children, which makes it difficult to choose between the "linguistic artefact" and the "cultural background" explanations.

Yet the overall tendency of the data was in favour of the "cultural background" hypothesis. It is interesting, however, that the cultural factors mentioned are selective and predominantly target children at school age. British and Russian preschoolers (4- and 5-year-olds) produced similar

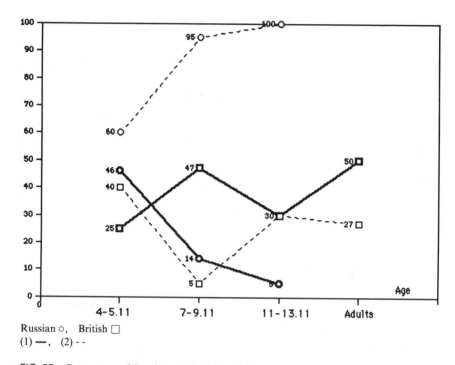

Russian ○,   British □
(1) ─ ,   (2) - -

FIG. 25.   Percentages of Russian and British subjects who (1) thought that an individual's "I" (Self) remains after the death of that individual's body, with the remainder not believing so, and (2) thought that the physical pain experienced by an individual does not affect the state of that individual's "I" (Self), with the remainder believing that it does.

answers and revealed a rather poor awareness of the distinction between "I" ("self") and body, whereas British adults showed results that were quite close to those of Russian schoolchildren. Another interesting fact is that British adults (as well as British schoolchildren) were significantly more "dualistically minded" in their discussion of the ontological relationships between "self" and "body" than the Russian schoolchildren; suffice it to say that 50% of British adults stated their belief in the posthumous existence of the individual's "self". This may suggest that the general cultural background in Britain, which is deeply rooted in Christian mythology, encourages "ontological dualism" to a significantly greater extent than "conceptual dualism", whereas the materialistic and atheistic cultural background of the former Soviet society stressed conceptual dualism while suppressing ontological dualism.

On the whole, two tendencies could be traced in children's judgements about the relationships between the body and mental phenomena. On the one hand, the children's growing awareness of the autonomy of mental entities and of their relative independence from the state of the body (i.e. illness and physical pain) became more apparent with age. The school-children, and the older ones in particular, began to regard mental phenomena as non-physical, ideal entities which are not subject to the body's distress, although they are capable of reflecting it. At the same time, the children developed the idea of a subjective type of distress, which is fundamentally different from physical distress.

On the other hand, along with the development of notions about the relative autonomy of mental phenomena, the tendency towards comprehension of the indissoluble connection between the existence of the body and the existence of the mind became more distinct with age. Whereas the preschoolers and first graders admitted the possibility that individual mental phenomena could continue to exist after the death of the body, almost none of the older children believed this.

Thus, with regard to the relationships between the categories of the corporeal and mental, there was a quite clear tendency towards differentiation between these categories in the children's consciousness, a breakdown of syncretic unity and a delimitation of notions about the body and mental phenomena as opposites. However, when the children reasoned about the "existence" of the body and the mind, it was just as apparent that they were becoming more and more aware, as they grew older, of the inseparable unity between the body and mental phenomena.

With respect to the latter assumption, there is one fact in the data that needs explanation; namely, that most schoolchildren admitted the possibility that a living body could exist temporarily independently of mental phenomena (sleeping without dreams). This contradictory fact can find a plausible explanation if one takes into consideration that the correct answer to the question (that is that for the subject in this special condition both mind and body cease to exist) requires a strong capacity for decentration and for a distinction to be made between the position of a subject who actually is in this state and one who is talking about the subject sleeping without dreams. It can be assumed that in reasoning about the possibility of the body of a sleeping subject existing during sleep without dreams, none of the children were able to place themselves in the position of the subject in question—one more manifestation of the characteristic of the child's mind described by Piaget as "egocentrism" (Piaget, 1986). Instead, the children based their responses on their actual position of an observer, for whom, of course, the body of the person sleeping without dreams does exist.

However, with regard to the question of a body that dies, decentration of the mental position relative to the body was no longer necessary since, with death, the body disappears not only subjectively (for the sleeping subject) but objectively (for other people) as well. This also eliminates the possibility of justifying the further existence of subjective phenomena by referring to their connection to the body (to the memory or to the brain)—a possibility which the children used when they acknowledged that a person who is sleeping without dreams still has subjective reality, but it is just lost "temporarily". Hence, in answering the question, the only possibility of "preserving" mental entities after the body's death may rest on the implicit assumption that "Death is a property of material things, subjective phenomena are not material, hence they are immortal." This argument, explicitly used by Descartes, in children's judgements took the form of placing the "I" (thoughts) in the "air", "space", and so on.

Nevertheless, with respect to the children who argued that "I" and thoughts remain after a person's body has died, an alternative interpretation is possible, according to which these paradoxical replies might have been caused by the special way the young children understand death. As has been shown elsewhere (Childers & Weiner, 1971; Nagy, 1948; Weininger, 1979), for the majority of 3- to 5-year-olds death is not an irreversible state in which all corporeal life stops, but rather a concealed life, a temporary and revocable state. It is possible that for these children "death" is also the state when the "I" and thoughts of a dead person are still alive, whereas for older children, who have a more adequate conception of death, these spiritual entities die at the same time as the body. This assumption needs to be clarified.

Following the pioneering study of Nagy (1948), a number of researchers attempted to study the development of children's conception of death. Most analysed some specific details of children's responses to questions about death, including their ability to understand the characteristics of death, its irrevocability and universality, as well as the fact that death brings about the cessation of corporeal functions (Koocher, 1973, 1974; Safir, 1964; Weininger, 1979; White et al., 1979). The studies (Koocher, 1973; Weininger, 1979) revealed that of the answers children give to the question "What will happen when you die?", some are relevant to the idea of reincarnation (i.e. spiritual immortality). However, in these studies, questions about death and life referred to human individuals as a whole; specific questions about the death of the body or about the death of mental capacities were never asked. Hence, it was unclear whether the children's answers (e.g. "going to heaven") to the above-mentioned question referred to a child's mind (soul) alone or to a child's body as well. It was also unclear whether the "reincarnation" type answers were not a consequence of the children's misconception of death as some kind of concealed life, a misconception that was typical for more than 80% of 5-year-olds and 60% of 9-year-olds (White et al., 1979).

In contrast to the studies discussed above, in this study the question was put in a different way, asking the children about the death of the body and the death of the mental entities separately. If the children's answers were based on the above-mentioned misconception of death, they should have reasoned along the lines that the "I" and thoughts of a dead person remain in the person's dead body (head, brain, etc.). In fact, however, there were only a few such answers; in most of the "reincarnation"-type answers it was suggested that the "I" and thoughts of the dead person "go out" of the body or that they can't die because, unlike the body, they "don't really exist". It should be borne in mind, however, that the study was undertaken in 1980 in a culture with strong atheistic views; no wonder, therefore, that among the "reincarnation"-type answers there was no single answer that would suggest that the "I" or thoughts of a dead person "go to heaven". All this makes the alternative interpretation of the causes of children's specific ("reincarnation"-type) answers most unlikely. It is much more plausible to assume that the children's answers were dictated by the implicit reasoning which was close to that put forward by Descartes. If that were so, why were such answers so rare among the children older than 7 years?

It should be noted that reasoning which implies the idea of "immortality of mind", although quite natural and the foundation of many religious systems around the world, is strongly at odds with the materialistic and physicalistic world outlook. According to the latter, the mind and its manifestations are nothing but products of the activity of the brain, hence they must cease to exist with the extinction of this activity. The installation of materialistic views in children's minds during school education might be responsible for the fact that children advanced in age abandon the idea of the indestructible nature of the human mind.

Another possible explanation is that with age children become more sensitive to the distinction between "the mind" as a concept (a conceptual aspect) and "the mind" as the mind of a concrete human individual (an ontological aspect). As can be seen from Fig. 11, the number of children who view the "I" and thoughts as a reality, distinct from the body (so distinct that even illness or physical injury do not, actually, affect the mental entities), grows with age, whereas the number of children who think that the "I" and thoughts can exist after the death of the body decreases rapidly. If older schoolchildren view the "I" and thoughts as pure products of brain (body) activity, they should have acknowledged that physical illness or injury would affect the mental entities to a much greater extent than was actually the case. If this explanation is correct, then their refusal to accept the idea of the posthumous existence of the "I" and thoughts must have been based on their more "ontological" interpretation of the question of what would happen to the mental entities if the body died. Indeed, formally speaking, neither the "I" nor thoughts can die, since death (the cessation of the body's functions followed by decomposition) is a physical phenomenon and mental entities are non-physical ones. However, personal experience convinces us that the states of our mind do depend on the states of our body, experience which suggests that our mind, possibly, cannot exist without our body. The growing awareness of this "conceptual versus ontological" distinction may have caused the older schoolchildren's contradictory answers to questions regarding the implications that illness and injury on the one hand, and the death of the body on the other, have for the "I" and thoughts. This contradiction (which doesn't exist in 4-year-olds and is much less apparent in 5-year-olds) is far from being a specific characteristic of children's concepts of the relationship between the mind and the body, though; rather, it reflects the real contradiction inherent in our general understanding of the relationship between mind and brain, which are viewed as mutually dependent yet different entities.

DIALOGUE 5: DEFINITION OF THE CRITERION OF TRUTH AND CLASSIFICATION OF TYPES OF KNOWLEDGE

The next step in the chain of Descartes' meditation is the one in which he discusses the problem of finding the truth criterion. In developmental psychology, children's developing ideas of true knowledge acquired through the senses has been studied in a number of aspects, in particular their developing capacity to distinguish between "appearance" and "reality". This problem first appeared in connection with specific (non-conserving) answers that most children before the age of 7 give in response to Piaget's famous "conservation tasks". In particular, Brain and Shanks (1965) showed that 5-year-old children were able to distinguish between what "really is the case" and what "only appears to be the case" if the questions asked stressed this kind of distinction ("Does it seem to be X?", "Is it really X?"), but performed significantly worse on the tasks if the questions were put in a neutral form ("Is this X?").

Developing this line of study further, Tailor and Flavell (1984) suggested that two basic types of incorrect answers could be distinguished in children's responses to tasks concerned with "appearance" and "reality". The first type of errors (phenomenalistic errors) appeared in tasks in which children were asked about objects' real and apparent qualities (like colour or size), and repeatedly named the apparent quality which was available in their perceptual field. The second type of errors, "intellectual realism", dominated the children's responses to tasks about objects' real versus apparent identity; for example, the children insisted that a sponge that looked like a stone did in fact look like a sponge. It was also shown that both types of errors were systematic and invariant with regard to certain cultural, semantic and memory variables (Flavell, 1986). It is not until children reach 11–12 years of age that they are able to cope with "appearance–reality" tasks. It was hypothesised that the reason for such mistakes among younger children is their inability to grasp the idea that an object can be represented simultaneously in different ways (i.e. what it appears to be and what it is "really and truly"). The development of an appreciation of the "appearance–reality" distinction was also linked to the development of conservation, visual perspective-taking ability and other psychological factors (Flavell, 1986; Russell & Mitchell, 1985). An alternative interpretation of the development of the "appearance–reality" distinction views this development as children's changing capacity for "existence attribution", rather than as the development of their cognition and thinking only (Subbotsky, 1993a).

This "non-cognitively based" interpretation was based on a series of experiments in which it was shown that the sheer intellectual discovery of certain "truths" about objects' spatial or causal relationships is insufficient for nullifying the effect that these apparent relationships have on children's behaviours in real-life practical situations (Subbotsky, 1990b). In one experiment, children aged 4–6 years were shown rulers equal in lengths and framed in the shape of the Müller-Lyer illusion. The children were then asked to remove the rulers from the display and compare them by putting them together. After all the children acknowledged that the rulers were of equal length, the rulers were returned to the board and each child was given a practical task of getting an attractive object which was beyond his or her reach. After a few unsuccessful trials, the children were allowed to use one of the rulers to reach the object; it was assumed that if their phenomenal perception of one ruler being longer than another was still active in their minds, despite their newly acquired knowledge about the rulers' equality, then the number of children using rulers from the dove-tailed part of the array would exceed 50%. This was exactly what happened.

In another experiment, children were introduced to the phenomenon of changing water colour (i.e. clean water becomes red when poured from two beakers into a third one), which they attributed to the influence of a red cardboard cylinder that had been placed over the third beaker. Despite the fact that the children were later told the real cause of the colour change (they were told a pseudoscientific illustrated story in which molecular effects were depicted in a form accessible to them), they still used the cylinders in the subsequent task with the aim of reproducing the effect. These and other studies show that children's ideas about the relationships between "true" and "false" knowledge undergo a complex development and are affected by a variety of contextual factors.

The studies reviewed, however, concentrated on a particular aspect of the relationship between "truth" and "falsity", in the sense that the children's judgements about various perceptual arrays, rather than about concepts of "truth" and "falsity", were the focus. This aspect, however, important, cannot replace an examination of children's developing notions about "true" and "false" knowledge.

Previous studies of children's developing ideas about the concept of truth can be divided into two groups. The first group concentrated on the development of children's judgements about empirical (or functional) truth, including those on the "appearance–reality" distinction and those on children's ideas about certainty and uncertainty (Byrnes & Beilin, 1991). The emphasis of the second group of studies was on children's understanding of necessity, in particular the way children begin to realise that some true facts (statements) *must* be true (Murray, 1990; Piaget, 1954).

However, the problem remains of how and when children begin to distinguish between empirical (or functional) true knowledge and necessary (modal) knowledge (Smith, 1993). It is this distinction that was the focus in Dialogue 5.

Specifically, the aims of Dialogue 5 were to determine to what extent children are able to (1) point out that the intuitive clarity and distinctive character of a piece of knowledge is the only reliable criterion of truth; (2) acknowledge the distinctions between various types of knowledge, such as knowledge about the fact of one's own personal existence, problematic knowledge (experimenter's claim that he has a cigarette lighter in his pocket), and dogmatic knowledge (knowledge about objects' names); and (3) acknowledge that our senses can deceive us. The questions were as follows:

Part 1. The relationships between true knowledge and probabilistic knowledge

1. So, we found that you exist in this world, didn't we? Are you sure about this?
2. Why are you sure that you exist?
3. Is there anything in the world about which you are not as sure as the fact that you exist? What is this?
4. For instance, are you sure that I have a cigarette lighter in my pocket?
5. If I said that you exist, would this be true or not? And if I said that you didn't exist, would this be true?
6. And if I said that there is a cigarette lighter in my pocket, would this be true or not?
7. So, by what means can truth be distinguished from falsehood? What is truth? What is falsehood?
8. How can you find out whether you were told something that was true or false? For instance, if I said that there is a cigarette lighter in my pocket, how can you find out whether I am telling the truth or a falsehood?

Part 2. The relationships between true knowledge and dogmatic knowledge

9. You already know many things; for instance, you know how objects around us are named. Whom did you learn the names from? Did you learn them from adults?

10. If so, then the adults could have deceived you if they wanted to; for instance, they could have named some objects wrongly, couldn't they?

11. For instance, if everyone agreed to try and convince you that an elephant is called a "cat", would you believe this or not? Why?

12. Well, is there anything in the world that nobody could deceive you about?

13. Tell me, what if all the people in the world agreed to try to convince you that you don't exist in the world, would you believe them or not? Why?

14. If you are very hungry and all the people kept telling you that you are not hungry, would you believe this or not?

15. If you can see the sun in the sky but all the people keep telling you that it's midnight and there's no sun in the sky, would you believe this or not?

Part 3. The relationships between true knowledge and knowledge acquired through the senses

16. Tell me, where do your thoughts about objects (for instance, about this table or about the sun) come from?

17. And if you can see a certain object (for instance, this table), does it really exist or is it merely your imagination?

18. And what do you think about this: if you can see a certain object, for instance the sun, is that object exactly the same as you see it or is it different in reality?

19. How big is the sun? Is it big or small in reality? Can you cover it with your palm?

20. But the sun as you see it is a small object and you can easily cover it with your palm. Therefore, it doesn't look like a real sun, does it?

21. Does this mean that human eyes don't always see objects in the right way? Can human eyes make errors?

22. And if you can see a certain object from a distance and it seems to you that it is a fountain pen, but other people say that it is a pencil, would you believe them or not? Why?

In response to Question 7 about what is truth and what is falsehood, two major types of answers were obtained. With the first type of answer (given mostly by third to seventh graders), truth was defined as a statement of something that really exists in the world ("Truth is something that if you say this—it really exists, and if you say something and there is no such thing— this would be falsehood"; "Falsehood is when there is no something, and truth is when there is something"; "Truth is when a person says something and it becomes reality, and falsehood is when a person says that it exists, but really it doesn't"; "Truth is if this exists really and truly, and falsehood is when there can be no such thing"; "Truth means to say something, that it is, that it is exactly what it is, that it exists. Falsehood is the opposite thing, what doesn't exist, or it is a half of something that exists and a half of another thing that doesn't exist"). The number of such answers increased with age (6 years to 9 years: $\chi^2 = 13.57$, $P < 0.001$) (Fig. 26).

With the second type of answer, the definition of truth was linked with moral duty or responsibility ("Truth is not to deceive people"; "Truth is when people are honest"; "Truth is when a person never tells lies"). Most preschoolers, however, were unable to provide any sort of definition of what truth is.

Answering Questions 6 and 8 about the relationship between truth and probabilistic knowledge (the experimenter's claim that he had a cigarette lighter in his pocket; see Fig. 26), most preschoolers considered it superfluous to check the information ("Yes, it is truth . . . Is there really a cigarette

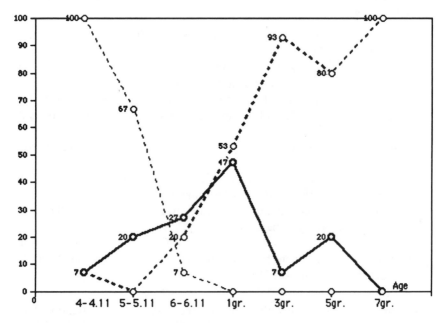

Children who defined truth (1) as something that really exists in the world (- -o- -), (2) as honesty (—o—).
Children who believed that the experimenter's suggestion that he had a cigarette lighter in his pocket did not need checking through their personal experience (- -o- -), with the rest of the children thinking that it did.

FIG. 26. Percentages of children producing answers in response to questions regarding the definition of truth (Question 7) and the relationship between true and probabilistic forms of knowledge (Questions 6 and 8).

lighter there?"; "If you say so, it is true"); most schoolchildren, however, thought that the information is problematic and should be checked through personal experience in order for its truth or falsity to be determined ("It's not true, because your pocket is rather flat, it would be convex if there were a cigarette lighter there"; "You can't be sure unless the person shows it to you"; "You have to ask the person to show the cigarette lighter to you"; "You have to check it", etc.) (increase 5 years to 6 years: $\chi^2 = 9.18$, $P < 0.01$).

As in Dialogue 3, none of our subjects doubted the fact of their personal existence (Question 13) and the fact of having personal experiences (the experience of hunger in Question 14 and the fact of seeing the sun in the sky in Question 15) (Fig. 27). Question 13, which required the children to justify their own personal existence, produced responses similar to those to

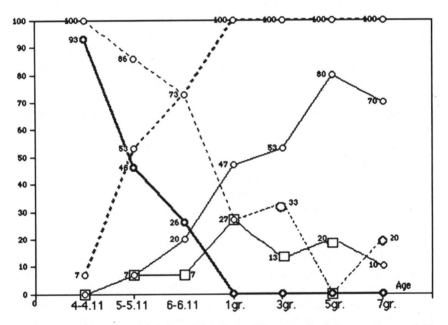

Children who believed that their knowledge about their personal existence was true and (1) produced no justifications of this (- -o- -), (2) justified this view by pointing out to the clarity of their subjective experiences (—o—), (3) said that it was not possible for a person to be aware of anything and not exist in the world (—□—).
Children who thought that their knowledge of having certain subjective experiences was true and (1) produced no justifications of that (—o—), (2) justified the view by pointing out to the clear and obvious character of their subjective experiences (- -o- -).

FIG. 27. Percentages of children producing answers in response to questions regarding knowledge of their own existence (Question 13) and knowledge of certain subjective experiences (Questions 14 and 15).

Question 3 in Dialogue 3. Regarding having certain personal experiences (Questions 14 and 15), most children simply stated the clear and obvious character of these experiences. Most children stressed that they were the only ones who could judge their own personal experiences ("I wouldn't believe that I am not hungry, because it is myself who wants to eat"; "I wouldn't believe that I don't see anything, because if I see anything—then it exists"; "No, I wouldn't believe them, because it's myself who wants to eat and not some other person"; "If I see the sun and adults say that I don't, it means that they just want to see it in a different way"; "You can try to reassure me that I am not hungry, but I will still be hungry").

Responding to Questions 10 and 11 regarding the relationship between true knowledge and knowledge dogmatically acquired from other people (knowledge about objects' names), the children split two ways. First, some children (most preschoolers and first to fifth graders) stated that knowledge about objects' names was true. Two major justifications were provided. Most preschoolers thought that the knowledge was true because it was received from adults and adults cannot tell lies ("No, I wouldn't believe that objects can have different names, because I was taught the names by my parents"; "No, names are all true because adults don't like to tell lies") (decrease 4 years to 6 years: $\chi^2 = 5.71$, $P < 0.02$).

However, most older children suggested that objects' names were true not because of the high moral standards of adults, but simply because the names were the only possible ones that fit the objects—a phenomenon identical to that described by Piaget as "ontological realism" which, according to Piaget, persisted in children until 10 years of age (Piaget, 1929/1983). Characteristically, Piaget found that even if a child agrees that objects can be renamed, he or she still considers names not to be arbitrary but to reflect some object's inherent properties (for instance, the child can think that the name "sun" involves the ideas of shining, of roundness, etc.). It is not until the age of 12 that children start to view names as strictly conventional and detached from the physical properties of their prototypes. Similarly, our data showed (see Fig. 28) that it was not until 13 years of age (seventh grade) that most children started to accept the idea of objects being renamed. Before that age most subjects were sure that renaming was not possible, and even if somebody were to tell them the wrong name of an object, they would quickly find out about it by just comparing the name with the real object or reading about the right name in a book ("It would be false if an elephant was called a cat"; "No, I won't believe that an elephant can be called a cat, because an elephant has a trunk and a cat hasn't"; "No, I won't believe it, even if all people call an elephant a cat, because an elephant isn't a cat". *Experimenter:* "But how would you find out that an elephant is called an elephant if everyone calls it 'a cat'?" "Because an elephant doesn't have a moustache, it has a trunk"; "They could try to persuade me that an elephant

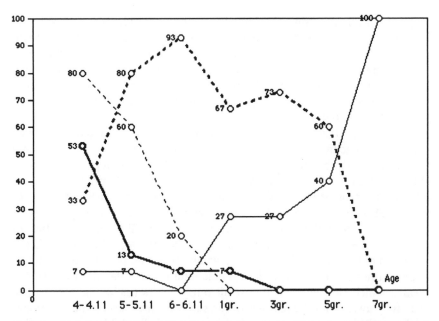

Children who believed that knowledge about object's names is (1) true because adults can not tell a lie (—o—), (2) true because objects and their names are one and the same thing (--o--), (3) problematic because objects' names are conventional and can be misunderstood or deliberately distorted (—o—).
Children who thought that the knowledge that we acquire through senses is true because sense organs cannot deceive us (--o--), (2) problematic because our senses can be wrong (the rest of the subjects).

FIG. 28.   Percentages of children producing answers in response to questions regarding the relationship between true knowledge and (1) dogmatic forms of knowledge (Questions 10 and 11) and (2) knowledge acquired through the senses (Questions 21 and 22).

should be called a cat, but then I would have a look and see for myself that it was an elephant, that's it"). However, half of the children in this group added that they would have accepted different names if they were smaller ("No, I wouldn't believe that objects have different names, but if I were very small and couldn't understand very much, I could have believed it"; "I could have believed, but not now when I already know the names, but at that time :.. when I didn't know").

The second group of children were completely aware of the fact that objects' names are conventional and do not reflect the objects' physical properties ("Of course I would believe, because I wouldn't know that the elephant is called an elephant, I would call it 'a cat' "; "I would not agree at first, but if I then go to the zoo and 'a cat' is written on the label, I'd believe it"). This type of answer was only predominant among the eldest subjects (increase 6 years to 11 years: $\chi^2 = 4.47$, $P < 0.05$).

Lastly, while assessing the knowledge about the identity between subjective images and objects that evoked them, most 4- to 6-year-olds thought that the images were correct because their eyes couldn't make mistakes. Even though most children acknowledged that the visible image of the sun was smaller in size than the real sun, it was not enough to make them doubt that the image was a strict copy of the object (decrease 5 years to 7 years: $\chi^2 = 10.15$. $P < 0.01$).

This is of particular interest, since it highlights the discrepancy between children's capacities to understand mechanisms of human perception and their conception abut true or false knowledge. As shown in previous studies (Flavell et al., 1981; Pillow & Flavell, 1986), young preschoolers are notoriously proficient at understanding some perceptual mechanisms. For instance, Pillow and Flavell (1986) reported that 4-year-olds (but not 3-year-olds) are able to understand whether an object should be moved farther or nearer in order to decrease or increase in apparent size; children of this age were also able to indicate how a circular object should be rotated to make it appear either circular or elliptical. These data are in concordance with our results, which showed that almost all our subjects (including 4-year-olds) were fully aware that the real size of the sun was much larger than the image of the sun they could see. Nevertheless, many of the children thought that the image was a true representation of the real object.

The rest of the children assessed knowledge acquired through the senses as problematic, since the perceptual organs could go wrong ("An object can be different in reality. If I can see the sun small, I know that in reality it is big"; "If the visibility is poor, our eyes can be wrong, but if it is good—they cannot"; "The sun is different in reality, it is big and hot, but it seems to me that it is small and slightly warm"). Such answers predominated among older preschoolers (Fig. 28).

In sum, the results show that during the primary school years, children's judgements about truth and various types of knowledge undergo noticeable changes. First, at approximately 9 years of age most children develop the notion of truth as knowledge which is identical to existence. In their view, the judgement is true only if the subject of this judgement really exists in the world and it is through personal experience only that the truth can be established. Interestingly, there is a gap between the age at which children are able to formulate the notion of truth and the age at which they realise the appropriate ways of finding the truth; 53% of 6-year-olds and 73% of first-graders were sure that true knowledge can only be established through personal experience (Fig. 17), whereas only 23 and 53% of them, respectively, were able to provide a definition of truth which they saw as a fact that really existed in the world (Fig. 14). The difference between the number of children on both sides of the above-mentioned gap as a proportion of the total number of subjects was significant ($z = 4.24$, $P < 0.01$).

Despite the fact that most preschoolers were unable to formulate any concept of truth, the identification of truth with existence was present in their judgements about their personal existence and about their subjective experiences. Thus, most 6-year-olds realised that what made their knowledge about their personal experiences so doubtless was the mere fact that they were so clear and obvious.

In contrast to the unanimous and stable tendency of children to acknowledge the true character of knowledge about their personal existence and personal experiences, with age they became increasingly cautious about trusting other types of knowledge. Probabilistic knowledge was the first to evoke such scepticism: most 6-year-olds not only acknowledged the unclear nature of the knowledge about the experimenter having a cigarette lighter in his pocket, but they also doubted knowledge acquired through the senses. These types of knowledge are typical of the kind of knowledge children acquire through their independent practical activities. In contrast, knowledge about objects' names is normally acquired from adults as a part of the "package" of culturally determined conventions people have about the world. Dissonance between this type of knowledge and what children acquire through their independent exploration is highly unlikely. Perhaps because it is not impossible to "check through experience", dogmatic knowledge is seen to be true knowledge as far as most preschoolers and primary schoolchildren are concerned. The discovery of a name's conventionality can only be the result of practice and experimentation with language (for instance, with foreign languages), which can only be achieved at a relatively advanced age.

DIALOGUE 6: JUDGEMENTS ABOUT THE ALMIGHTY SUBJECT

The idea of the existence of a Divine Subject who is a creator and guardian of the laws of the universe is deeply rooted in the Western rationalistic world outlook. It is discussed in the works of Descartes, Kant, and other prominent ideologists of rationalism, but it dates back to the famous ontological proof of the existence of God created by the Archbishop of Canterbury in 1078, St. Anselm.

· Yet the way contemporary children and adults brought up in Western cultures view and treat this famous logical puzzle has not been investigated by psychological means. Psychological studies of developing conceptions about God (Basett, Miller, Anstey, & Crafts, 1990; Nye & Carson, 1984; Zuberi, 1988) show that with age children's ideas about God become more complicated and adequate; however, these studies targeted children's dogmatic beliefs about God which are imposed on children by their culture and religious tradition rather than the children's independent thinking about the Supreme Being.

With this in mind, St. Anselm's ontological proof is of special interest, as it appeals not to sheer beliefs or faith but to the independent autonomous thinking of an individual about the necessity of the Supreme Subject's existence. It was with the aim of studying children's and adults' independent ideas about the Supreme Subject, that this dialogue was undertaken. It was an adaptation of Descartes' version of the ontological proof (i.e. meditating about the existence of a Supreme Being proves that a Supreme Being must exist) (Descartes, 1988). One particular problem with this dialogue was finding an appropriate term for Descartes' traditional wording "the Supreme Being". The term used had to meet at least three criteria: (1) it had to reflect the characteristic of "almightiness", which is one of two key features of the Supreme Being; (2) it had to appear in children's everyday dictionaries; and (3) it shouldn't interfere with the religious tradition of the culture to which the children belonged. The latter criterion was the most important, since it was children's independent thinking and not their acquired knowledge about religious dogmas that was the major aim of the dialogue.

The selection of the term "almighty wizard" may be questioned by readers. Indeed, if Descartes in his studies was interested in proving the existence of God, why not employ the term "God" in dialogues with children? The answer to this question lies in the specific cultural meaning the term "God" has for a child educated in any Christian culture, or even in an atheistic European culture like the former Soviet Union was. If asked directly about the existence of God, children are likely to reveal their socially accepted beliefs about God, rather than their independent and autonomous thinking of the necessary existence of the Supreme Being. Thus, children brought up in a Christian culture are tempted to say that God exists, as they have been taught by their families and teachers to think this, whereas children educated in the atheistic tradition are more likely to deny God's existence on the same grounds. Hence, children's answers that reflect their conformity to the prevailing views can easily be mistaken for their independent appreciation of the existence (non-existence) of God. Therefore, employing the term "God" would have introduced external social control into the children's answers, thus violating one of the most important principles of the dialogues as laid down in the Introduction (i.e. the children should have no reason to mask or conceal their views on the problems they were asked about). This made the use of the term "God" unacceptable.

Instead, in the search for an appropriate substitute, the term "almighty wizard' was selected. Of course, having selected the term, I was fully aware of the possible difficulties here, specifically that the term "wizard" may have undesirable connotations—a fictitious character, someone who is evil or at least mischievous. However, the second connotation is characteristic to

English culture, and doesn't exist in Russia, where a "wizard" (*volshebnik*) has no negative moral connotations. To account for any possible misrepresentation of the term by the British children, similar dialogues were conducted with British adults who were told in preliminary interviews about the conventional nature of the term "wizard" as employed in the dialogues. As the answers supplied by the British adults didn't differ from those given by the British or Russian children, it was unlikely that undesirable connotations of the term "almighty wizard" had played any significant role in the children's judgements of the Supreme Being.

All of these considerations made the term "almighty wizard" most suitable. First, it eliminated any possibility of the children displaying their religious ideas of God (if they had any), which are acquired in the main dogmatically (see, for instance, Nye & Carson, 1984). Second, the term appears in dictionaries used by the average child. Third, although the concept of "almighty wizard" was not identical with the notion of the "Supreme Being", reflecting only one side of the latter (that is, almightiness and omnipotence) and leaving aside its other important aspect (moral perfection), it was just the characteristic of "almightiness" that was of main interest for this dialogue, since it is the "almightiness" that is crucial for determining the link between having an idea of the almighty person and acknowledging that person's real existence.

Therefore, the aim of this dialogue was to examine to what extent children of various ages are capable of acknowledging this conclusion. The following questions were asked:

1. Tell me, do you know many things? Do you know everything in the world? Who knows more than you do?
2. Can you do everything that you want? Who can do more things than you can?
3. Is there anywhere in the world a person or a fairy tale wizard who knows everything and can do everything he or she wants? Can such an almighty wizard exist in a fairy tale? Can he or she exist in an imaginative play?
4. Tell me, is this almighty wizard capable of creating you or somebody like you?
5. Is this almighty wizard capable of creating a planet like Earth?
6. Can this almighty wizard come out from a fairy tale or our imagination into the real world?
7. Can you imagine such an almighty wizard who would even be able to come out from your imagination into the real world?
8. Can you imagine such a wizard right now?
9. But if you have the idea of the almighty wizard in your mind, does this wizard exist in your mind?

10. But if this wizard is almighty and he or she exists in your mind, can he or she jump out from your mind into the real world, for instance, into this room and sit down over there on the chair? Why do you think so?

The dialogue comprised three stages of discourse. In the first stage (Questions 1–3), we examined whether the children were inclined to acknowledge the real existence of the almighty wizard in the domain of everyday reality and in the domains of fairy tales and imaginative play. The aim of the second stage was to examine the children's notion of "the almighty wizard" (Questions 4–7), in particular whether they thought that almightiness included the capacity for the wizard to "come out" from play or an individual's imagination into the real world. In the third stage (Questions 7–10), the children were put through a series of steps in an attempt to make them aware of the link between the acknowledgement that the imaginative wizard is almighty and the acknowledgement that such a wizard can come out of the imagination; that is, the wizard had to really exist, not just in the imagination.

The results of the first stage (see Fig. 29) showed that a few 4-year-olds acknowledged the existence of the almighty wizard, identifying him with a fairy tale wizard who lived "in the forest", "in the woods", "on another planet". Obviously, this acknowledgement was based on the children's dogmatic acceptance of fairy tale characters as the real thing and had nothing to do with an acknowledgement based on the ontological argument. The overwhelming majority of the children denied that the almighty wizard could really exist in the world (increase 4 years to 6 years: $\chi^2 = 6.70$, $P < 0.01$). At the same time, all the children acknowledged that such a person could exist in play and imagination.

Further questioning revealed that some of the children did not acknowledge the almighty wizard's ability to create a boy or a girl. The most typical explanation for this was that the wizard couldn't do this because he really didn't exist ("He is in a fairy tale, and I am not"; "How can he create me or someone like me? He is not alive, wizards don't really exist"; "No, these wizards ... there are stories about them, but they don't exist in reality"). However, these children also agreed that "inside a fairy tale" the wizard can create everything, including a living child.

In response to Question 6, all but three children denied that the imaginary wizard could come out of fairy tales into the real world ("No, he cannot, because it's just a play"; "No, because he is in a fairy tale"; "No, he is simply drawn on paper"; "No, because a fairy tale is just ... words for children to make their life happier").

Question 7, whether or not the children could imagine a wizard in whose power it was to come out from their imagination (which played a crucial role in the "ontological argument"), proved to be too difficult for 4-year-olds,

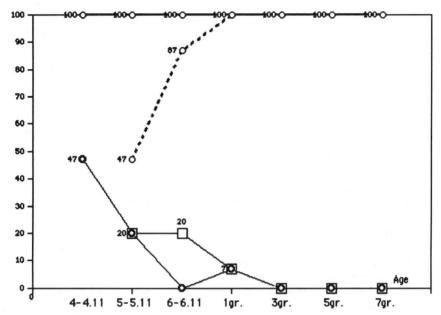

Children who believed (q. 3) that the almighty wizard did exist (1) in the real world (—o—), (2) in fairy tales (—o—).

Children who (1) acknowledged that it was possible to imagine a wizard in whose power it would be to come out of our imagination into the real world (q. 7, - -o- -), (2) either denied that this was possible or gave no definite answer (the rest of the children).

Children who acknowledged (q. 10) that the almighty wizard did exist in their imagination and (1) indeed was able to come out from their imagination into the real world (—□—), (2) was unable to come out of their imagination (the rest of the children).

FIG. 29. Percentages of children producing answers in response to questions regarding the possibility of the "almighty wizard" existing in the real world.

who were unable to produce sensible responses or denied that such a wizard can be imagined. Nevertheless, 47% of 5-year-olds, 87% of 6-year-olds, and all of the older children responded in the affirmative (increase 5 years to 7 years: $\chi^2 = 8.35$, $P < 0.01$). However, in the third stage of the dialogue, almost all of them crucially refused to agree that such a wizard has to really exist.

In order to make sure that the children's negative answers were not situational judgements, the contradiction in their judgements (that is, the fact that the wizard in whose power it was to leave the domain of our imagination was unable to do so) was pointed out to them in a subsequent discussion. The discussion took the form of strengthening and emphasising the ontological argument ("OK, now let us imagine wizard number two, who is even more powerful than wizard number one and who really can jump from our imagination into this room. Can you do this?"). However, even when the circle was reproduced up to five times with each child, it failed to shatter the children's firm belief that the almighty wizard could only exist in their imagination. Here are a few examples:

Natasha (girl aged 6 years)
E: If this wizard can do everything he wants and even come out from our imagination into the real world, can he jump from your mind into the real world, for instance, in this room and sit down here on the chair?
N: No, because he can only exist in our thoughts or in books, but he can't go out into the real world.
E: Therefore, he is not almighty, is he?
N: No, even if they write in books that he can do everything, it is not true, it is just for fun.
E: OK, but can we think of such an almighty wizard who can really come out of our imagination into the real world?
N: Yes, we can think, but he won't be able to come out of our thoughts.
E: Therefore, he isn't almighty?
N: They write in books that he is almighty, but in reality he isn't and he doesn't exist.

Nastija (girl aged 7 years)
E: If we agreed that this wizard is really almighty and he is even able to go out from our thinking, then can he really go out and sit down on this chair?
N: Yes.
E: Therefore, if we think of him strongly will he come out and sit down here in front of us?
N: No, because he can't go out, he has no power enough to go out of our thoughts.

Oleg (boy aged 7 years)
E: Well, if the wizard is almighty and he exists in our thinking, can he now go out and sit down right here?
O: No. We are just thinking of him and imagining that such a person exists, just like those people who believe that there is a God in the world, but in reality there is no God.

Artiom (boy aged 9 years)
E: Look, if the wizard exists in our thoughts and can go out of our thinking into the real world, he will go out and sit down here, won't he?
A: No, he is only in our thinking, but not outside it.
E: But can we think of such an almighty wizard who is even more almighty than the first one and who can really go out into the real world?
A: We can, but this is only fantasy. In reality he, however powerful, cannot go out of our thoughts, because he doesn't exist, he can only be conjured up.

E: Therefore, he is not almighty?
A: He is not. He is almighty, but only in his own way, in a fairy tale way.

In contrast to the majority of the children who merely acknowledged the existing contradiction in their judgements, some of the children made an attempt to overcome the contradiction by rejecting the earlier accepted premise about the wizard's almightiness. For instance, Ania (girl aged 13 years) at first acknowledged that we could think of the almighty wizard:

E: So we can think of such an almighty wizard, one who is even able to come out of our thoughts and sit down here in the chair?
A: Yes.
E: And can he now come out and really sit down here on the chair?
A: No, we cannot think of such a person.
E: But we are thinking and talking of him now, aren't we?
A: Yes, but he still won't come out. We cannot think of the almightiness. You can think, but he won't be almighty.
E: Therefore, when we think of the almighty wizard, he is not really almighty?
A: No. When you think of him … no, we cannot think of the almighty wizard.
E: Yet we are talking of him right now?
A: Yes, but he can't come out; therefore, he is not almighty.

Only a small number of 5- and 6-year-old children believed it possible that the almighty wizard could come out into the real world. Here are some examples:

Polija (girl aged 6 years)
E: Therefore, such a wizard can exist in the real world?
P: Yes, both in fairy tales and in the real world.
E: Can he come out of our thinking into this room and sit down here?
P: Yes, he can. I am very fearful that it would occur to him to come out, I don't like wizards.

Roman (boy aged 6 years)
E: And this almighty wizard can now come out into the real world?
R: Yes, he can.
E: Why can't I see him then?
R: I don't know. Perhaps, he doesn't want to.

Summing up the results of Dialogue 6, we can see that children between the age of 5 and 6 years come to appreciate the distinction between various domains of reality; namely, the domain of everyday reality, in which no personified almighty subject is possible, and the domains of unusual realities (such as fairy tales, imagination, and fantasy), in which the almighty wizard can exist. It is noteworthy that the boundary between these domains of reality is viewed by most children older than 5 as being impermeable to the wizard. They refuse to let the almighty imaginative subject through the boundary even under pressure from the ontological argument; that is, being aware of the fact that the wizard in question was not an "ordinary fairy tale wizard" but an almighty subject whose real existence had to be acknowledged on the grounds of the sheer fact of thinking of him (imagining him). It was also obvious that even the few young children who acknowledged the almighty wizard's real existence did it on the basis of their dogmatic beliefs in fairy tale wizards' reality, rather than on the grounds of understanding the logical necessity of the "ontological argument".

It needs to be made clear at this stage that in philosophical terms, the logical validity of the "ontological argument" can be (and often has been) questioned. One well-known objection to this argument was put forward by Kant, who argued that "Time and labour ... are lost on the famous ontological (Cartesian) proof of the existence of a Supreme Being from mere concepts; and a man might as well imagine that he could become richer in knowledge by mere ideas as a merchant might claim that he had improved his financial position by adding a few noughts to his cash account" (Kant, 1966, p. 88). Similar objections were provided by later commentators (e.g. Kenny, 1968). The weakness of the Kantian counterargument is that he puts the idea of the Supreme Being on the same plane as all other ideas (such as the ideas we have about physical objects, fantastic creatures, angels, etc.), which requires the *a posteriori* proof to be acknowledged as really existing and not only an imaginary product, although Descartes stated quite clearly that whereas all other ideas can be created by a subject himself or herself (who, therefore, is uncertain about their real existence), the idea of the Supreme Being cannot. However, it is not my objective here to raise deep philosophical and theological disputes. What was of interest in this study was the psychological preparedness of a philosophically unsophisticated mind to accept the ontological proof, and as the children's answers clearly indicated, they were definitely unwilling to do so. Instead, the vast majority of the children produced objections similar to that created by Kant.

As the analysis of the answers showed, the resistance of the children to the "ontological argument" was unlikely to be caused by their insensitivity to the key features of the argument; that is, by a lack of awareness that there was a logical contradiction in their judgements. The discussions that the experimenter had with the children revealed quite clearly that although all those of school age were quite aware of the contradiction, they preferred to accept the contradiction rather than to allow for the possibility of the almighty wizard's real existence.

This makes it more plausible to assume that the denial of this possibility was caused by a combination of two factors. On the one hand, the children (and most adults, as later studies have shown) were incapable of distinguishing between the idea of the almighty creature and all other imaginary products which do not include the characteristic of "almightiness". On the other hand, from their primary school years (and even before this), children in Russia at the time of the research were constantly pressured to accept the physicalistic view of the world, which is inherently hostile to the idea of the real existence of magic or superhuman spiritual forces of any kind.

In order to test the possible role that an atheistic background may have played in the overwhelming resistance of Russian children to the ontological argument, the dialogue was replicated in Britain, a country where religious education has always been part of the school curriculum. It was assumed that if cultural background (atheistic versus religious) had no real role to play, then the British children would be equally unwilling to accept the ontological argument (which appeals to the subject's rational thinking and the acknowledgement of the logical necessity of the Supreme Being's reality, and not to the dogmatic belief that such a being really exists), since as far as the idea of the Supreme Being is put on the same plane with other possible ideas (such as the idea of money, of a cucumber, or a dragon), it immediately becomes a subject for the empirical "check on reality", and such a check with respect to the Supreme Being (the almighty wizard) is theoretically impossible.

The procedure followed in Britain was a strict replication of that employed in the original Russian study. The subjects comprised 4-year-olds ($n = 15$, $\bar{x} = 4{:}5$ years), 5-year-olds ($n = 15$, $\bar{x} = 5{:}5$ years), 6-year-olds ($n = 15$, $\bar{x} = 6{:}6$ years), 9-year-olds ($n = 15$, $\bar{x} = 9{:}3$ years), 11-year-olds ($n = 15$, $\bar{x} = 11{:}9$ years), and 13- to 14-year-olds ($n = 15$, $\bar{x} = 13{:}11$ years). There were approximately equal numbers of boys and girls in each group. The results of the comparative study in Britain are shown in Fig. 30.

A logistic regression model was run for age (4) and nationality (2) for the Russian and British 6-, 9-, 11- and 13-year-old children's answers to Question 7 and Question 10 separately. No main effects were found. This showed that there were no statistical differences between the Russian and British children's answers about the almighty wizard's existence, with the overwhelming majority of children of both nationalities saying that the almighty wizard could exist in the imagination but could not leave its bounds.

This would suggest that both British and Russian children conceived the almighty wizard as an imaginary and not real creature. Among the British children there were only two (one 4-year-old and one 9-year-old) who acknowledged that the almighty wizard could come out of our minds into the real world. This was in concordance with the results of the Russian study, apart from the fact that Russian 4-year-olds were significantly more often inclined to admit the real existence of the almighty wizard than their

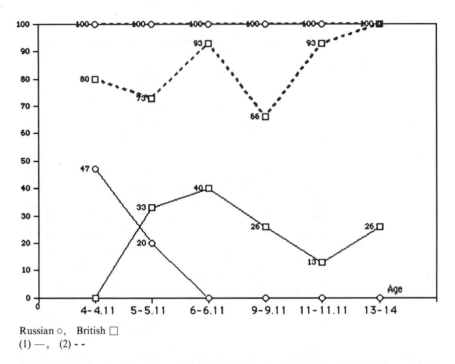

Russian ○,   British □
(1) —,   (2) - -

FIG. 30.   Percentages of Russian and British children who believed that the "almighty wizard" exists (1) in the real world and (2) in fairy tales.

British peers. This result can be explained by the relatively greater popularity of themes about wizards and magicians in Russian folk tales for small children in comparison with those in British folk tales.

Because unlike the original study the replication in Britain did not involve any subsequent discussion of the logical contradictions in the children's judgements, the fact that there were fewer British children than Russian children who acknowledged the almighty wizard's capacity to come out of our minds into the real world could be a consequence of this methodological difference. To account for this possibility, another replication study was conducted in the UK. Seventeen 6-year-old children (8 girls aged 6:1–6:9 years, $\bar{x}$ = 6:5 years; 9 boys aged 6:2–6:10 years, $\bar{x}$ = 6:4 years) and sixteen 9-year-olds (8 girls aged 9:0–9:10 years, $\bar{x}$ = 9:2 years; 8 boys aged 9:1–9:7 years, $\bar{x}$ = 9:4 years) participated in the study. All the children were native English speakers and attended a suburban school in the north-west of England.

In this second replication study, the questions asked of the British children were slightly modified so as to avoid the ambiguity that was present in some of the original questions. They were as follows:

Preliminary questions

1. Would you mind if I talk to you a bit about wizards?
2. Tell me, is there in the world a man or a wizard who knows everything and can do anything he wants, yes or no?
3. Can such an almighty wizard exist in a fairy tale, yes or no?
4. Can this wizard create a mouse, yes or no?
5. Can this wizard create a planet like Earth, yes or no?

If all these questions except for Question 2 were answered in the affirmative, key questions followed. If not, the preliminary questions were repeated in a different form in order to obtain positive answers. If the child continued to deny the existence of a fairy tale wizard, he or she was excluded from further analysis.

Key questions

1. Tell me, is it possible to think of a wizard who is so powerful that he can even go out of your thinking and into the real world, for example, into this room, yes or no? [If the answer was "no", an additional question was posed, "Can we talk about such a wizard?"]
2. Let us think (talk) about such a wizard right now. Does he exist in your mind while you are thinking of him (in our conversation while we are talking of him), yes or no? [If the answer was "no", the experimenter repeated the question in a different form in an attempt to persuade the child that everything we are thinking or talking about exists in the form of thoughts or words.]
3. Well, as this wizard is so mighty and he exists in your mind (in our conversations), can he now go out from your mind (from our conversation) into this room and sit down in this chair, yes or no? [If the answer was "no", the additional question "Why?" was asked. The purpose of this was to list the reasons the child used to support his or her refusal to allow the almighty wizard to come out of the mind. If the answer was "yes", the following question was posed: "Then why can't I see him?" The aim of this was to ascertain if the child's positive answer was sensible and conscious. The expected answers included "He doesn't want to go out", "He might be invisible", and "He might be hiding somewhere in the room".]

The results of this modified study (see the comparisons between the Russian and British children in Fig. 31) showed that although a significantly larger number of British 6-year-olds than British 9-year-olds acknowledged the possibility of the wizard coming out into the real world ($\chi^2 = 4.497$, $P < 0.05$), the differences between the Russian and British

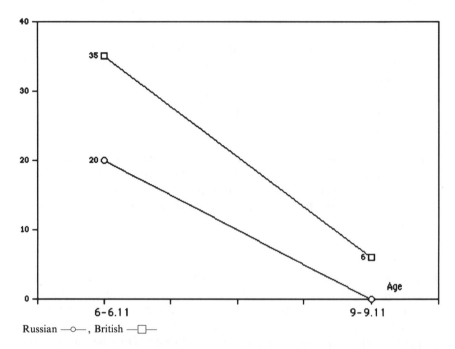

Russian —o—, British —□—

FIG. 31. Percentages of Russian and British children who acknowledged that the "almighty wizard" who existed in their imagination could materialise in the real world, with the remainder denying that this was possible.

children of the same age groups were not statistically significant. This confirms that it is between the ages of 6 and 9 years that children in both cultural groups start to resist the idea of the almighty wizard's real existence.

The reasons British children gave for their denial that the wizard could come out of their thinking was similar to those given by the Russian children ("Because he is not real", "He is not really here, he is in our minds, I can only think about him"; "Because a spirit can't go out of a person's mind"; "He is almighty only in my brain, but he is not so almighty to go out of my brain"). The seven 6-year-olds and one 9-year-old who acknowledged the possibility of the wizard coming out into the real world stated that "you can't see him", "he might be invisible", "because he is a ghost, and ghosts can't be seen", "he's gone somewhere", grounds very similar to those given by Russian children in the original study.

The results of the replication study did not support the expectation that the resistance to the possibility of the almighty wizard's real existence in Russian children might have been caused by their predominantly atheistic cultural background; as can be seen from the data, British children were equally unwilling to accept this possibility. An alternative possible explanation for this unwillingness is to assume that children view the almighty wizard as a fantastic creature from the world of fairy tales and do not distinguish it from other imaginary objects whose existence is confined to the limits of the imaginary world. If this were the case, then the characteristic feature of the almighty wizard (i.e. its almightiness, which is a sufficient condition for its real existence) was not meaningful enough to have any impact on the children's judgements. It could be expected, however, that if adult subjects were asked the same questions, they would appreciate that the almighty wizard they were being asked about was a metaphorical way of talking about the Supreme Being and not a "fairy tale" character in its literal sense.

To examine this possibility, the same set of questions was put to adult subjects. Eight male (aged 19–23 years, $\bar{x}$ = mean age 20:8 years) and nine female (aged 18–27 years, $\bar{x}$ = 21:3 years) Lancaster University students participated as subjects. The questions asked were the same as put to the British children; however, if a negative answer was given to the final key question, the experimenter drew to the subject's attention the fact that there seemed to be a logical contradiction between the statement that the wizard was almighty and the fact that he or she could not yet go out of the mind. An additional question was then put to the subject: "Do you agree or disagree that there is a logical contradiction in what you have said?" If the answer was "yes", the subject was asked: "Do you prefer simply to accept this contradiction, or would you like to reconsider your opinion that the wizard is unable to come out of your mind and into this room?"

The objective of these questions was to emphasise a major strength of the ontological argument; that is, the fact that the almighty being, once it is acknowledged that he or she exists in any form (even in the form of an image or a spoken word) has to be ascribed a real physical existence too. If the subject cannot see the necessity of the link between "almightiness" and "real existence", then nothing more can be done about it. If, however, the subject does acknowledge this link (and, therefore, the fact that his or her former denial of the almighty subject's capacity to come out of the imagination was based on a logical contradiction), he or she still has two options: either simply to accept the fact of the contradiction without changing his or her opinion on the almighty subject's existence, or to change their opinion and accept the conclusion that the almighty wizard could, in fact, come out of his or her mind into the real world.

The results of the study showed that only one of the 17 subjects (a man) acknowledged the fact of the wizard's real existence ("He is here, but we can't see him. He's not giving any light waves"), with all the others emphatically denying this. Of the other 16 subjects, 11 (5 men, 6 women) saw no logical contradiction in their judgements, and 5 (2 men, 3 women) said that there was a contradiction but they preferred to accept it rather than change their minds on the wizard's "existential status".

As the results show, the denial of the almighty subject's real existence was not a specifically children's way of reasoning but it was revealed by the overwhelming majority of adult subjects. Since it was unlikely that the adult subjects simply saw the almighty wizard as a fairy tale character (as might have been the case with the children), it became clear that there was some reason that made it very difficult (and in fact impossible) for most of the subjects to draw a link between the "imaginary almightiness" and "real existence". It was also clear that this reason was psychological rather than logical; indeed, five adult subjects preferred to acknowledge and accept the logical contradiction in their judgements than to abandon their views on the impossibility of the wizard "coming out of the mind".

In order to investigate this, a separate study with adult subjects was undertaken. Four experiments were conducted. The experiment described above was used as a preliminary experiment (referred to here as Experiment 1). The experiment merely confirmed the fact that had previously been established in experiments with Russian and British children, most of whom showed strong resistance to the ontological argument. Experiments 2–4 examined the possible psychological causes of this resistance. The dialogue presented in Experiment 1 was reproduced at the end of every experiment as a control dialogue.

One reason why most subjects refused to acknowledge the almighty subject's capacity to go beyond their thinking could be because they saw "getting out of the mind into the room" as a causal event, in which they viewed their thinking as the cause and the almighty wizard as the consequence. In so far as the almighty wizard is, by definition, much more powerful than the subjects themselves, the subjects may have felt that they were being forced to acknowledge something unnatural and impossible (i.e. a succession in which a cause creates an effect that exceeds the cause in all respects).

To prevent this kind of feeling (or reasoning) occurring in Experiment 2, a preliminary dialogue about the almighty wizard was run, which was immediately followed by the dialogue as in Experiment 1. The purpose of this preliminary dialogue was to help the subjects indirectly come to terms with the fact that it was not they themselves who caused the almighty subject to "go out of their minds"; on the contrary, it was in fact the almighty wizard him or herself, who may have "settled down" in their minds in the form of their thinking (speaking) about him. This understood, the almighty wizard's "coming out" of the subjects' minds would no longer be perceived by them as an "inverted causal sequence"; rather, it should be viewed as the wizard's own action (i.e. the wizard leaving the subjects' minds to go back into the external world from which he or she had originally entered their minds). If the reason for the resistance to the ontological argument in Experiment 1 was the subjects' ideas about cause–effect relationships, then at the end of Experiment 2 there should be more subjects acknowledging the wizard's real existence than at the end of Experiment 1.

The questions posed in the preliminary dialogue were as follows:

1. Now I'd like to talk to you about wizards. Have you ever heard or read something about them? What have you heard or read?
2. Tell me, if a wizard is almighty, can be create a human individual, yes or no?
3. And can this almighty wizard create a person like yourself?
4. And can this almighty wizard create some thoughts in your mind; for instance, can he make you think about an almighty wizard, yes or no?
5. And can this wizard, if he is almighty, turn himself into your thoughts, enter your mind and settle down there, yes or no?
6. If this occurred, would you know that it was the wizard who settled down in your mind or would you think that it is you who produced thoughts about this wizard?

If the answers to some of Questions 2–5 were negative, the experimenter reassured the subject and tried to persuade him or her that the almighty wizard was indeed able to create somebody like himself or herself, to create his or her thoughts and even to settle down in his or her mind. If a subject answered Question 6 as follows, "I would think it was myself who produced this thought about the almighty wizard", the questions used in Experiment 1 were asked. If the answer was "I would know that the wizard settled down in my mind", the following question was asked: "How would you find out about it?" If the subject insisted on his or her view, he or she no longer participated in the experiment.

Six men (aged 18–30 years, $\bar{x}$ = 22:0 years) and nine women (aged 18–21 years, $\bar{x}$ = 19:1 years) took part in the experiment. All of them acknowledged in a preliminary dialogue that it was possible for the almighty wizard to have created thoughts about himself in their minds. One male subject gave a positive response to the question about the almighty wizard's capacity to come out of the subject's mind into the real world. Other subjects gave negative answers to this question; eight of them refused to see any contradiction in their judgements, and six subjects acknowledged and accepted the contradiction without changing their minds. The justifications for the negative answers given by the subjects in this experiment were similar to those given in Experiment 1. As can be seen from the results, it was not the "inverted causal succession of events" that deterred the subjects from acknowledging the real existence of the almighty subject.

Another possible psychological reason for the subjects' refusal to allow for the almighty wizard's capacity to come out of their minds could be the "anthropomorphisation" of the almighty wizard by the subjects. It is possible that the subjects viewed the almighty wizard as a humanlike creature with a physical body and, therefore, it seemed odd to them to admit that a physical object like that could be "materialised" by their sheer will power.

In order to prevent (or at least to weaken) the possibility of this "physicalisation" of the almighty subject's image, a special preliminary dialogue was run in Experiment 3. In this dialogue, it was made clear to the subjects that the almighty wizard could be invisible and not necessarily human. If the reason for not allowing the almighty subject into the real world was the anthropomorphisation of the wizard's image by the participants, then the number of subjects who insisted on their denial of the almighty subject's real existence in this experiment should be significantly less than in Experiment 1.

The questions posed in the preliminary dialogue were as follows:

1. Now I'd like to talk to you about wizards. Have you ever heard or read something about them? What have you read or heard?
2. Tell me, please, is it necessary that wizards should look like human beings, or they can look different?
3. Can a wizard be invisible, yes or no?
4. Can a wizard turn him or herself into various animals and objects, yes or no?
5. Can a wizard be in the air or in the walls of this room, yes or no?

If the subject's answers to some of Questions 1–5 were in the negative, the subject was immediately reassured by the experimenter who reminded him or her of passages from books and fairy tales (like "The lamp of Aladdin"), which showed that a wizard could in fact take any shape and look different from humans, be invisible and enter various objects. Final question then followed:

6. So, if the wizard is almighty, he or she will not necessarily be visible and may hide in various objects in this room, yes or no?

If the answer was "yes", the questions used in Experiment 1 were followed.

Eight men (aged 18–23 years, $\bar{x}$ = 20:1 years) and 10 women (aged 18–22 years, $\bar{x}$ = 20:9 years) participated in this experiment. All of them acknowledged the wizard's capacity to take the shape of various objects and to be invisible. Three of the subjects responded "yes" to the question about the wizard's capacity to come out of their minds into the experimental room;

they justified the apparent absence of the wizard in the room by the wizard's wish to remain invisible or be "elsewhere". Of the 15 subjects who denied the wizard's capacity to become real (giving arguments similar to those given by the subjects in Experiment 1), 7 did not see any logical contradiction in their judgements; the other 8 accepted their contradiction without changing their minds about the wizard's inability to come out into the real world.

The results of Experiment 3 did not differ significantly from those of Experiment 1. This suggests that it was not the almighty wizard's anthropomorphisation that prevented the subjects from acknowledging the wizard's real existence.

Finally, there was one more psychological factor that could have compelled the subjects to deny the possibility of the almighty wizard coming out of their minds. This was an awareness of the subjects of the impenetrable boundary that exists between mental and physical realities. Indeed, as has been shown in experimental psychology (see Subbotsky, 1991, for a review), a person who believes in the permanence of physical objects has to maintain certain rules, and in particular the "non-creation rule", which states that a non-physical object like a thought, a mental image, or a spoken word cannot turn into a real physical object without certain conditions being observed (like it having some "primary matter", applying special efforts to the matter with the aim of creating the object).

Since the almighty wizard was seen initially as an imaginary creature existing in the subjects' thinking, the subjects may have viewed it as any other imaginary object (like an imaginary car or a "flying saucer") and applied the "non-creation rule" to it. This hypothesis gains support from the fact that, according to our data, a systematic denial of the ontological argument by the overwhelming majority of children appears between the ages of 6 and 9 years, and it is exactly at this age that the idea of object permanence is finally established in children's minds on the level of representational intelligence (Piaget, 1986b).

In order to investigate this hypothesis, Experiment 4 was conducted. In this experiment, the subjects were individually shown a trick in which an object conjured up by the subject would spontaneously turn into a real thing. In our previous studies (see Subbotsky & Trommsdorff, 1994), this trick proved to be quite efficient in weakening children's and adults' beliefs in object permanence. If it was a belief in object permanence that prevented the subjects from acknowledging that the almighty wizard could come out from their imagination into the real world, then after Experiment 4 the number of such subjects should decrease significantly. The procedure of Experiment 4 was as follows.

Each subject was invited individually into the experimental room in which there was a table and an empty wooden box measuring

15 × 11 × 11 cm with an open lid. The box was constructed such that if the lid was closed, a metallic plate separated from one of the inside walls and sunk to the bottom silently revealing a postage stamp that had earlier been placed between the plate and the wall of the box. The special construction of the lid and a system of magnets incorporated in the side and bottom of the box ensured that the box could be manipulated (i.e. turned upside down) without giving up the secret of its construction.

The experimenter asked the following:

- Now I'd like to show you something. Tell me, if you imagine some object, for example a nice postage stamp, and if you want this stamp to appear here on the table, will it appear or not? Why?
- Now, have a look in the box and see whether it is empty. [The experimenter than asked the subject to close the lid of the box. He then placed a postage stamp on the table and continued.]
- Tell me, if you conjure up this stamp in your mind very strongly and want this stamp to appear inside this box, will it appear or not? [After the subject had answered this question, the stamp was covered with a sheet of paper, and the experimenter continued.]
- Now let's try it. Please, try and conjure up this postage stamp in your mind and wish as strongly as you can this stamp to appear in the box.
- Now, please, open the box.

When the subject opened the box he or she would find the postage stamp inside. The experimenter answered the subject's questions without revealing the secret of the trick, and then asked the subject the questions asked in Experiment 1.

Six men (aged 19–30 years, $\bar{x}$ = 21:8 years) and six women (aged 18–21 years, $\bar{x}$ = 19:3 years) participated as subjects. All of them were noticeably surprised to see the stamp "materialise" and asked for an explanation. The experimenter provided an explanation that did not divulge the secret of the trick. In the dialogue that followed, one subject answered "yes" to the question about the wizard's capacity to come out of their minds, with the rest of the subjects emphatically denying this on grounds similar to those given in Experiment 1. When asked about the logical contradictions in their arguments, two female subjects denied any contradictions, five subjects (two men, three women) confirmed that there was a contradiction but refused to change their minds, and four subjects (three men and one woman) acknowledged the contradiction and changed their minds, saying that now they believed the almighty wizard could come out of their minds. When asked why no wizard was in the room, four subjects said that the wizard might be invisible ("He won't let us see him"; "He can't be visible, but can be real") and one subject said that it was up to the wizard's will when and where he would show himself.

As can be seen from the subjects' answers to the first round of questions regarding the wizard's real existence, the results of Experiment 4 did not differ significantly from those in previous experiments. However, the second round of questions (which followed the subjects' judgements about the logical contradictions in their arguments) detected a significant change in the subjects' opinions: 9 out of 11 subjects in Experiment 4 acknowledged that there was a contradiction in their judgements, 4 of whom changed their minds on the almighty wizard's capacity to come out of their minds. A summary of the data in Experiments 1–4 is shown in Fig. 32.

Two logistic regression models were run for experiment (4) and sex (2), with acknowledgement of logical contradictions or acceptance of the ontological argument in the first and/or the second round of questioning as dependent variables. They showed only marginal effects for experiment $[(\chi^2(3,56) = 7.478, P < 0.05$ for the first model; $\chi^2(3,63) = 7.524, P < 0.05$ for the second model]. However, when six logistic regression models were run in which the data from each of Experiments 2–4 were compared with

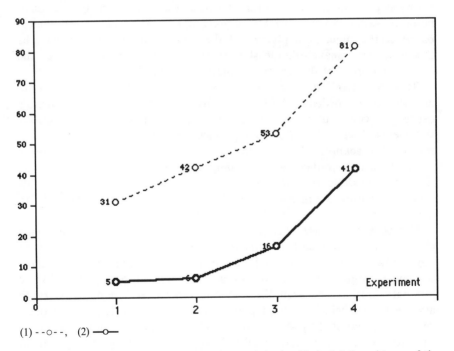

(1) --o--,   (2) —o—

FIG. 32. Percentages of subjects in Experiments 1–4 who (1) denied the existence of the "almighty wizard" in the real world during the first round of questioning, but who acknowledged that there was a logical contradiction in their judgements, and (2) acknowledged that it was possible for the "almighty wizard" to materialise in the real world during the first or second round of questioning.

the data from Experiment 1 (with acknowledgement of logical contradictions and acceptance of the ontological argument in the first and/or the second round of questioning as dependent measures), only Experiment 4 yielded main effects. There were main effects of experiment for the acknowledgement of logical contradiction [$\chi^2(1,27) = 9.187$, $P < 0.01$] and main effects of experiment [$\chi^2(1,29) = 5.662$, $P < 0.02$] and sex [$\chi2(1,29) = 4.616$, $P < 0.05$] for the acceptance of the ontological argument.

Only in Experiment 4 (not in Experiments 2 and 3), therefore, were a significant number of subjects prepared to acknowledge that by denying the almighty wizard's existence they logically contradicted themselves, and only in Experiment 4 did a significant number of subjects in the end accept the ontological argument. It is also noteworthy that the majority of these subjects were those who had changed their minds regarding the existence of the almighty wizard after they acknowledged that there was a logical contradiction in their judgements, and they were predominantly men.

This suggests that it may have been the subjects' strong belief in object permanence (and not the "inverted causal succession" or the "anthropomorphisation" of the almighty subject) that was the major psychological barrier to the subjects complying with the ontological argument. As soon as this belief was weakened, the shift in the subjects' attitude towards the ontological proof of the supreme subject's existence became apparent.

This shift manifested itself in the fact that the subjects became more inclined to acknowledge the fact that by denying the almighty wizard's capacity to come out of their minds they were contradicting their previous statements about the subject's almightiness. However, as Experiments 1–3 showed, this acknowledgement alone was not enough to make the subjects reverse their final verdict about the almighty wizard's real existence. For this to become possible, the subjects needed some additional "push", and this "push" was provided in Experiment 4 by weakening the subjects' belief in object permanence.

If this was the case, then the coincidence between the age at which children's beliefs in object permanence are finally established on the level of representational intelligence, and the age at which children start resisting the ontological argument (i.e. between 6 and 9 years) can be explained by the internal "kinship" between the two phenomena. It is not necessary to assume that a belief in object permanence is consciously used by older children and adults to justify their refusal to accept the almighty wizard's capacity to come out of their minds. However, a strong feeling that an imaginary object can never become real "on its own" and without special productive actions on the part of the subject can definitely hinder the "logical power" of the ontological proof, which simply does not work unless the belief in object permanence is shattered. It is only when this belief is weakened that the subjects become susceptible to the logical appeal of the ontological argument.

DIALOGUE 7: THE DISTINCTION BETWEEN PHYSICAL OBJECTS AND THE SUBJECTIVE IMAGES THEY PRODUCE: JUDGEMENTS ABOUT DREAMS AND REALITY

Dialogue 7 was the last in the series and examined the children's capacity to accept two major characteristics of the rationalistic world outlook: the fact that subjective images of objects are different from the objects "in their own right" and the distinction between dreams and reality. The following questions were asked:

1. If you can see a red pencil but I tell you that you have nothing in front of you, would you agree with me or not?
2. If other people—your friends, parents, and grandparents—told you the same thing, would you believe them?
3. If you were told, "OK, you can see the pencil, but this is nothing but your imagination, there is no pencil in front of you in reality", would you believe it or not?
4. And if you burned your hand in a fire and it hurt terribly, but somebody told you that it didn't hurt, would you believe them?
5. And if you were told the following: "It does hurt, but in reality there was no fire and the pain simply emerged in your hand on its own", would you believe it or not?
6. Look at this red pencil in front of you [the child is shown a red pencil lying on the table]. Can you see it? Tell me, please, this redness of it, where is it—in the pencil or in your brain (in your eyes)?
7. You know, there are some people whose vision is damaged and they see this red pencil as being coloured green. If you and such a person were looking at this pencil, it would seem red to you and green to the other person. What colour is it really and truly?
8. Let's imagine that a certain radiation permeated Earth from space and all people but you have had their vision changed by this radiation, so that they see the pencil as green and you see it as red. What colour is it really and truly?
9. So, can you tell me where is the colour—in the pencil or in your brain (in your eyes)?
10. And what about the heat that comes from the fire, where is it situated— in the fire or in your brain (in your hand)?
11. Tell me, if you pricked your finger with a needle and your finger hurt, where would the pain be, in the needle or in your brain (in your hand)?

12. So you think that you are not asleep at the moment and everything that you can see and hear exists really and truly?
13. And why do you think that you are not asleep right now?
14. Can it be that it only seems to you that you are in a vigilant state, whereas in reality you are still asleep? Why?
15. Can you tell me how people who you can see in your dreams differ from real people?
16. And how do objects which you see in your dreams differ from real objects?
17. How do you know in the morning that you are awake and are no longer asleep?

The link between subjective phenomena (i.e. images of physical objects, such as whiteness or redness, coldness or warmness, lightness or heaviness, etc.) and the external causes of these phenomena (i.e. objects in their own right, traditionally described in special terms of physical theories, such as the field theory of colours, a molecular theory of thermal processes, gravitational theory or mass and weight, etc.) can be viewed from different aspects. First, it was necessary to determine whether the children could allow for the possibility of the independent existence of subjective images without them being caused by certain external objects. If a child thought this was impossible, it was necessary to further enquire whether the child could really distinguish between the image of the object and the object in its own right and did not confuse the two.

Second, the permanent link that exists between subjective images and the real objects that initiated them is a characteristic feature that distinguishes the real world (or, to put it differently, the domain of everyday reality) from the dreams where such a link is missing.

The results showed that the overwhelming majority of children thought it impossible to have a subjective image of pain without any external cause of that pain ("No, I won't believe that there was no fire, pain cannot emerge from the thin air"; "No, pain can't emerge on its own, you have to burn your hand or hit it"; "No, I won't believe that there is not a real pencil in front of me, I can see it with my own eyes; if you took it away, I could conjure it up but I won't be able to see it").

Even most young preschoolers considered the link between subjective images and their physical causes as necessary. The only exception was four schoolchildren who acknowledged that subjective images could exist without external objects being the cause ("This may be autosuggestion, I can believe that there is something which really doesn't exist") (see Fig. 33).

Next the question of the children's capacity to appreciate the role of sense organs (the brain) was examined. As basic subjective phenomena, colour (redness), warmth and pain were selected.

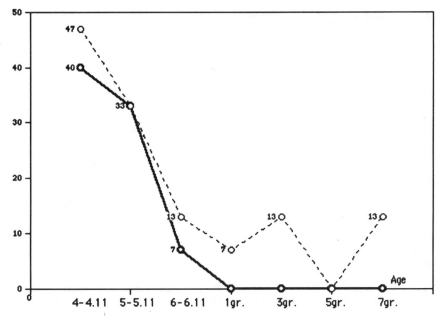

Children who believed that a subjective image of a pencil could appear without having been initiated by a real physical object (q. 3, —o—).
Children who acknowledged that pain could emerge without having been caused by an external physical object (q. 4, --o--).

FIG. 33. Percentages of children producing answers in response to Questions 3 and 4 regarding the possibility of subjective images not initiated by external objects.

Answering Question 6 (whether "redness" belongs to the pencil's physical body or to the subject's brain), the children produced three types of answers. All the preschoolers (except one) and a considerable number of first- and third-graders were sure that the "redness' belonged to the pencil ("The redness is in the pencil", "it is in the paint", "it is in the core") (see Fig. 34). In response to Questions 7 and 8, used to point out indirectly that perceptual organs play a part in the perception of colour, all the children acknowledged that different people can see the same object as having a different colour; most of the children believed they themselves who would see the "right" colour, whereas the other person (or even all people on Earth) would be wrong. Even the discussion used by the experimenter to question the child's view failed to provide any appreciation of the role of the sense organs (the brain) in the perception of "redness". Here are two examples:

Tanija (girl aged 9 years)
   T: The pencil will still be red ... it's their vision, it only seems to them that it's green, but in reality it is red.

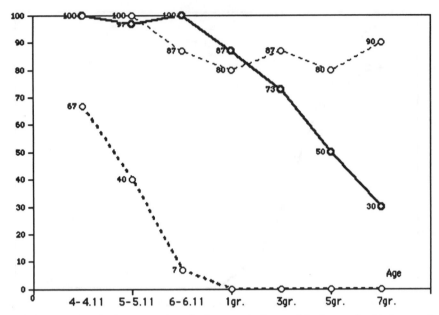

Children who thought that a sensation of redness was in the pencil (q. 6, —o—), with the rest of the children thinking that the sensation of redness was in the subject's eyes (brain) or in the eyes (brain) and in the pencil together.
Children who believed that a sensation of warmth was in the fire (q. 10, --o--), with the rest of the children thinking that it was in a subject or in the subject and in the fire together.
Children who thought that pain was in the needle (q. 11, --o--), with the rest of the children believing that pain was in a subject.

FIG. 34. Percentages of children producing answers in response to Questions 6, 10, and 11 regarding links between physical objects and the subjective images they produce.

E: But wouldn't they think it is you who have the abnormal vision.
T: Well, then I could explain this to them.

Vasia (boy aged 7 years)
V: It'll still be red, you can't change the colour by words.
E: But the other people would think that it's you who sees the pencil as having the wrong colour.
V: Well, I will try to prove they are wrong.

Other children acknowledged that the sensation of colour belongs to the subject's eyes (brain) ("The redness is in my brain ... I can see it and know that it is red"; "Perhaps the redness is in the pencil ... or in my eyes. Perhaps it is in my eyes, because if this radiation hits my eyes they would view the pencil as green"). Finally, some children thought that the redness was both in the pencil and in their eyes (their brains) ("Well, colour can be ... in the pencil and in my eyes"; "Well, it looks as though the redness is in my eyes ... at first it is in my eyes, I can see it, but then when you start drawing it is in the pencil"; "Redness is both there, in the pencil, and in my brain ... there is redness in my brain because the pencil is red"). The number of children who can appreciate the role of the perceptual organs increases among third-graders and older subjects (increase 7 years to 13 years: $\chi^2 = 6.8$, $P < 0.02$) (see Fig. 34).

Similar types of answers were provided regarding the sensation of warmth. A different pattern, however, was revealed with respect to pain. The children who identified pain with a physical object (a needle) were few in number and all preschoolers (decrease 4 years to 6 years: $\chi^2 = 9.18$, $P < 0.01$). Most 5- and 6-year-old preschoolers and all the schoolchildren expressed a strong belief that pain was a product of the perceiving subject and did not belong to the object that had initiated it ("Pain is in me, because it's me who pricked my skin with a needle and not the other way round"; "Pain is in me. The needle has only a sharp end, but it's me who has pain"; "Pain is in me. There is no pain in the needle, it is not alive"). This appreciation of the subjective character of pain co-existed in the main with projecting other subjective qualities (warmth and redness) into external physical objects. However, the experimenter's attempts to make the children see this as a contradiction in their judgements failed. Here are some examples:

Anija (girl aged 9 years)
 E: So what is the difference between heat and pain? If, as you are saying, heat is in the fire, then pain must be in the needle too?
 A: No, the needle is made from iron, it can feel nothing, but human skin, and human flesh, and human blood can be pierced through and it hurts, it hurts.

Lena (girl aged 7 years)
 E: Look, heat too is felt by you in a similar way as pain is. Why are you saying then that heat is in the fire and not in your hand or in your brain?
 L: It is me who feels pain, because the needle doesn't know whom it pricked, it simply is sharp, but heat ... it is in the fire.

Mitija (boy aged 9 years)
 E: Why do you think that heat is in the fire and pain is in you? What is the difference between heat and pain?
 M: Because heat ... it is in the fire. If it were in me I would not exist, I would melt as steel in a blast-furnace, but pain—it is in me because it's me who pricked himself with the needle.

Gena (boy aged 11 years)
 G: Pain is in me, because the needle has pricked my skin, and I feel the pain, but heat ... it is just warmth from fire.

E: But pain also comes from the needle, doesn't it?

G: No, it's me who was pierced by the needle and it is my finger where the pain is.

E: And heat too is in your body and not in the fire?

G: No, it is in the fire.

The boundary that the children drew between pain and two other sub-jective qualities was particularly obvious when a special "imaginative experiment" was conducted with a selected group of five 6-year-olds, six 9-year-olds, ten 11-year-olds, and ten 13-year-olds. The experiment was designed as a continuation of the discussion that followed the children's answers to Question 11 and included an imaginative situation. The children were asked to imagine that the Earth had been hit and a stream of harmful rays from space had killed all living creatures—people, animals, and plants. The children were then asked whether the pencil would remain red, the fire hot, and the needle "painful" after the event. The experiment showed that the overwhelming majority of children confirmed that colour and warmth would remain, whereas pain would disappear. Here are some examples:

Petija (boy aged 11 years)

E: Tell me, if the harmful radiation kills all the living creatures on Earth, will the pencil still be red?

P: Yes, it will.

E: Will the fire still be hot?

P: Yes, it will.

E: And pain, will it stay on Earth or it will disappear?

P: Pain will disappear.

E: Why will it disappear?

P: Because all people and animals will die.

E: And what about redness and heat?

P: Redness will stay and heat will stay also.

Anija (girl aged 13 years)

E: Tell me, if all the living creatures disappeared on Earth, would fire still be hot?

A: Yes, I think it would stay hot.

E: And the needle, would it still be painful?

A: No, to whom would it be painful if there was nobody?

E: So, if there are no living creatures on Earth, pain would disappear?

A: Yes, it would, because there is nobody to experience it.

E: And heat would disappear too, wouldn't it?

A: Heat? In a human being it would, but on Earth it wouldn't. For instance, there is nobody on Venus, but the temperature there is 800°C.

Misha (boy aged 11 years)
E: Would redness stay or disappear?
M: It would stay.
E: And heat?
M: It would stay too.
E: And pain?
M: It would disappear because pain can only be experienced by living creatures, and if they don't exist...
E: And who can experience redness then?
M: Redness is seen by living creatures too.
E: And if they all disappear?
M: Well, redness will stay anyway.
E: But if pain disappears, why should colour remain?
M: Well, if living creatures disappear, there won't be redness for them any more.
E: And in general?
M: In general, colour will stay.

Only 3 of 31 subjects gave a different kind of answer: two preschoolers thought that pain would remain on Earth together with colour and warmth, whereas one 14-year-old boy, (Petija), thought that all of the subjective phenomena would disappear:

E: Would pain stay or would it disappear?
P: It would disappear.
E: And redness?
P: It would disappear too, because there would be nobody to see redness.
E: And what about heat?
P: It would disappear too, because there would be nobody to experience heat.

The imaginative experiment showed quite clearly that redness and warmth were not considered by most children to be subjective phenomena; in the children's view, they were identical to the physical causes that evoke them. Although many of the children may not have been acquainted with the physical theories of colour and thermal processes, they successfully filled this gap in their knowledge by pointing out that redness is something that belongs to the physical body of the pencil and is, therefore, independent of the subjects who may experience it. The same was true with respect to warmth (which was almost invariably identified with temperature), but not to pain, which was treated as a subjective phenomenon by most children older than 4 years. The discrepancy between the way the children perceived pain on the one hand, and warmth and redness on the other, shows that although the distinction between the physical cause and the subjective experience is understood by most children of 5 years and older, it is not transferred to such subjective qualities as warmth and redness—a fact that may have deeper roots in the structure of human perception of various modalities than the present study was concerned with.

Regarding the concluding part of Descartes' procedure, in which a comparison between dreams and reality is made, the results were as follows. Question 14, which prompted the children to come up with criteria that distinguish dreams from reality, yielded four types of answers. In the first type of answers, the children's strong beliefs in a difference between dreams and reality were not supported by any sensible justifications. In the second type of answers (increase 6 years to 9 years: $\chi^2 = 6.57$, $P < 0.02$), the clarity of self perception in the domain of everyday reality, if compared with the lack of such clarity in dreams, was put forward as a criterion ("It is not a dream now, because I am sitting here and can see ... it does not only seem to me but I really can see my body, my dress and these books, toys, this heating radiator... In dreams something seems to me, for instance, I want to touch it and there is no such thing"; "Because I can see only what really exists, and in my dreams I can see things that do not exist and what I only think of").

A few children distinguished between dreams and reality using the criterion of magic being possible or impossible (the third type of answers): "It is not a dream now, because there is logic here, here we are talking to one another, arguing, thinking, and I never noticed that I could think in my dreams ... everything flows on its own there ... and there are various magic transformations, something improbable, impossible"; "You can have something in dreams that is impossible in reality"; and "There are wizards in dreams, but in reality there are not". Lastly, in the fourth type of answers, the children appealed to the fact that everyday reality is continuous and stable and the stream of our life moves constantly ahead, whereas dreams contain short-lasting and occasional images which are often unconnected with one another (*Experimenter:* "Does it seem to you that you woke up but in reality you are still asleep?" "No, because many years have passed, I was small, then I became older and there are still years ahead ... a dream cannot be as long as this"; "No, dreams are different all the time, they are changing, and what I can see here now—this school, this blackboard, these streets around me—this I see every day"; *Experimenter:* "How can you tell that you are awake and not in a dream?" "Because there is daylight outside, and mum wakes me up and I get up"; "Because I can see a different reality ... in which books have no legs and arms"; "Mum switches on the light, I open my eyes and I do my physical exercises"; "Because I get up and see that there is this table here, with this lamp on it, and everything is real and I can touch the lamp and switch it off"; "I can see around me everything that I see every day and that is real. All objects around are normal, and people are normal as usual"; "Because the chain of events changes abruptly: if I saw one thing in my dream, then when I wake up I can see that I am in my bed"). Such answers, given by only a few children in response to Question 14, which encouraged them to make a theoretical distinction between dreams and reality, dominated their responses to Question 17, which focused on the practical criteria the children use every morning to find out that they are awake (increase 5 years to 11 years: $\chi^2 = 13.57$, $P < 0.001$) (Fig. 35).

In response to Question 15, most children denied that people they see in their dreams differ in any way from people they see during a vigilant state of mind. Those who acknowledged that there were some differences justified this by appealing to the stronger clarity of people's images in reality if compared with those in dreams ("Those people in dreams, they are hollow." *Experimenter:* "What do you mean?" "Just that ... I can only see them and imagine, that is all, and if I see a person and he has everything, then the person is real"; "Those people in dreams, they are merely in my head, and these real people ... they walk around ... you cannot touch those people in dreams and these people—you can touch them"; "Those people in dreams—

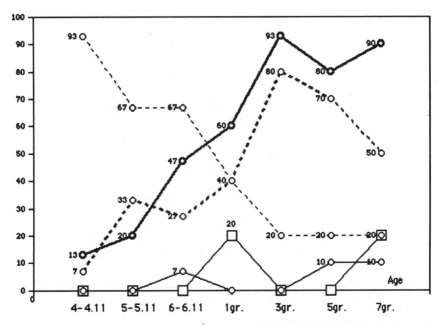

Children who thought that dreams were different from reality and (A) justified their view by pointing out that (1) in reality sensations are clear and distinctive, and in dreams they are not (q. 14, - -o- -), (2) magic is possible in dreams, but not in reality (q. 14, —o—), (3) in reality there is a permanent stream of consciousness, and in dreams, thoughts and images are bizarre and chaotic (q. 14, —□—; q. 17, —o—).
(B) provided no justification - -o- -

FIG. 35. Percentages of children producing answers in response to Questions 14 and 17 regarding differences between dreams and reality.

they have only silhouettes, but they have no bones, nothing"), or by the fact that people in dreams may have an unusual character and behaviour ("Sometimes you can see a person in your dream with a character from another person"; "They can be different in dreams. For instance, we have a girl in the classroom who likes to be bossy, but in dreams she seems to be a nice girl"). Another group of children noted that dream people have unusual appearances ("A person may be old, but it seems in a dream that he is still young"; "Real people are nice, but in dreams they can seem ugly, with big noses"; "Those people in dreams, they are completely different . . . they may have an alligator's snout. I had such a dream once—they can have tails and long necks like a giraffe"). Lastly, some children said that in dreams people can be subject to magical transformations (Fig. 36).

Similar justifications were given regarding the differences between dream and real objects. Some children thought that the two types of objects do not

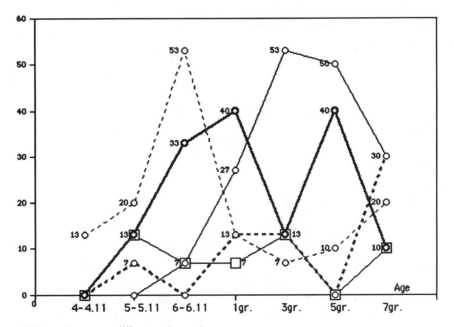

Children who saw no differences (- -o- -).
Children who thought that there were differences and argued that (1) in dreams the images are vague and unclear and in the vigilant state they are clear and distinct (—o—), (2) in dreams people have unusual characters and behaviours (- -o- -), (3) in dreams people can undergo magical conversions (—□—), (4) in dreams people can have unusual appearances and clothes (—o—).

FIG. 36. Percentages of children producing answers in response to Question 15 regarding differences between images of people we have in our dreams and those we have of them in a vigilant state of mind.

differ at all; others noted that dream objects have vague and hazy shapes and look unreal ("The objects in dreams disappear quickly, and real objects—they don't disappear"; "Real objects—you can touch them, but in dreams you cannot touch them, your hand would go through them"); still others pointed out that dream objects had unusual shapes, colours and appearances ("They can be of a different colour and have an unusual shape. What I think about them—they will take this shape, and real objects—they are as they always are"). Lastly, some children thought that in dreams objects can undergo a magical conversion ("Well, in dreams you can put a curse on them, they can be of any shape") (Fig. 37).

The replication study in Britain showed that British 6- and 9-year-olds were significantly more inclined to think that a visual image could appear without an appropriate external initiation than their Russian peers; however, there was a significantly smaller number of such answers among the

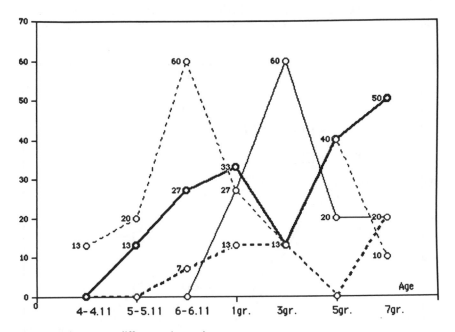

Children who saw no differences (- -o- -).
Children who thought that there were differences and argued that (1) in dreams the images are vague and unclear, and in the vigilant state they are clear and distinct (—o—), (2) in dreams ordinary objects can have unusual shapes and colours (—o—), (3) in dreams objects can undergo magical conversions (- -o- -).

FIG. 37. Percentages of children producing answers in response to Question 16 regarding differences between images of objects we have in our dreams and those we have of them in a vigilant state of mind.

British schoolchildren (Fig. 38). There were no significant differences between the British and Russian children regarding whether sensations of redness and warmth belong solely to external objects (a pencil and a fire) or whether they also belong to the mind (sense organs) (Fig. 39).

However, while significant numbers of Russian 4- and 5-year-olds attributed pain to external objects, none of the British children felt this way (Fig. 39). With regard to the difference between dreams and reality, the British children provided justifications identical to those given by their Russian peers, with the most popular justification being the clear character of sensations in everyday reality versus the vagueness of those in dreams. Although the majority of British children in all age groups acknowledged that dreams were different from reality, significantly more British 4- and 5-year-olds thought that there were no differences between people seen in dreams and real people. Also, compared with their Russian counterparts, significantly more 4-, 5-, and 9-year-old British children thought there were no differences between objects seen in dreams and real objects (Fig. 40). The fact that the British children were so reluctant to acknowledge differences

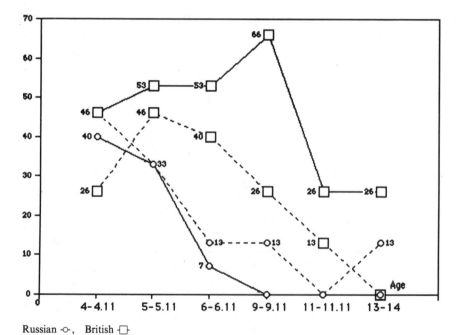

Russian -○-, British -□-
(1) —, (2) - -

FIG. 38. Percentages of Russian and British children who thought that (1) a subjective image of a pencil can appear without being initiated by a real pencil and (2) pain can emerge without having been initiated by an external physical cause.

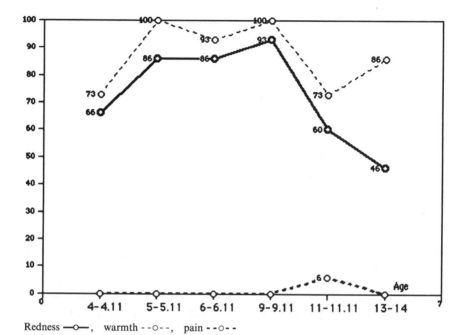

Redness —o—,   warmth - -o- -,   pain - -o- -

FIG. 39.   Percentages of British children who thought that sensations of redness, warmth, and pain belonged only to the external objects which initiated them, with the remainder acknowledging that the mind (sense organs) also plays a part in producing them.

between real and dream entities and lagged far behind Russian children in that respect is unusual and warrants further investigation, especially in light of the study that showed an early appreciation of the differences between real and dream entities in American 3- and 4-year-olds (Woolley & Wellman, 1992). However, the British children who did see a difference between people and objects as they were viewed in dreams and in reality provided justifications similar to those of the Russian children.

In sum, although all the children were aware that there are differences between dreams and everyday reality, it was mainly schoolchildren who were able to produce sensible criteria which distinguish the two domains of reality. The criteria included clarity of sensations and self-perception in a vigilant state (versus the obscurity of the latter in dreams); the strange and bizarre characteristics that people and objects have in dreams compared with those they have in everyday reality; violations of physical causality due to magical transformations, which are possible in dreams but not in everyday reality; and the presence of a permanent and steady stream of consciousness in everyday reality versus the absence of such permanence and constancy of thinking in dreams.

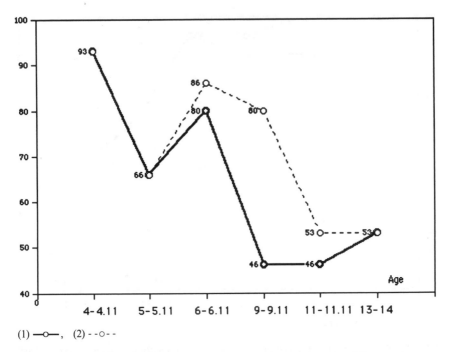

(1) —o—,   (2) - -o- -

FIG. 40. Percentages of British children who thought that there were no differences between (1) the people seen in one's dreams and in reality and (2) the objects seen in one's dreams and in reality.

These results are in accordance with the study of Woolley and Wellman (1992), who showed that 3- and 4-year-old American children can distinguish between real and dream entities, viewing dream entities as private and non-physical and real objects as public and physical. Among the justifications offered by the children were some which referred to the different existential status of real and dream entities ("because it's real", "because it's only pretend"). When asked about real entities ("an ant crawling on the ground") and fictional entities ("ant riding a bike"), most children of both age groups showed an understanding of the fact that, in contrast to everyday reality, dreams can contain both real and fictional objects.

In general, the criteria offered by Russian and British children seem very close to those put forward by Descartes and none of the children's criteria look incompatible with the rationalistic view of the boundary between dreams and everyday reality outlined by Descartes.

As can be seen from Figs. 34 and 39, most 4- to 9-year-old Russian and British children confused the subjective sensations of colour and the physical basis of colour perception, the concept of which is embedded in contemporary physical theories of the atomic structure of nature, electro-magnetic fields, etc. The result of this confusion was that children attributed subjective sensations of colour (redness) to the physical body of the object which initiated the sensation (to the pencil, the paint on it, the core of the pencil, etc.). Even many 11- to 14-year-old children make this mistake.

This may suggest that children (and, in fact, many educated adults) have a poor awareness of the distinction between sensations produced by external objects in the human sense organs on the one hand, and the physical properties of the objects "in their own right" on the other. If this is the case, then scientific education (both at secondary and high schools) is failing to achieve its main aim; that is, to create in students a special kind of the "double vision" of reality, according to which the same objects can be described in terms of sensations (like redness, warmth–coldness, hardness–softness, heaviness–lightness) and in terms of the physical characteristics behind the sensations (like light rays, temperature, consistency, weight, etc.).

Indeed, as has already been mentioned, the double character of reality is a fundamental idea which is deeply rooted in Western rationalism. Thus, Descartes wrote regarding the psychological and physical description of sound: "Most philosophers believe that sound is only a vibration of the air impinging on our ears; thus, if our sense of hearing conveyed to our thought a true image of its object, instead of giving us the ability to perceive sound, this would compel us to perceive the movements of the particles of air that at the time happen to be vibrating near our ears" (Descartes, 1950, p. 174; see similar theories with regard to light in Descartes, 1988). This classic view of Descartes is far from out of date. In fact, according to contemporary scientific theories, a physical object is viewed as a complex entity consisting of physical characteristics (Duncan, 1987; King, 1962), whereas human sensations are interpreted as qualities produced by the human mind and sense organs whenever they are affected by the above-mentioned physical characteristics of objects (Geldard, 1972; Wyszecki & Stiles, 1967).

However, our results suggest that for most 4- to 9-year-olds (and for many older children too), it is not their sense organs and minds that produce sensations of "redness, warmth and hardness", but it is the objects in their own right that are red, warm, and hard.[11] This confusion, however important it is for the creation in a person of the feeling of the outer world's reality, nevertheless contradicts the scientific representation of objects as combinations of physical bodies and fields. In fact, one of the important implicit objectives of a scientific education is the creation of this distinction between subjective and objective ways of describing objects. Thus, in a GCSE textbook on physics (Duncan, 1987), light is described as light rays entering human eyes, colour as a composition of light rays, sound as a kind of vibration that travels through the air to our ears and which we can hear, the weight of a physical body as the force of gravity combined with the resistance of other objects, temperature as a measure of average kinetic energy of the molecules of a physical body, and so on.

In order to further examine this phenomenon, four experiments were conducted in the UK that, unlike the other studies reviewed in this book, had analysis, rather than phenomenological description, as their major aim and complied with the requirements of a traditional statistically oriented study (Subbotsky, 1996). The objectives of Experiment 1 were to examine to what extent 6- and 9-year-old children and adults were able to (1) appreciate the fact that sensations that they have about objects are produced by their minds (sense organs) and are not physical properties of objects; (2) acknowledge that all types of sensations (and not only some kinds of sensations) should be attributed to the human mind (sense organs); and (3) appreciate the role of the human mind (and not only human sense organs) in sensory processes.

Sixteen children in each of the two age groups and 16 adults participated. The younger (8 boys aged 6:0–6:10 years, $\bar{x}$ = 6:4 years; 8 girls aged 6:1–6:9 years, $\bar{x}$ = 6:5 years) and older (8 boys aged 9:1–9:7 years, $\bar{x}$ = 9.4 years; 8 girls aged 9:0–9:10 years, $\bar{x}$ = 9:3 years) groups of children came from a mixed socioeconomic background, recruited from a suburban school; the adults (8 males aged 18–27 years, $\bar{x}$ = 21:3 years; 8 females aged 18–31 years, $\bar{x}$ = 21:6 years) were students at Lancaster University

A red pencil, a small bell, a piece of cotton dipped in perfume, a piece of chocolate, a metallic 1 lb disc, and a cigarette lighter were employed as materials.

The children and adults were questioned individually, and there were eight separate periods of questioning. Each set of questions comprised a few preliminary questions and two key questions which targeted one of seven sensations involved. Six of the seven sets of questions were accompanied by demonstration of each of the sensations; the remaining set concerned pain which was addressed only theoretically by asking the subject to imagine how he or she would feel at the moment when a doctor performed an injection with a syringe.

For instance, with respect to colour the procedure was as follows. A subject was shown a red pencil lying on a table and asked the following preliminary questions: "Can you see this pencil?" "What colour is it?" This was followed by the key questions: "Where do you think this redness of the pencil is, in the pencil or in your mind?" (the order of the words "pencil" and "mind" was randomised) and "Where do you think this redness is, in the pencil or in your eyes?" (the order of the words "pencil" and "eyes" was also randomised). In order to control the role of the order of the key questions, the key questions were given in the reverse order for half of the subjects.

The questions were put in such a way that the mind and sense organs were not presented as alternatives (i.e. they were put as alternatives to the object but not to one another), though it was possible to assess the subjects' preferences with regard to locating sensations mainly in the mind or in the sense organs.

The third possible variation of the localisation question ("Is redness both in the pencil and in the subject's mind or eyes?") was not included so as to avoid providing the subject with an opportunity to escape from searching for a correct solution by simply opting for a compromise. However, if the subject produced this type of answer spontaneously (which happened very rarely), it was registered as a correct answer in which the role of the mind (sense organs) in producing sensations was understood.

Spatial terminology (where is the redness, the ringing, the warmth, the hardness, etc.) was used in the study instead of more precise and philosophically sophisticated wording (i.e. "To which of the two realities does the sensation belong: to the reality of the mind and senses, or to the physical structure of objects?"). This was done because the philosophically accurate wording would be inaccessible for most children and many adults. The wording selected, although metaphorical, was nevertheless not incorrect, because for the layperson it is just through spatial terms that the distinction between psychological and physical realities is represented, with psychological qualities (such as thoughts, sensations, feelings) being viewed as resting "in the mind", "in the head", "in the eyes" and physical qualities (temperature, weight, light, etc.) being embedded in external objects. It was assumed, therefore, that the spatial location employed in the questions (i.e. "in the mind" or "in the pencil") would portray the distinction between the subjective and objective realities in a philosophically unsophisticated mind. It was further assumed that children who, for example, associate warmth with the mind (or the hands) rather than with a fire, mean that warmth is a subjective rather than an objective (physical) quality.

The questions regarding the rest of the sensations included auditory sensations ("the ringing of a bell"), olfactory sensations ("the odour of perfume"), taste sensations ("the sweetness of chocolate"), thermal sensations ("the warmth of fire"), tactile sensations ("hardness *vs* softness" of a physical object), sensations associated with weight ("heaviness *vs* lightness" of the object), and the sensation of pain ("the pain caused by a needle or a syringe"). The questions were asked in the same manner as those regarding colour.

The major objective of the questions was to establish a general picture of the subjects' views on the allocation ("in the subject" *vs* "in a physical object") of various subjective qualities. It was expected that the adults and older children, who were more advanced in their scientific education, would be more likely to appreciate the role of the mind and sense organs in producing sensations than younger children. It was also assumed that the subjects would allocate sensations to sense organs more often than to the mind; the reason for this expectation was that for many children and adults "the mind" is a more obscure and vague notion than are the "eyes", "ears", and other sense organs.

As the comparative study has already shown (see Figs. 34 and 39), there were no significant differences between Russian and British 6- and 9-year-olds' responses to the allocation of redness to the external object or to the subject's mind (sense organs), with more than 70% of children in both cultural groups allocating redness to the external object. With regard to other perceptual qualities, the number of children in the analytical study who showed an awareness of their subjective nature was also quite small (between 20 and 50% of the total sample for most of the sensations) (see Fig. 41).

A statistical analysis of the British subjects' responses revealed no overall age effect regarding their tendency to allocate sensations to the subject rather than to the object. This means that adult subjects show no significant improvement in their understanding of the distinction between the psychological and physical terms of describing an object when compared with 6- and 9-year-old British children (Subbotsky, 1996).

There were, however, significant age changes when using some scales. Thus, 6-year-old boys showed a significantly stronger tendency to allocate sensations to the subject than did 6-year-old girls; there were no such sex

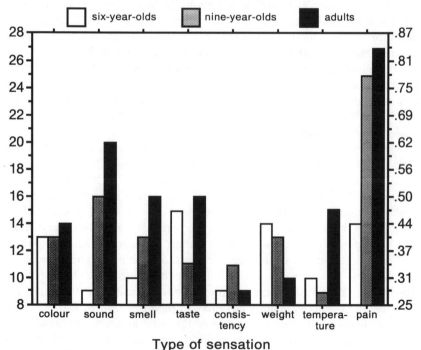

FIG. 41.   Numbers (left) and proportions (right) of answers (out of 32) in which sensations were localised to a subject and not to an object.

differences observed among the 9-year-old children and adults. There are two possible explanations for this. First, it could be assumed that 6-year-old boys are more sensitive to the distinction between subjective and objective properties of objects than 6-year-old girls; second, 6-year-old boys may appreciate the role of the mind and sense organs in producing sensations more than their female peers. Both explanations point to the greater effect that elementary physical science education has on 6-year-old boys compared with girls, a differential effect that disappears with age.

The second major age effect was related to the preference that children of both age groups had for the attribution of sensations to the human sense organs rather than the mind. This result is concordant with that expected and indicates that children of both age groups viewed the sense organs as a more appropriate locus for psychological attributes than the mind. The fact that such a difference was not found in the adult subjects may suggest that adults have a more adequate idea about what the mind is, as well as a better appreciation of the role the mind plays in sensation.

Although the adults and 9-year-old children showed no clear improvement in the "within-subject" allocation of sensations compared with the 6-year-olds, there was nevertheless an indirect indicator of such an improvement. This indicator was the emergence of the differential treatment of various types of sensations by adult subjects who preferred to allocate the "ringing of a bell", and especially the pain in a subject significantly more often than other types of sensations. The reason for this selective appreciation of the subjective character of pain is not yet clear. One possible explanation may be that pain is normally inflicted through direct physical contact between the pain-causing substance and a subject's body (like the one employed in this study), whereas many other types of sensations (vision, hearing, olfactory sensation) are aroused by distant objects.

Yet, despite these indirect indicators of an age-related improvement, most subjects from all groups considered sensations to be inherent properties of external objects, which contradicts modern science's image of the world and that reflected in educational programmes and textbooks (Duncan, 1987). However, this contradiction is not explicitly stated in most textbooks for beginners, which provokes further explanation of the matter in more advanced guides. Thus, in a book for students who "had attended an excellent course in elementary college physics", definitions of temperature involving the physiological sensations of hotness and coldness were qualified as "utterly unreliable", since "a piece of iron may *feel* colder than a block of wood though the two are at the same temperature as determined by any one thermometer" (King, 1962, p. 2). Instead, temperature was defined as "that property of a system which determines whether the system is in thermal equilibrium with other systems" (ibid., p. 2). In a guide on colour concepts, colour stimulus is defined as "radiant energy of given intensity and spectral composition, entering the eye and producing a sensation of colour" (Wyszecki & Stiles, 1967). With respect to the other senses (hearing, taste, sense of pressure, etc.), similar distinctions between physical stimuli and sensations proper are made (Geldard, 1972).

This way of representing modern scientific knowledge is expected to destroy the child's initial naive identification between sensations produced by objects and the objects described in physical terms, and induce in the child's mind the double picture of the world which consists of physical bodies and their subjective images. However, our present knowledge does not allow us to estimate the extent to which the above-mentioned separation really takes place in children's and adults' minds as a result of scientific education.

To examine this, a series of intervention experiments was conducted in which the effects of various kinds of intervention on children's and adults' capacity to appreciate the difference between sensations and the physical characteristics of objects were examined. The interventional strategies used were as follows: direct explanation (Experiment 2), cognitive conflict treatment (Experiment 3), and "personal views conflict treatment" (Experiment 4).

Experiment 2 employed the same subjects as Experiment 1. Three types of sensation (colour, sound, and smell) were selected from the initial sample involved in Experiment 1. Each subject was tested individually. The interventional session consisted of telling a subject a short story in which physical causes of the subjective qualities were described; the story was accompanied with a picture illustrating it. After the story, the subject was asked to reproduce it by answering the experimenter's questions. If the reproduction was satisfactory, questions were asked that were identical to the key questions in Experiment 1. For example, with respect to colour the procedure was as follows:

The story: "You know of course, that different objects have different colours, don't you? Now I'd like to explain to you how people can see colours, OK? Have you ever seen waves on the surface of water? You should know that each object produces a special sort of waves—the light waves. Look at this picture [Fig. 42]. These waves—here they are. They are not coloured themselves, but if they come into human eyes, people can see colours. Now look. Some of the objects produce big and slow waves, the others produce small and quick waves. If big and slow waves come into our eyes, we can see a red colour, and if small quick waves come into our eyes, we can see a green colour.

After a few preliminary questions in which it was ensured that the subjects understood the story correctly, a set of key questions was asked as in Experiment 1. It was expected that if the treatment affected the subjects' tendency to identify sensations with the objects that produce them, then the

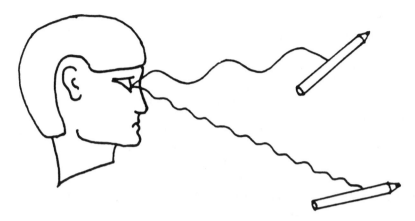

FIG. 42.   Picture used for the demonstration of light rays based on the theory of colour perception.

number of answers making this identification was expected to be significantly smaller after the interventional treatment than before it.

The results showed that direct explanation has proved to be ineffective regarding 6- and 9-year-old children, and only moderately beneficial for adult subjects who showed a significant improvement with regard to sensation of smell after the interventional treatment but not with regard to colour or the auditory senses. Since the original number of adult subjects' correct and incorrect answers in the pre-test (see Experiment 1) were equal (16 *vs* 16) and the only change in the post-test affected incorrect answers, this change cannot be explained by the mere fact of the repeated questioning. Indeed, if the latter were the case and the subjects changed their opinions in the post-test merely because of the fact that they were repeatedly asked the same questions and thought their original answers were wrong, then the change should have affected both correct and incorrect answers. This was not the case, however, the change was unidirectional (that is, caused the transition from incorrect to correct answers only). This indicates that the intervention affected subjects in a selective way and the improvement in answers observed in the post-test should be attributed to the intervention as such and not to the test questions being repeated.

The selective partial success of the direct explanation treatment with respect to adult subjects (and not to the children) can be explained by the fact that adult subjects were intellectually prepared to benefit from the explanation to a greater extent than the children. However, an alternative explanation can be suggested according to which the adult subjects simply benefited from their superior linguistic capacities. Although the children's answers to the check questions showed that they understood the story correctly, their capacity to benefit from this explanation may have been significantly less than that of the adults. Whatever the correct explanation, it is clear that the direct explanation treatment was to a large extent linguistically biased. In order to eliminate the verbal and abstract character of the interventional treatment and to make it more "tangible" for the children and adults, the "cognitive conflict treatment" was employed in Experiment 3.

Sixteen 6-year-olds (8 boys aged 6:1–6.10 years, $\bar{x}$ = 6:8 years; 8 girls aged 6:2–6:9 years, $\bar{x}$ = 6:5 years), sixteen 9-year-olds (8 boys aged 9:1–9:10 years, $\bar{x}$ = 9:5 years; 8 girls aged 9:1–9:10 years, $\bar{x}$ = 9:3 years), and thirty adults (15 men aged 19–26 years, $\bar{x}$ = 21:6 years; 15 women aged 18–29 years, $\bar{x}$ = 21:6 years) participated in the experiment. The children were recruited from another suburban school, and the adults were students at Lancaster University.

A yellow pencil and a multicolour plastic film measuring 42 × 21 cm were used, with one-third of the film being transparent, one-third red, and one-third blue. A metallic disc employed in Experiment 1 for testing subjects' judgements about sensations of weight and consistence, a heavy hammer, and a one-penny coin were also employed in the experiment.

Each subject was tested individually. The pre-test procedure was identical to that in experiment 1 for colour and weight sensations. In the intervention session which followed the colour sensation pre-test, the subject was shown a yellow pencil placed first under the transparent part of the film, then under the red part (which made it look orange) and, finally, under the blue part (which made it look green). Each time the subject was asked what colour the pencil was. After the subject acknowledged that the pencil had changed colour, the following questions were asked: "But you told me earlier that the pencil was [the previous colour of the pencil]"."Have I painted the pencil [the new colour of the pencil]?" "If I didn't, is the pencil [the previous colour] and [the new colour] at the same time?" "If it is not, what is its real colour?" Independently of the subject's answers and immediately after the treatment, he or she undertook a post-test that was identical to the pre-test.

Next, the "weight" pre-test was conducted. In this pre-test (identical to that for "weight" in Experiment 1), the subject was given the metallic disc and asked whether it was heavy or light. Then the subject was asked whether the "heaviness" ("lightness") was in the disc or in the subject's hand (mind). The order of the words "disc/hand" and "disc/mind" was randomised, and the order of the key questions (one giving the mind and the other giving the hand as the alternative to the disc) was reversed for half of the subjects. The pre-test was followed by the intervention session, in which the subject was asked to keep the disc in one of his or her hands and a heavy hammer (which was many times heavier than the disc) in another hand. The following questions were then asked: "How does the disc feel now: is the disc heavy or light?" "Is it heavier or lighter than the hammer?" "But you told me before that the disc was heavy, so how can it be that that disc is heavy and light at one and the same time?"

Next, the subject was asked to replace the hammer with a one-penny coin, and the same set of questions was repeated, this time highlighting the heaviness of the disc in comparison to the coin. The intervention session was followed by the post-test, which was identical to the pre-test.

The assumption behind this interventional treatment was that the clash between the knowledge that an object can have only one colour (or weight) and the fact that the object was actually changing its colour (or weight) would help the subject to realise that the properties of the object they were being asked about were an illusion and, as with any illusion, belonged to the subjects' mind (sense organs) rather than to the object in its own right.

It was thought that this type of treatment would only be successful with subjects who had an idea about the constancy of an object's physical characteristics in contrast to the changeable and situation-biased nature of sensations; therefore, the procedure wasn't expected to affect 6-year-olds. However, there were reasons to believe that 9-year-old children and adults might benefit from the intervention. Indeed, some studies (Light, 1986; Piaget, 1952) have suggested that 6-year-old children are not proficient enough in distinguishing between situation-biased properties of objects (such as, for instance, shapes of liquid substances) and their constant physical characteristics (such as the amount of liquid), whereas children older than 7 (and of course adults) are aware of this distinction. Since the colour and weight of a physical object belong to its stable characteristics, any demonstration of a change in them might help subjects to think that it was not the physical basis of colour and weight but rather their subjective (and changeable) "prints" that they were being asked about.

As in Experiment 2, in this experiment the intervention proved to have only a partial effect: after the treatment, the adult subjects allocated sensations of "heaviness/lightness" to the subjects' mind (sense organs) significantly more often than before the treatment. As in Experiment 2, the change cannot be explained solely in terms of the repeated questioning, since the change obtained was predominantly unilateral: 11 of the 27 incorrect answers in the pre-test were replaced by correct answers in the post-test, whereas only 2 of 33 correct answers in the pre-test were replaced by incorrect answers in the post-test; the difference between the two samples was significant ($z = 2.65$, $P < 0.05$).[12]

The results, however, showed no indication that either 6-year-olds or 9-year-olds benefited from the cognitive conflict treatment, and the adults' tendency to ascribe colour sensation to the object didn't change either. In other words, the varying of the object's perceived colour and weight was not viewed by children (and with regard to colour, by adults) as the proof the subjective character of sensations.

A possible explanation of this failure is that the treatment didn't highlight the changeable and situation-biased nature of sensations on the one hand, and the permanent and situation-independent nature of physical characteristics of objects on the other, with an implicit assumption that this kind of knowledge had already been acquired by the subjects. However, it might have been the case that the children and many adults lacked an appreciation of the fact that what is subject to changes and illusions must necessarily be ascribed to the subject's mind or sense organs; instead, the children and adults may have thought that the physical characteristics of objects could also be transformed into illusory forms under certain conditions (such as covering the pencil with a coloured film). If this was the case, then acknowledging that a pencil could change its colour and the metallic disc could change its perceived weight was not viewed by the subjects as sufficient grounds to ascribe these variable characteristics to the subject's mind (sense organs) and not to the object in its own right.

In order to overcome this kind of confusion between "changeable" and "physical" characteristics of objects, Experiment 4 made it clear to the subjects that the variations in characteristics of objects employed in the experiment could only be attributed to a subject's senses (subject's mind), and the physical prototypes which produced the variable sensations were permanent and independent of the subjects' views or conditions.

To achieve this, the subjects were subjected to the "individual views conflict" treatment, in which one and the same object was perceived and measured by various individuals. In so far as this type of treatment involved intellectual strategies that were unlikely to be present in children (such as comparisons between perceptions of various individuals on the one hand, and measurements made by the same individuals on the other), only adult subjects were involved in Experiment 4.

Sixteen subjects (8 males aged 20–35 years, $\bar{x} = 26{:}1$ years; 8 females aged 19–58 years, $\bar{x} = 27{:}1$ years), all students at Lancaster University participated as subjects. A yellow pencil and a metallic disc were employed as materials.

The same two sensations as in Experiment 3—colour and weight—were employed in this experiment. The pre-tests were identical to those used in Experiments 1 and 3. After the pre-tests, the intervention procedure followed, in which various individual judgements about sensations received from the same objects were contrasted with the unanimity of judgements of the same individuals if the judgements were made about measured physical properties of objects. For instance, with respect to colour, the subjects were asked the following questions:

1. Do you know what makes you perceive this colour as yellow and not, for instance, as green or pink? The sense of this particular colour is produced by light waves with a certain wavelength, so that light waves which produce the sensation of yellow colour have different wavelengths from those that produce the sensation of red colour, OK? [Fig. 42 is shown to the subjects during the explanation.]
2. Now, do you know that there are people who have abnormal colour vision and either cannot see colours at all or see this yellow pencil as green or pink?
3. Now, if you and those people with abnormal colour vision were asked to measure the wavelength of the light waves that come from this yellow pencil [Fig. 43a is shown to the subjects] with a special physical device, would you all come to the same conclusion or to different conclusions?
4. Now, if you and those people were just shown this pencil [Fig. 43b is shown to the subjects] and asked what colour it is, would your answers be the same or different?

A similar type of treatment was used with regard to weight. This time the subjects were prompted to realise that various individuals can perceive the same metallic disc as either light or heavy, but they would agree about its physical weight if they measured the weight on a pair of scales. The post-tests (identical to the pre-tests) were carried out immediately after the intervention.

It was assumed that the treatment would help the subjects to realise the difference between the sensory qualities of objects (which are individually biased) and their physical qualities (which are universal and invariant with regard to the individual characteristics of subjects' perceptual organs), and subsequently acknowledge that sensory qualities belong to the subjects' mind (sense organs) rather than to the objects in their own right.

The "individual views conflict" treatment proved to be more effective than either the "direct explanation" or "cognitive conflict" kinds of intervention with respect to colour sensation, for which a main effect of intervention was found and the effect approached significance with regard to the sensation of weight. This suggests that for some reason it was more difficult for the subjects to appreciate that "heaviness" and "lightness" are properties of an object which are different from the object's physical weight than to acknowledge that "yellowness" or "redness" could be various subjective manifestations of one and the same kind of light rays. No plausible explanation of this differential effect of the "individual views conflict" treatment with regard to colour and weight sensations can be offered for the moment; obviously, the effect warrants further investigation.

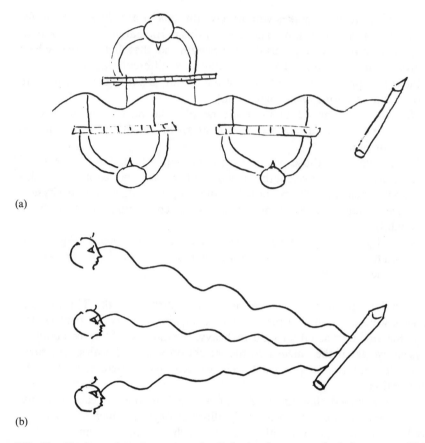

(a)

(b)

FIG. 43. Picture used to demonstrate the distinction between a physical measure of light wavelengths and the sensation of colour.

One important result of this study was that there was no significant improvement in the understanding of the subjective nature of sensations in adults compared with 6- and 9-year-old children. This result is not surprising if one considers that there is no programme of psychological education either in schools or on most university courses (apart from psychology and related courses). The resulting effect is that the confusion between the scientific and psychological terms used to describe physical objects and events, which are typical of young children, remain largely intact as a person goes through the "channel of scientific education".

Thus, Levin, Siegler, Druyan, and Gardosh (1990) reported that both schoolchildren and university students revealed poor knowledge of the fact that various parts of an object rotating around its axis don't move with the same speed. With respect to the distinction between subjective and objective facets of an object's description, a traditional school education does even less than it does to acquaint children with the physical qualities of rotating objects, since the distinction between subjective and objective is often viewed as unimportant. However, even if the distinction is indeed unimportant in some areas of everyday life, it becomes important if scientific education is to be based on firm theoretical grounds.

Nevertheless, the data in this study reveal certain age-related differences. Thus both 6- and 9-year-olds showed a tendency to localise sensations in the sense organs rather than in the mind, whereas adults did not. This can be viewed as a growing appreciation among adults of the role that the mind and thinking play in sensory processes. This may be a result of the wider knowledge that adults have about the functions of mind and "higher mental processes", which they receive both from popular scientific literature and from their empirical self-observation.

Various types of interventional treatment applied to children and adults with the aim of increasing their understanding of the distinction between the subjective and objective facets of an object's description yielded variable results. The "direct explanation" treatment applied in Experiment 2 proved to be mainly ineffective: the only effect was that of test for sensation of smell in adult subjects. A slightly more notable effect was achieved for the "cognitive conflict" treatment (Experiment 3); however, in this study (unlike Levin et al., 1990, who reported cognitive conflict to be an effective mode of intervention) the effect was very limited, in that it only showed an improvement in adult subjects' judgements about the sensation of weight but not about the sensation of colour. The most effective treatment proved to be the "individual conflict" treatment which, due to certain limitations which make it difficult to apply it to children, was applied to adult subjects only.

It can be seen, therefore, that the direct explanation of the distinction between subjective and physical descriptions of objects (which is most likely to be used in classroom teaching) turned out to be the least effective method. This poor effect can be explained by at least two factors. First, the illusion which causes the confusion between the subjective and objective descriptions of an object is usually very strong and difficult to overcome by means of explanation alone. It should be noted, however, that the strength of the illusion varies depending on the kind of sensation; for example in adult subjects, the illusion proved to be very strong with respect to the sensation of colour but was completely absent with respect to pain. Second, the cognitive benefit of making the distinction between the subjective and objective ways of describing an object is not that obvious; even some professional psychologists think that it doesn't actually matter whether "redness" or "heaviness" are viewed as sensations of the subject or as physical properties of an object.

Indeed, in ordinary life, some sensations can quite successfully represent their physical prototypes, which makes direct reference to these prototypes superfluous. However, in science, such confusion between the subjective and physical descriptions of objects can create inconsistencies and paradoxes (see Subbotsky, 1993a), and even in everyday life the lack of a proper understanding of this distinction can enhance in individuals an egocentric confusion between their feelings and views about certain objects and events, and the objects and events as they "really are".

Moreover, it is assumed that acknowledgement of the subjective character of sensations is not an isolated cognitive achievement on the part of an individual, but rather is a particular manifestation of a more general ability to appreciate the double character of reality in which almost every object has two separate manifestations: a subjective image (the visible image of a cube, for instance) and its rational construction (the same cube as a physical body with such unchangeable characteristics as magnitude, shape, molecular structure, etc.). Much of psychology has been devoted, for example, to the examination of the development of understanding of rational constructions by children (e.g. the development of various types of conservation). One of the most obvious demonstrations of the double character of reality is the phenomenon of an object changing in size as it is moved away from (or closer to) the observer. Children should be able to understand the double character of reality if they are able to acknowledge two things at once: that an object becomes smaller the further it is moved away from the observer and yet it remains the same at the same time (i.e. it retains its physical shape and magnitude, *not* to be confused with an understanding of constancy of shape and magnitude). In the light of this, it would be interesting to examine in future research whether children's capacity to distinguish between the subjective and objective terms of reality with regard to sensations would positively correlate with their ability to distinguish between other types of phenomenal images and rational constructions, such as objects' visible (versus real) shape and size.

Returning to the results of the present study, it can be seen that the "cognitive conflict" treatment (Experiment 3) also produced a very moderate effect. It was not until adult subjects were made to realise that individuals' sensations with respect to the same object could vary (the "individual views conflict" treatment in Experiment 4), that many subjects were prepared to acknowledge that the "redness" or "heaviness" of objects were produced by subjects' senses (minds) and were not physical properties of the objects. Although limited, the change, nevertheless, demonstrated that to a considerable degree human sensations are conventional and situation-biased psychological units in contrast to physical properties of objects which are universal and invariable. It was this contrast between the situation-biased nature of sensations and the universality of physical properties of objects that our subjects were most sensitive to. This suggests that the "socioconstructive" approach to human sensations and psychological functions can be a most powerful educational means of dealing with common illusions, such as the confusion between human sensations and the physical properties of objects that initiate these sensations.

CONCLUDING REMARKS: CHILDREN'S REASONINGS ON THE METAPHYSICS OF THE WORLD

Within the age range 4–14 years, children acquire definite and sensible solutions to many metaphysical problems and many of these solutions are close to those given by Descartes. Thus, at the beginning of the dialogues, the children of all age groups produced a number of statements which they viewed as being unquestionable and flawless. The statements included claims about the existence of the external world, the personal existence of the child, the adequacy of the subjective images of objects for the objects in their own right, the existence of subjective experiences (visual sensations, sensations of pain and hunger) and their necessary links with the external objects that initiated them, and the distinction between the everyday reality and dreams.

When encouraged to doubt their statements in the course of the subsequent conversations, most children agreed that some of the statements could be viewed as unreliable. The first type of knowledge to be questioned was probabilistic knowledge (the experimenter's statement that he has a cigarette lighter in his pocket), which was doubted by children as young as 5; this was followed by the belief that our sensory images of objects are identical to what the objects are "really and truly" (this was questioned by most 6-year-olds and older children). Interestingly, scepticism about these types of knowledge was expressed even by those children who were unable to produce any sensible definition of true and false knowledge.

At a later age, the children acquired a capacity to question some more stable and firm beliefs, such as the belief that our images of objects (including images that we have of our bodies) correspond strictly to the objects as they are in their own right. With respect to the image of the body, it was not until the children reached 9 years of age that most of them accepted the idea that the shape of their bodies could be different from that they thought their bodies had ("Maybe, in reality, I live on a different planet and my body resembles that of an octopus"). Regarding images of external objects, it was notable that even many 5-year-olds were able to acknowledge that our sense images differ from the objects they represent (the sun as we see it is unlike the sun in its own right, which is "much bigger and hotter"). However, most children younger than 11 refused to accept the idea that subjective images may be totally different from what real objects are; there had to be a general resemblance between the images and the objects being viewed.

However, some beliefs could not be changed, including the children's beliefs in their own personal existence, in the existence of the external world, in the existence of the children's personal experiences (sensations and feelings), in the fact that these experiences have been evoked (initiated) by some real external objects (a pencil, a fire, a needle). Another was the belief that the "almighty wizard" could not exist in the real world.

All the subjects stressed their strong belief in their personal existence. More than that, most 6-year-olds and older children were able to produce a proof of this which was similar to Descartes' "cogito ergo sum". According to this proof, being and thinking (imagining, doubting, being in any of the active conscious mental states) is one and the same thing; or, to put it differently, the mere awareness by an individual that he or she has mental activity is a necessary and sufficient indication of the individual's personal existence.

At a slightly older age (around 7 years), most children become aware of yet another fundamental rationalistic idea, that there is an identity between existence and truth (truth is a statement about something that really exists, and falsehood a statement about something that doesn't exist). At approximately the same time, the children become aware that to ensure that a certain piece of knowledge is true, it has to be checked through personal experience.

Something else that appeared not to be open to question was the children's inability to separate object and subject. This was manifested in the children's refusal to accept that it was possible to doubt the real existence of the external world ("Where would I be if there were not the world?") and the existence of subjective phenomena (like pain, redness, warmth) without the existence of external objects (a needle, a pencil, a fire) that initiated the phenomena. However, the capacity to justify this primary intuition didn't appear until age 11, significantly later than the capacity to justify the identity between existence and thinking (which appears in children around 6 years of age). This suggests that the idea of the "thinking–being" identity is more fundamental and intuitively obvious for children than the idea of the "subject–object" inseparable unity—a fact that fits well with the "subordination" between the fundamental ideas made by Descartes. Another distinction that seemed to be clear for most children was the distinction between everyday reality and dreams. The criteria produced by the children were close to those generated by Descartes.

In contrast to the above-mentioned ideas, such an important element of rationalist metaphysics as the acknowledgement of the real existence of the Supreme Being on the mere grounds of the idea that such a being exists, seems to be totally alien to the overwhelming majority of children. Although some of the youngest subjects were quick to acknowledge the "almighty wizard's" real existence, this did not appear to have been caused by a real understanding of the "ontological argument"; rather, in their judgements, the children were guided by their uncritical attitude towards certain fairy-tale characters whom they were happy to let into everyday reality. However, all 6-year-olds and older children emphatically denied that the almighty wizard could exists outside their imagination. The stubborn resistance the children revealed towards the "ontological argument" can be explained by the combination of at least two factors.

The first factor may stem from a certain emotional resistance to the idea of the real existence of the almighty subject. First, education (especially an atheistic education, as in the Russia of the 1980s) helps children to develop a strong distinction between everyday reality and the unusual realities such as dreams and fairy tales (see Subbotsky, 1993a), which prevents fairy-tale characters (which, most probably, the "almighty wizard" was for the children) from permeating the domain of everyday reality. Second, the traditional image of the wizard in folk and fairy tales depicts him or her as a capricious and despotic creature who is likely to violate the laws of nature, rather than as a wise guardian and protector of those laws. All this makes the idea of the real existence of such an extraordinary creature highly undesirable for children.

The second factor may have a cognitive, rather than emotional, under-pinning. It is the incapacity of the children to get to grips with the impli-cations of the "almightiness" of the imaginative subject. In contrast to all other possible imaginative ideas whose existence in our imagination is not sufficient for them to be acknowledged as really existing things, the idea of an "almighty subject", according to Descartes, cannot possibly be produced by ourselves and therefore makes us acknowledge the real (and not only imaginative) existence of the object (or subject) to which the idea refers. As a long history of attempts to overthrow the "ontological argument" shows, an understanding of the logical necessity of a link between the idea of the Supreme Being and the Supreme Being's real existence has always been notoriously difficult. No wonder, therefore, that our subjects lacked this understanding too.

However, an analytical study of British children and adults (who proved to be as resistant to the ontological argument as the children) showed that it was not cultural differences or a misrepresentation of the image of the almighty wizard for a human-like creature that made the idea of the almighty wizard coming out of our minds so unacceptable. In fact, the subjects' resistance had nothing to do with logical arguments but was engendered by psychological causes. Specifically, it was the subjects' strong belief in object permanence [i.e. the impossibility for an imaginative entity to spontaneously acquire real (physical) existential status] that was the major obstacle to an acceptance of the ontological argument. Not until the belief in object permanence was weakened in a special experimental condition did a significant number of subjects begin to accept the ontological argument.

Finally, one further fundamental aspect of European rationality that was evolving in these children's minds was the distinction between mind and body. At the age of 4–5 years, these categories are often confused by children. Although the body and its attributes (shape, spatial location, weight, nourishment, accessibility to sense organs, divisibility, etc.) are more tangible for children than are mental attributes (thinking, imagination, etc.), it is the former that attract children's attention most of all. For many preschoolers, something is real only if it can be perceived through the senses, whereas psychological entities like "I" and thoughts simply "don't exist". While being aware of the body's attributes, most children of 4 and 5 relate them not only to the body but also to psychological entities. It is not until children reach the age of 6 that psychological phenomena become free of most physical qualities.

Another important feature which children use to distinguish between body and mind is their belief in the independence of psychological entities ("I" and thoughts) from the body. This belief becomes apparent in children aged 4–6 years of age and manifests itself in statements in which illness or physical injury don't affect the "I" and thoughts, although the former can be reflected in the latter. Even pain is not related to the class of mental entities by many children ("thinking can only think about the pain, but it's the body that feels it"). Lastly, many schoolchildren develop a purely rationalistic view of the individual having direct access to his or her mental entities which are, therefore, easier to cognise than is the body which is not "directly" open to the individual ("Thoughts are easier to study than is my body. My soul is somehow open to myself, I know my soul, and my body . . . it has yet to be studied").

The confusion between mental and physical properties that was a characteristic feature of thinking in 4- and 5-year-olds doesn't mean that children of this age are aware of the inseparable unity which exists between the mind and the body of a real human individual. The controversial nature of the children's judgements was just this striking combination of ascribing physical properties to the mental entities ("I" and thoughts) on the one hand, and viewing them as totally independent from the body (that is, not vulnerable to physical injury, illness or even death) on the other. This type of reasoning, which was very close to Descartes' idea of the independence of the mind from the body, almost disappears among 9-year-olds and older children, for whom death of the body also means death of all mental manifestations of the individual. It may be assumed that the idea of the "immortal nature of mind", which is a classic element of Cartesian metaphysics (but which can also be seen to be incorporated in many religious systems around the world) is a consequence of confusion between the conceptual and ontological planes of viewing the relationship between body and mind. With the onset of the physicalistic theories and views which are part of the European school of education, the ontological plane of the body–mind relationship becomes more salient for most children who gradually abandon the view of the individual mind's immortality.

Thus, along with the typical rationalistic metaphysical ideas and solutions which appear in children of the age studied here as constant and permanent views, some solutions were found which seemed to be ousted from the children's minds as they grew older (the idea of the immortal nature of human "I" and "thoughts", the idea of the real existence of the almighty wizard). Although these solutions were naive and cannot be held to be on the same plane as those of Descartes (which were the result of sophisticated philosophical meditations), their meaning was very close to those proclaimed by Descartes.

At first glance, this looks somewhat strange and runs counter to the theories that portray cognitive development as a steady process. However, a closer look at the structures mentioned above reveals that in children they either have an intuitive ("'I' cannot die because it does not exist") or dogmatic ("The wizard lives in the forest") character which makes them contextually quite different from ideas of Descartes. In this regard, abandoning these beliefs at a later age may be a result of children's intellectual growth rather than a sign of the weakening of their precocious "philosophical capacity". In order to gain a genuine understanding of the "immortality of soul" and the necessity of the existence of the Supreme Being, these abandoned naive preconceptions must reappear as a part of mature thinking and experience. According to our results, this never happens in children of the age studied here, and with regard to the necessity of the Supreme Being's existence, this is even beyond the understanding of most adults.

There were also a few ideas in the "Cartesian group" which failed to appear even in the older children. The limits to our subjects' reasoning were manifested in the children's strong belief that certain subjective qualities (warmth, redness) belong to the physical bodies of objects and not to the subject's brain or the subject's perceptual organs. In a separate analytical study, this belief was proved to be true with regard to many other subjective qualities, and it was shared by Russian and British children as well as British adults. The application of special interventional methodologies showed that the confusion between subjective and physical qualities of objects was very strong and resistant to either a direct explanation or an indirect "perceptual conflict" treatment. It was only under the "social views conflict" treatment that this confusion was partially overcome in the majority of adult subjects.

Most children also failed to get to grips with the idea that names of objects are conventional and don't reflect an object's physical properties.

The comparative study in Britain showed that, with a few exceptions, British children manifested the same phenomena that the Russian children did, including the illusion of independently acquired knowledge, allowance for the possibility of doubting the shapes that our bodies and external objects seem to have, the unquestionable belief in our own existence and the existence of the external world, the growing awareness of the fundamental difference and yet inseparable unity between body and mind. The British children also provided justifications for their beliefs similar to those of the Russian children. Like the Russian children, the British children experienced the illusion that subjective qualities of objects (like redness or warmth) belong to external objects and not to subjects' minds (sense organs); they also unanimously denied the possibility of the almighty wizard coming out of our imagination into the real world. All this suggests that the development of metaphysical judgements in Russian and British children follow the same path.

Of course, cultural differences did affect certain aspects of this development. Thus, the earlier beginning to the intensive school education in Britain compared with Russia may account for the earlier realisation among British children that part of their knowledge is acquired from other people. The different "cultural stress" when talking with young children about magic and magicians, could have been responsible for the differences between Russian and British 4-year-olds in their beliefs about the real existence of the almighty wizard. Yet these and other differences cannot disguise the fact that the development of metaphysical thinking in Russian and British children is much the same, which supports the assumption about the fundamental and uniform character of metaphysical beliefs that exist within one type of rationality.

In general, the study revealed that as children advance in age, the solutions they give to cartesian metaphysical problems approach those suggested by Descartes, with the most sensitive period for the acceptance of rationalistic views being around 6–7 years of age. As far as most of these rationalistic solutions (such as the view that there is an identity between being and thinking, between being and truth, the appreciation of the inseparable unity between mind and body, etc.) are beyond the limits of the school curriculum, it is reasonable to assume that they appear spontaneously in the course of the child's life and everyday experience. It is quite obvious that European languages, thinking habits, social and moral norms, the ways of creating and handling human artifacts, fine arts, and other facets of the contemporary European culture, implicitly (if not explicitly) incorporate major structures of European rationality. It is not implausible to assume that in the course of various activities and education, children absorb ideas which lay the foundation for their metaphysical world outlook.

It can be further hypothesised that these rationalistic structures, which appear as latent and unconscious consequences of the child's everyday experience and independent thinking, later begin to exercise a feedback effect on the process of learning, providing the child with a special "language" to help him or her get to grips with many areas of European culture (such as sciences, fine arts, law, etc.), which are, whether we like it or not, biased by the history of European rationality. The way this backward influence affects children's development and education will, however, be the subject of a special study.

NOTES

1. The answers given by the children were then classified and presented in a descriptive form (the name of the class and examples of the children's judgements or justifications) and in pictorial form. As some of the children failed to produce answers to certain questions and some of the answers were impossible to interpret, the percentage of children in any age group answering a particular question may not equal 100%.

2 This study was undertaken by Nikki Ratcliff as part of her BSc research project (see Ratcliff, 1995).

3. This study was undertaken by Sharon Bland as part of her BSc research project (see Bland, 1994).

4. When the results of the original Russian study are being discussed, I use the terms "subjects", "children", "schoolchildren", or "preschoolers"; when the results of the replication study in Britain are being discussed, I use the terms "British children", "British adults", "British subjects", or "adults" (as there were no adults in the original Russian study).

5. Only the average numbers of answers to the key questions are presented in the figures; the other questions in each dialogue were included to prepare the children for the key questions or to repeat the key questions in a different form. The children's answers to some of the non-key questions are analysed in the text.

6. For convenience, differences between age groups will be shown as follows: "(increase [decrease] x years to y years: $\chi^2 = 0.00$, $P < 0.00$)". The comparisons were made using the chi-squared test with continuity correction.

7. For the assessment of "within-subjects" differences, McNemar's z-test for dependent samples was used (Glass & Stanley, 1970).

8. The term "I" was employed in the Russian study, whereas the term "self" was used in the replication study in Britain as it is a traditional equivalent for "I" in the English language.

9. If the key question consisted of more than one actual question, the line in the figure represents the average number of one particular type of answer, calculated on the basis of all the answers to questions related to the key question. For example, Questions 6–8 relate to one key question examining whether children attribute shape to the body only, to mental entities only, or to both the body and mental phenomena.

10. The replication was carried out by Sharon Bland as part of her BSc research project (see Bland, 1994).

11. This is not to be confused with the famous illusion of confusing "reality" with "appearance", according to which an object that possesses certain subjective qualities (e.g. an apple made of plastic) can be mistaken for another object which produces similar sensations but

has a different function and chemical structure (e.g. a real apple) (see Brain & Shanks, 1965; Flavell, 1986; Tailor & Flavell, 1984).

12. A McNemar's z-test for independent measures was used to assess the difference between the changes in answers in the post-test compared with the pre-test (see Glass & Stanley, 1970).

3

Children's Judgements About the Metaphysical Aspects of a Human Being

In addition to metaphysical problems related to reality as a whole, there is a special group of problems which emphasise what might be called "human reality". It is very difficult to distinguish between "human reality" and "reality proper" in general terms, since reality can only be conceived as reflected in an individual human being or, as Kant (1965, p. 85) put it, "reason can see only what it created according to its own plan". Nevertheless, since antiquity human reality has been studied as a separate reality, as a "microcosm" in which the "cosmos" of the external world is reflected and provided with sense and meaning.

Recently, developmentalists have become increasingly interested in children's judgements about human psychology. This resulted in a series of studies which concerned children's understanding of perception (Flavell et al., 1981), of human feelings (Carroll & Steward, 1984; Donaldson & Westerman, 1986), of emotions (Bullock & Russell, 1984; Harris, 1989), defence mechanisms (Dollinger & McGuire, 1981), and so on. Most of these studies, however, concentrated on those particular aspects of human psychology which are confined to the realm of scientific expertise.

As is the case with metaphysical problems of external reality, metaphysical problems of human reality (which might also have been called "metapsychological problems" had they not touched upon many aspects of physical reality) intersect with problems traditionally studied by such sciences as psychology, physiology, and sociology. They are different from scientific problems, however, in that they go beyond the realm of traditional scientific thinking and scientific experiment. This does not mean that no definite solutions to the problems are possible; it only means that the solutions will depend very much on certain fundamental beliefs about human beings rather than on any established and verified facts. Thus, for instance, a newborn infant (or even a fetus in the mother's womb) is the subject of many sciences; however, no scientific discipline is prepared to answer the question whether the infant (or fetus) has a personality with all sorts of complex emotions and a developed "inner world", or is just an organism similar to subhuman organisms. It is this inability of the sciences to answer this fundamental metaphysical question about the bonds between the human organism and the human "spirit" that generates complicated social dilemmas, such as those concerning euthanasia and the legality of abortion.

The same is true with respect to the causal determination of human actions. Scientific investigation can trace the smallest actions and movements of a criminal up to the moment of the crime itself; however, it is unable to answer the basic question whether the criminal acted as a "free agent" and is therefore personally responsible for the crime, or whether his or her actions were predetermined by certain external circumstances. Paradoxically, this final judgement rests upon the shoulders of a jury of laypeople.

It is such problems that were the subject of most of the dialogues in this chapter. It starts with a dialogue about the "threshold" that has to be crossed by newborn infants before being attributed with "understanding" and "self-realisation" as well as the capacity to generate moral feelings. This dialogue, mostly "psychologically' oriented, is followed by dialogues that investigate more difficult metaphysical problems, including the freedom of an individual action (Dialogue 2, "Freedom"), the fundamental "incompleteness" and "unfinished nature" of human passions and wishes (Dialogue 3, "Faust"), the role of the unconscious in human conscious actions (Dialogue 4, "The unconscious"), the borderline between the human mind and that of animals and plants (Dialogue 5, "Inner world"), the fundamental human need to go beyond the limits of one's individual lifetime (Dialogue 6, "Lifetime"), and the limits which everyday reality lays upon human wishes and thoughts (Dialogue 7, "Reality").

Altogether, 73 children took part in this study: seventeen 5-year-olds (mean age 5:3 years) and fifteen 6-year-olds ($\bar{x}$ = 6:6 years) were recruited from a kindergarten in Moscow, and 11 first-graders ($\bar{x}$ = 7:4 years), 10 third-graders ($\bar{x}$ = 9:7 years), 10 fifth-graders ($\bar{x}$ = 11:7 years), and 10 seventh-graders ($\bar{x}$ = 13:3 years) were recruited from Moscow schools.

The procedure was the same as in the study of children's metaphysical judgements presented in Chapter 2.

DIALOGUE 1: "PSYCHOLOGY"

The structure of this dialogue was based on the tract by the 18th-century French philosopher Condillac (1969) and on the model of psychological development created by Russian psychologist Lev Vygotsky (1981). Condillac (who was also one of the founders of the rationalist view of human beings) created a model suitable for the investigation of children's judgements about the capacities and the limitations of the human infant's sensations. Vygotsky produced a model which, far from being alien to the general rationalist view of human beings, stresses the role of language as a means of converting human lower mental functions (e.g. the primary sensations, perceptions, etc., which are similar to those of other species) into higher mental functions which are specific to humans and are subject to reflective contemplation and voluntary control.

The aims of this dialogue were to determine to what extent children are capable of understanding that a newborn human infant is unable to: (1) reflect its sensations mentally; (2) distinguish between sensations and the objects which cause them; (3) relate its sensations to its own person; (4) know names of objects; and (5) understand that the acquisition of speech and knowledge about objects' names and moral norms by a child does not bring with it knowledge about the social functions of those objects and the capacity to conform to moral norms. The dialogue had three parts: "sensations and perception", "names and functions of objects", and "moral knowledge and behaviour".

In the replication study of this dialogue in the UK, 4-, 6-, 9-, and 13-year old children took part as subjects; there were 20 children in each age group, which were made up of equal numbers of boys and girls.[1]

Each subject was interviewed individually. The child was shown a plastic doll whose eyes, ears, nose, and hands were covered with pieces of plasticine. There were also a red ball and a blue cube made of plasticine, a door key, a coin, and a little bell on the table. The instructions were as follows: "Look at this doll. Let's imagine that it is a child who's just been born, OK? The child is alive but it is not yet able to see anything, to smell, to hear, to move, or to touch anything with its hands—look, its eyes and ears and hands are covered with plasticine. Neither can it speak or know anything at all, OK?

Part 1. Sensations and Perceptions

After a few questions to check that the child understood what had been said about the doll, the plasticine was removed from the doll's nose and the following questions were asked:

1. Now that I have removed the plasticine from the infant's nose, it can smell odours, OK? Tell me, if I place a piece of tissue dipped in perfume under the infant's nose, will it be able to smell the perfume?
2. And will it know that it is the odour of perfume and not the odour of, say, a rotten potato?
3. And will it be able to know that it is the infant itself, and not some other person, who smells the perfume?
4. Will it realise that it is a small child?
5. Will it realise that other people exist in the world?
6. And this odour of perfume, will it be pleasant or unpleasant for the infant?
7. And if I place under the infant's nose an object with an unpleasant smell, will it smell a good odour or a bad odour?

The plasticine is then removed from the doll's ears:

8. Look, its ears are now open too and it can hear sounds, OK? If I ring a bell near its ear, will it hear the sound?
9. Will it realise that it is the sound of a bell and not, for instance, the sound that a fly produces?
10. And will it realise that it is the infant itself, and not some other person, who hears the sound?
11. And if I say "Hello, there", will it hear me?
12. Will it understand what I have said.
13. Will it realise that other people exist in the world?

The plasticine is then removed from the doll's hands:

14. Look, now it can move its hands and touch everything, OK? If I give this key to it to keep, will it be able to feel the key?
15. Will it understand that it is a key?
16. And if I give it my fur hat to touch, what will it feel?
17. Will it understand that this is a hat and not another object?
18. And if it puts its hand in hot water, what will it feel?
19. Will it understand that it is water and not sand, for instance?
20. Will it understand that other people exist in the world?

The plasticine is then removed from the doll's eyes:

21. And now its eyes are open and it can see things. If I show it this red ball, what will it see?
22. Will it be able to understand that it is a ball and that it is red in colour?
23. And if I show it this blue cube, will it see it?

24. Will it understand that this is a cube and that it is blue?
25. If I put the ball and cube next to each other, will the infant realise that they are different objects and look different?
26. And if I move this ball far away from the infant, will it be able to see it?
27. Will it realise that the cube is closer to it than the ball?
28. And if the infant looks at a human person, what will it see?
29. Will it realise that this is a human being and not a cat, for instance?
30. Will it realise that it is a human being itself?

Part 2. Names and Functions of Objects

The children were asked to imagine that the infant had been taught to speak and taught the names of all the things around it.

31. If I place the piece of tissue dipped in perfume under the infant's nose now, what will it smell?
32. Will it know that this is the smell of perfume?
33. Will it know what perfumes are used for?
34. And if I ring the bell near the infant, what will it hear?
35. Will it understand that this is the sound of a bell?
36. Will it know what bells are used for?
37. If I give the infant this coin to keep, will it know that it is a coin?
38. Will it know what money is used for?
39. And if the infant looks at a human being, what will it see?
40. Will it understand that it is a human being and not, for instance, a dog?
41. Will it understand that it itself looks like a human being?
42. And if I say "Hi, say Hello to me", will it understand what I have said? Will it answer me?
43. And if I teach the infant what a spoon and a cup are called, will it be able to eat with a spoon and drink from a cup?

Part 3. Moral Knowledge and Moral Behaviour

44. Let us imagine that our infant gets hungry and sees a piece of chocolate on the table. What will it do?
45. And if at this very moment another child comes to our infant and asks politely for a piece of chocolate, will our infant give the other child a bit or not?
46. And if our infant is hungry and sees another child who has a piece of chocolate in its hand, will our infant take the chocolate away from the other child or not?
47. Let us imagine that our infant is alone in the room and breaks an expensive porcelain vase. If the infant knows that it is likely to be punished, will it confess to the owners of the vase or not?

48. Does the infant know that it is good to share one's sweets with other children, that it is good to be honest and not to tell lies, or does it not know this?
49. And if we tell the infant what is right and what is wrong, will it share sweets with another child? Will it take the chocolate away from another child? Will it tell the truth about who broke the vase?
50. For our infant to do good things, is it enough to tell it what is good and what is bad, or is that not enough?
51. Are there children in the world who know how they should behave but they still don't behave?
52. But if they know how they should behave, why don't they behave?

Regarding the first part of the dialogue (sensations and perceptions), the results of the study showed that all the children acknowledged the newborn infant's capacity to experience olfactory, auditory, tactile, and visual sensations and to distinguish between various kinds of the sensations (i.e. between pleasant and unpleasant odours, between ringing of a bell and the sound a fly makes, between hard and soft, cold and warm, red and blue).

How children view the relationships between the senses and the objects that produce them was a more complex issue (see Fig. 44). Most preschoolers and some schoolchildren thought that although the newborn could not speak and had no personal experience it could, nevertheless, know what kind of objects produced these particular sensations, although it had not been specified in the question what this knowledge includes. The majority of the children grounded their opinions in such a way as to suggest that sensations alone contain information about the objects from which they are initiated and a newborn infant is capable of realising this ("The infant will understand that this is perfume, because it is the smell of perfume, and rotten potato has a different smell"; "He will touch the water, and the water is not hard and heavy, and the infant will realise instantly that this is water"; "He will understand that this is a cube, it has sides, and a ball—it is round shaped").

The number of children who attributed an inherent capacity to the infant to guess what objects are on the basis of mere sensations decreased significantly among the 11-year-olds compared with the 5-year-olds (χ^2 scores for various kinds of perceptions were as follows: olfactory, $\chi^2 = 4.58$, $P < 0.05$; auditory, $\chi^2 = 5.57$, $P < 0.02$; tactile, $\chi^2 = 1.63$, NS; visual $\chi^2 = 7.38$, $P < 0.01$). In general, the children were inclined to ascribe knowledge about sense-initiating objects to the infant's visual sensations significantly more often than to the infant's sensations of other modalities ($z = 5.57$, $P < 0.01$). The remaining subjects (mainly schoolchildren) refused to ascribe knowledge about sense-initiating objects to the newborn infant on two major grounds. Almost all preschoolers and first-graders pointed out that it was only visual sensations that could directly provide information

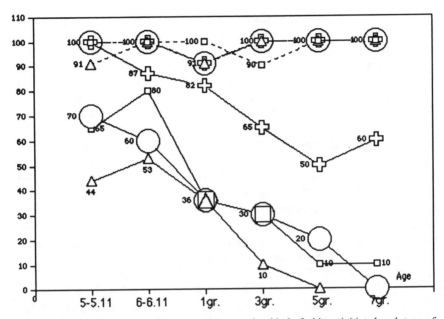

Children who thought that an infant would know what kind of objects initiated each type of sensation (1) before the infant acquired language (—) and with regard to olfactory sensations (q. 2, ○), auditory sensations (q. 9, □), tactile sensations (q. 17, △), and visual sensations (qq. 22 & 23, ✛), and (2) after the infant acquired language and learned objects' names (- -), with each type of sensations shown by the same symbol as above, qq. 32, 35, 37, and 40, respectively.

FIG. 44.   Percentages of children producing answers in response to questions regarding the infant's knowledge of objects that cause various sensations.

about the objects that initiated them, whereas sensations of other modalities could only be "object-related" if they were accompanied by visual sensations ("The infant won't be able to understand that this is a key, because his eyes are closed"; "He won't realise that this is the odour of perfume, because he cannot see anything"). The second type of justification which was produced by most 9-year-olds and older children stressed the absence of personal experience in the newborn child; according to this view, since the infant has just been born, it cannot know what kind of objects are associated with its sensations ("No, he won't be able to know, because he doesn't know what perfume is and what the odour of the rotten potato is"; "I think the infant won't understand this because the infant is only seeing the world for the first time in his life"). By providing such justifications, the children didn't suggest directly that it is necessary for the infant to communicate with other people in order to gain the experience it needs; however, this suggestion might have been present implicitly in their reasoning.

Almost all subjects stated that after the infant was taught to speak and taught the names of objects in its immediate environment, it would know what objects initiated the sensations (Fig. 44). Those children who had already claimed this simply reproduced their previous justifications, which they provided with regard to the prespeech infant; obviously, the fact that the infant had learned to speak didn't affect the children's judgements. Many of the children, who denied that the prelinguistic infant was able to know anything about sense-initiating objects, attributed such knowledge to the speaking child, providing two types of justification. Some of them thought that the infant could now see the objects and therefore must know what they are (the "priority of vision" type of argument) ("Now the infant will know that it is a bell ringing, because his eyes are open"; "He will know, he will see with his eyes that it is a bell that makes the sound"). Others believed that if the infant had been told the objects' names, then it was able to associate sensations with the objects ("If you come to the child and tell him that this is perfume, then he will understand that it is perfume that produces this odour"; "Well, she has been told the names, and now she will have a look at it, touch it, and, perhaps with some difficulty, she will tell that this is a key"). Overall, significantly more children attributed knowledge about sense-arousing objects to the speaking child than to the prelinguistic infant ($z = 6.4$, $P < 0.01$).

The replication study in the UK showed that significantly fewer British than Russian 6-year-olds attributed the capacity to know what kind of objects have initiated various types of sensations to prelinguistic infants, regarding the olfactory, auditory, and tactile sensations. Fewer British than Russian 4-, 9-, and 13-year-olds did this with regard to visual sensations (Fig. 45).

There were no significant differences found between the answers of the British and Russian children with regard to the attribution of knowledge about sense-initiating objects to an infant who has been taught to speak. This would suggest that although British children in general are less inclined to attribute the "inherent knowledge" about objects' names to prelinguistic infants than Russian children, this attribution was clearly present among British 4- and 6-year-olds, particularly regarding the auditory and visual sensations. However, if compared with Russian children, this attribution of precocious capacities to a prelinguistic infant decreased significantly among British children at an earlier age (6 years *vs* 9 years in Russian children), a finding that can be attributed to the earlier start of intensive school education in Britain. Why school education has this detrimental effect on British and Russian children's tendency to overestimate an infant's knowledge is yet to be established; however, it may be assumed that this is an indirect result of the growth in the intellectual capacity of children during school education, rather than a consequence of any specific growth in psychological knowledge.

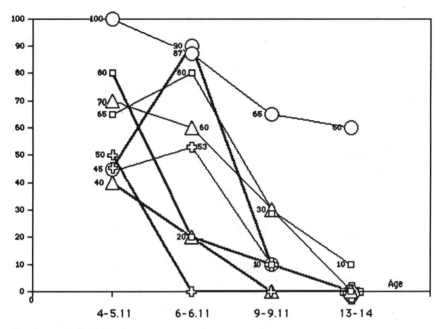

Russian —, British —
Olfactory △, auditory □, tactile ✠, visual ○

FIG. 45. Percentages of Russian and British children who believed that a prelinguistic infant knows what kinds of objects initiate olfactory, auditory, tactile, and visual sensations.

The majority of the children acknowledged that an infant who sees objects for the first time will be able to appreciate their relative distances from itself (Question 27); it followed from the children's justification that the capacity for depth perception was viewed as inherent in infants ("The infant will understand because it will be clear that the ball is at a greater distance from him than the cube is"; "He will understand this". *Experimenter:* "But how?" "I don't know how ... perhaps it is ... what is it called? ... instinct"). Some of the children remarked about the resolving capacity of vision or the law of perspective ("He will understand, because he will see the cube better than the ball"; "She will know this because when it is far away it looks very small, and when it is close—it is big"). Only a small number of subjects refused to attribute the capacity for "depth perception" to the newborn infant on the grounds that the infant, having no experience of manipulating objects, would be unable to appreciate distance.

With respect to the relationship between the names and functions of objects, most children believed that an infant who could speak and knew the names of objects would also be able to use the objects according to their specific functions (Questions 33, 36, and 38) (decrease 5 years to 7 years: $\chi^2 = 4.74$, $P < 0.05$). Some of the children argued along the lines that it was the objects' shapes that contained information about the objects' social functions. It followed from this that in order to gain knowledge of how an object is used, it is enough to have a look at the object:

E: Will the infant know what the bell is used for?
C: He will.
E: How will he find out?
C: Because he'll see that it is a bell.
E: But how will he learn what bells are used for?
C: Simply because he will see it as a bell.

Such reasoning obviously makes knowledge about the object's name superfluous.

Another type of justification appealed to the belief that knowledge about an object's function is contained in the object's name:

C: The infant will know as he will be taught that this is perfume.
E: But we only told the infant what perfume is called and then gave him a piece of cloth to sniff. How will he find out from this what perfume is used for?
C: He will know.

Some children argued that knowledge about an object's social function is gained as a result of personal experience the infant has with the object ("The child will know what money is used for. She used to go to the market with her mum and saw that people sell and buy things with money"). This group of children implicitly attributed more experience to the infant than the infant was supposed to have after only being given the names of objects (Fig. 46).

As can be seen in Fig. 46, the number of children who denied that the infant had a capacity to use objects according to their specific functions increased significantly between 7 and 9 years of age ($\chi^2 = 6.89$, $P < 0.01$). Typically, the children argued that the infant was still very small and could not possibly know what the objects are used for. Some of the children stressed that knowledge about objects' names didn't contain knowledge about their specific functions.

In answer to Question 43, regarding whether an infant who learns the names of a spoon and a glass will be able to use them for eating and drinking, most preschoolers and first-graders answered "yes" (Fig. 46), believing that knowledge about objects' names automatically brings with it the skills necessary to use the objects:

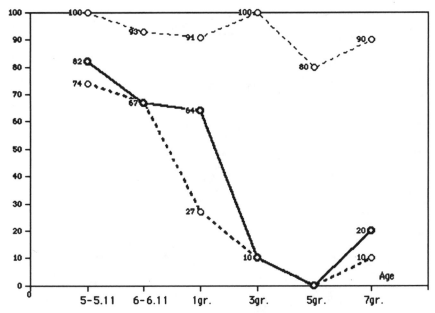

Children who thought that a newborn infant was capable of understanding that one object is closer to it than another one (q. 27, - -o- -).

Children who believed that the infant's knowledge of an object's name does (qq. 33, 36, & 38, - -o- -) or does not (the rest of the children) provide the infant with the knowledge about the object's specific practical functions.

Children who thought that the infant's knowledge of an object's name is (q. 43, —o—) or is not (the rest of the children) enough in order for the infant to be capable of using the object in accordance with its specific practical functions.

FIG. 46. Percentages of children who produced answers in response to questions regarding the infant's capacity for depth perception and an understanding of the relationship between an object's name and its practical function.

E: Will the infant be able to eat with a spoon and drink with a glass?
C: Yes, he will.
E: Why?
C: Because he knows what it is—a spoon and a glass.

Other children denied a direct link between objects' names and the skills needed to use them ("No he won't be able to use them, because he can't use them, he only knows the names"; "Names give nothing for practice") (increase 7 years to 11 years: $\chi^2 = 4.31$, $P < 0.05$).

The comparative study revealed that British children ascribe the capacity to appreciate depth to prelinguistic infants to the same extent as Russian children (see Fig. 47). There were no significant differences between the

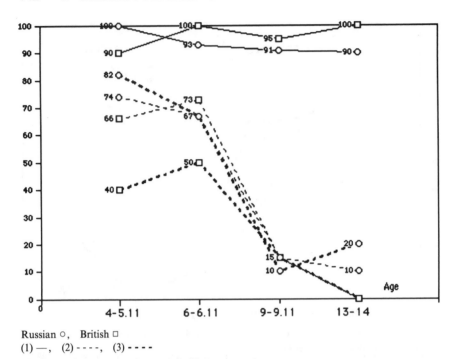

Russian ○, British □
(1) —,   (2) - - - -,   (3) - - - -

FIG. 47. Percentages of Russian and British children who believed that (1) a newborn infant is capable of perceiving the relative distances of objects, and that an infant's knowledge of the name of an object provides it with (2) knowledge of the object's practical function and (3) the skills necessary to use the object in accordance with its practical function.

British and Russian children's answers in their tendency to attribute the knowledge about an object's specific function to a child who was taught the object's name. However, British 4-year-olds were significantly less inclined than Russian 5-year-olds to attribute to the child the skills necessary for using an object in accordance with its proper function, a difference that was not observed among the older children. Therefore, the limited nature of knowledge about an object's name is understood at about the same age (i.e. 6–9 years) by British and Russian children.

Interestingly, most of the children thought that a newborn infant who cannot speak is able to understand the personal nature of its olfactory and auditory sensations (Questions 3 and 10; see Fig. 48). Some of the children (mainly preschoolers) were unable to ground their opinions, but most children argued along the lines that an understanding of the personal nature of sensations is inherent in the child: ("He will understand." *Experimenter: But how?*" "Well, he will feel it … I can't even find a proper word for it … He simply must be able to understand and feel that it is he who feels it"; "I

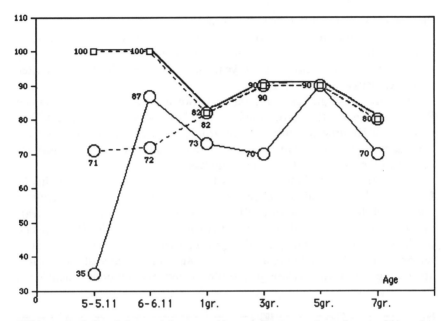

Children who believed that an infant was able to realise personal attachment of his or her olfactory (q. 3, —) and auditory (q. 10, - -) sensations before (○) and after (□) the infant acquired language.

FIG. 48. Percentages of children producing answers in response to questions regarding whether infants appreciate that their sensations belong to them and no-one else.

think she will get it, because she has a mind and any human being has a mind, and any living creature has a mind, even the smallest ant"). The subjects who denied the infant's capacity to grasp the personal nature of sensations justified this in two main ways. The first type of argument drew upon the idea that the personal nature of sensations can only be understood from personal experience which the newborn infant lacked ("No, she won't realise it. She hasn't yet had the opportunity to see herself in the mirror"; "No, when a person has just been born, he can understand nothing at all"). The second type of argument suggested that the personal nature of sensations can only be understood on the basis of knowledge of other people's existence and a comparison of other people with oneself ("I think, he won't get it. He came to life, but he doesn't know yet that there is somebody else in the world"; "No, he won't be able to understand this, because he can't tell who else can feel this, and nobody has yet told the infant that it is he who feels this").

With regard to the prelinguistic infant's capacity to understand the personal nature of his or her sensations, the replication study in Britain showed that there were no differences between British and Russian 6-year-olds. However, significantly more British 4-year-olds than Russian 5-year-olds attributed this capacity to the prelinguistic infant responding to olfactory sensations; British 9- and 13- to 14-year-olds did this significantly less often than their Russian peers (Fig. 49).

There were no significant differences between the answers of British and Russian children with regard to infants who have been taught to speak. The majority of children in both cultural groups were of the opinion that the "language-equipped" infant can understand that his or her sensations belong to him or her and not to anyone else.

What can be seen from Fig. 49 is that there was a major shift in the British children's opinions concerning a prelinguistic infant's capacity to understand the personal nature of its sensations, with 9- and 13- to 14-year-olds doing this significantly less often than 4- and 6-year-olds. There was no similar shift observed among the Russian children. This suggests that British senior schoolchildren acquire a more adequate and critical attitude towards attributing their own psychological sophisticatedness to a prelinguistic child

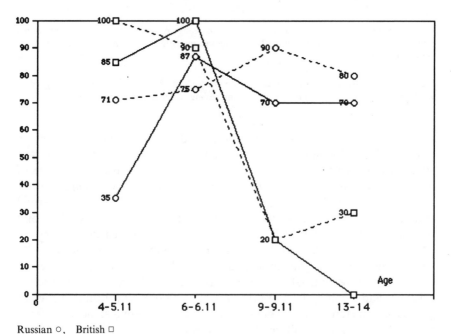

Russian ○,   British □
(1) —,   (2) - -

FIG. 49.   Percentages of Russian and British children who believed that prelinguistic infants are capable of understanding the personal attachment of their (1) olfactory and (2) auditory sensations.

than their Russian peers, a hypothesis that was suggested above on the basis of evidence showing that British children realise at an earlier age than Russian children that a prelinguistic infant is unlikely to know what kind of objects initiated his or her sensations (Fig. 45).

Questions regarding whether a prelinguistic infant is aware of the fact of other people's existence were asked after each type of sensation was introduced (Questions 5, 13, 20, 29). As Fig. 50 shows, only about 30% of preschoolers and first-graders thought that a prelinguistic infant would be aware of other people's presence if it were in possession of olfactory sensations; almost all older children denied this. The addition of hearing increased significantly the number of children who believed that the infant would be aware of others ($z = 5$, $P < 0.01$). The addition of tactile and visual sensations didn't change things to a significant extent. The only significant age trend was found for the number of children who attributed an

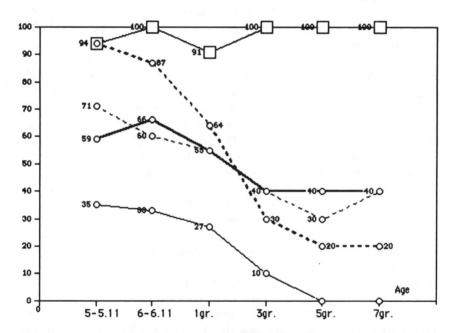

Children who thought that a newborn infant would be capable of understanding that there are other people around him/her if the infant had (1) only olfactory sensations (q.5, —o—), (2) olfactory and auditory senstions (q. 13, —o—), (3) olfactory, auditory and tactile sensations (q. 20, - -o- -), (4) olfactory, auditory, tactile and visual sensations (q. 29, - -o- -).
Children who believed that the infant was capable of understanding that there are other people in the world after he/she acquired language (—□—).

FIG. 50.   Percentages of children producing answers in response to questions regarding infants' capacity to understand that other people exist in the world.

awareness of other people's presence to the prelinguistic infant who was in possession of all four senses (decrease 6 years to 9 years: $\chi^2 = 6.62$, $P < 0.02$). In all cases, the children's argument was very similar ("He would be aware that there are other people around, because he would hear that other people talking"; "She would touch some person, and realise that there are other people in the world"). Those children who denied the infant's capacity to realise the presence of other people either referred to the fact that having this limited set of senses was not enough for that ("She wouldn't be able to realise this, she can't yet hear anything"; "He won't understand this because he can't see"), or pointed out that knowledge about other people's existence can only be acquired through life experience, which the infant lacked. Although the infant's acquisition of language significantly increased the average number of positive answers within the total sample of subjects ($z = 6.4$, $P < 0.01$), the children's arguments remained the same and didn't involve language as an indicator of other people's existence. Only a small number of fifth- and seventh-graders pointed out that knowledge about other people's existence could be acquired through linguistic communication and teaching.

The comparative study in Britain showed that the majority of British children, like their Russian peers, were certain that an infant would understand that other people were present as soon as the infant had acquired language. With regard to a prelinguistic infant who possessed only olfactory sensations, British children denied to the same extent as their Russian peers that the infant would realise other people's presence (i.e. between 70 and 100% of children in each age group answered in the negative). There were no differences between the answers of the British and Russian children on this question regarding prelinguistic infant who possessed olfactory and auditory sensations, and olfactory, auditory, and tactile sensations. However, significantly more British than Russian 13- to 14-year-olds ($\chi^2 = 7.6$, $P < 0.005$) acknowledged that a prelinguistic infant would realise other people's presence as soon as visual sensations were added to the others senses (Fig. 51), a fact that runs counter to previous findings about British children's generally more cautious attitude towards attributing precocious psychological capacities to a prelinguistic infant.

Most children of all ages thought that the prelinguistic infant would realise it had features in common with other people (Question 20). For this to be possible, it was enough for the infant to have a look at himself and at another person (Fig. 52). Many preschoolers and first-graders thought that the prelinguistic infant was also able to understand human speech (question 12), although the number of such children decreased rapidly with age (decrease 7 years to 11 years: $\chi^2 = 3.91$, $P < 0.05$). The children who answered these questions in the negative normally justified this by the infant's lack of experience and interaction with other people. As in many

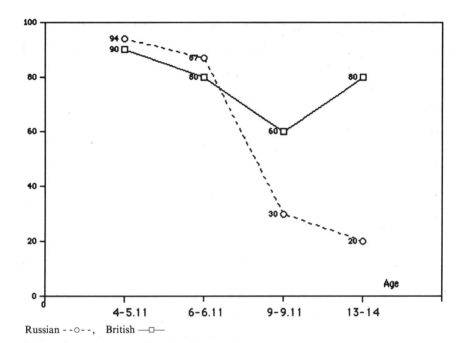

Russian - -o- - ,   British —□—

FIG. 51.   Percentages of Russian and British children who believed that newborn infants are capable of understanding that other people exist in the world if they possess olfactory, auditory, tactile, and visual awareness.

other cases, the fact that the infant acquired language (Questions 41 and 42, respectively) changed the results by increasing the number of positive answers (for the infant's capacity to understand human speech, the increase was significant: $z = 6.4$, $P < 0.01$ for the total sample).

In the comparative study, British 6-year-olds and older children were significantly more sceptical than their Russian peers regarding a prelinguistic infant's capacity to know that he or she was a human being. British 9- and 13-year-olds even extended this scepticism to include the child who was taught to speak (Fig. 53).

There were no differences between British and Russian children's judgements about the infant's capacity to understand human speech, apart from British 4-year-olds ascribing this capacity to a prelinguistic infant significantly less often than Russian 5-year-olds ($\chi^2 = 7.3$, $P < 0.007$) (Fig. 54). Despite all this, British 4- and 6-year-olds did reveal an "anthropomorphic" tendency to attribute a prelinguistic infant with precocious psychological capacities, although British 9- and 13-year-olds did this less often than did Russian children of the same age.

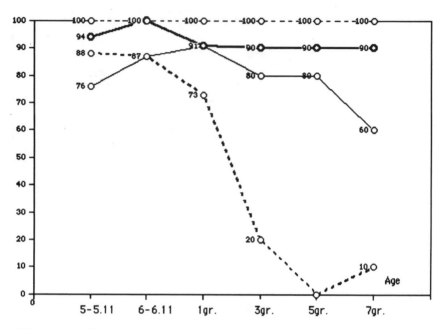

Children who believed that an infant was capable of identifying him- or herself with other people before (q. 30, —o—) and after (q. 41, —o—) the infant acquired language.
Children who believed that an infant was capable of understanding human language before (q. 12, - -o- -) and after (q. 42, - -o- -) the infant acquired language.

FIG. 52. Percentages of children producing answers in response to questions regarding an infant's capacity to identify itself with other people and to understand human language.

With regard to questions about the infant's capacity to manifest moral behaviour (Part 3 of the dialogue), most preschoolers and first-graders thought that an infant who was able to speak and knew objects' names could also observe certain moral norms (Fig. 55). Even among third- to seventh-graders, there were some who ascribed this moral capacity to the child. Providing grounds for this view, some children spoke as though moral motivation was inherent in the infant ("No, he won't take the chocolate away from a little child, because he is a good person"; "No, she won't take the food away from the infant, because if she did she would feel ashamed of herself"). Others stated that the infant would respect moral norms either because of the fear of punishment or in the search of rewards ("He would tell the truth that he broke it, because he would be punished if he didn't").

The children who denied that the infant would be able to uphold moral norms gave two main reasons for their belief: some of them pointed out that moral behaviour was based on a knowledge of the norms and on certain moral feelings which are absent in the infant ("He wouldn't share the

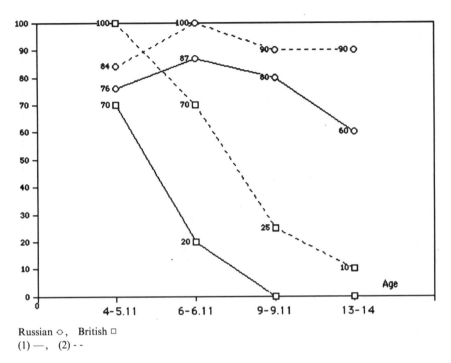

Russian ⟠,   British □
(1) —,   (2) - -

FIG. 53.   Percentages of Russian and British children who believed that infants are capable of identifying themselves with other people (1) before and (2) after the acquisition of language.

chocolate, because ... he doesn't yet know whom he should share things with". "She can take the chocolate away". *Experimenter:* "Why?" "Well, she doesn't know what is good and what is bad"; "Basically he must share, but ... he won't because he has no such feelings yet as kindness and compassion"); other children simply noted the fact that observing moral norms would be at odds with the infant's personal interests ("She would be deceitful because she has fear"; "He would take the chocolate away because he wants the chocolate"). In this group, eight children said that the infant wouldn't share its property and would take chocolate away from a smaller child but wouldn't deceive adults because it is still naive and is not aware of the possibility of concealing the truth ("He won't deceive, because ... he is still too small for this"; "The infant is naive and he doesn't know what a lie is"). The number of children who attributed to the infant the capacity to observe moral norms decreased with age: for the norms "generosity" and "politeness", the decrease was stable and significant (decrease 7 years to 11 years: $\chi^2 = 8.05$ for generosity, $\chi^2 = 6.89$ for politeness; both $P < 0.01$).

Almost all of the children acknowledged that after the infant acquired speech, it would observe moral norms. Significantly more children attributed

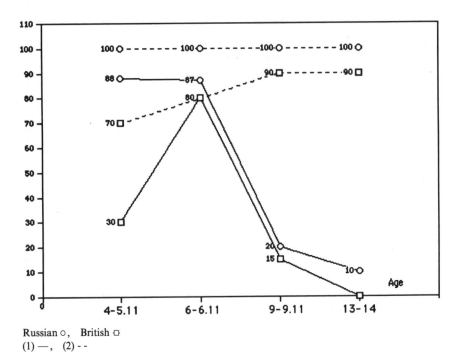

Russian o,   British ⊡
(1) —,   (2) - -

FIG. 54. Percentages of Russian and British children who believed that infants are capable of understanding human speech (1) before and (2) after the acquisition of language.

the capacity to observe moral norms to a speaking child than to a pre-linguistic infant ($z = 5.6$, $P < 0.01$ for the total sample). Together with the reasons given above, some of the subjects referred to the effect of learning on the infant ("He won't deceive, he is already taught properly"; "She was told that she must do this"). Only a few children believed that the infant wouldn't be able to observe moral norms even if told about them, but they were unable to justify their opinions ("He will still deceive." *Experimenter:* "But he knows to lie is a bad thing to do, so why would he still deceive?" "Because he doesn't understand").

The replication study showed that British children demonstrated the same age pattern of answers as their Russian peers with regard to the child's capacity to observe the norms of "generosity" and "politeness" before acquiring knowledge about those norms. Most 4- and 6-year-olds and about one-half of 9- and 13- to 14-year-olds thought that the child would observe the "generosity" norm, and about 30–50% of children of all age groups thought the same regarding the "politeness" norm (Fig. 56).

However, British 4- and 13- to 14-year-olds were significantly less likely than their Russian peers to attribute moral behaviour to a "morally

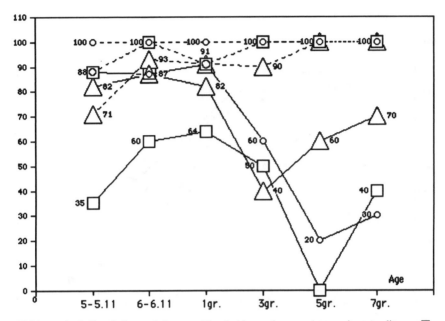

Children who believed that an infant would uphold moral norms (generosity ○, politeness □, and honesty △) before (qq. 45–47, —) and after (q. 49, - - - -) the infant acquired verbal knowledge about the norms.

FIG. 55. Percentages of children producing answers in response to questions regarding an infant's capacity for moral behaviour.

ignorant" child as far as the "honesty" norm was concerned; that is, more British than Russian children thought that the infant would be deceitful if it did not know that deception was bad behaviour. The majority of British and Russian children thought the infant would uphold moral norms as soon as it learned about them.

The pattern of answers to Question 49 was reproduced by preschoolers and first-graders in response to Question 50, which put the same problem but with special emphasis on how sufficient verbal knowledge of moral norms is for their proper implementation (Fig. 57). Most third-, fifth-, and seventh-graders did not believe that knowledge of moral norms alone by the infant would make it conform to those norms (increase 6 years to 9 years: $\chi^2 = 7.78$, $P < 0.01$). Most of these children thought that the infant would be able to observe the norms if it was shown positive moral models ("No, it is not enough to tell the infant what is good, you also have to show it how to do good"). Only a few children pointed out that in order to be able to observe moral norms, the infant needs something special in its character and personality ("No, it is not enough to tell a person what is good and what is

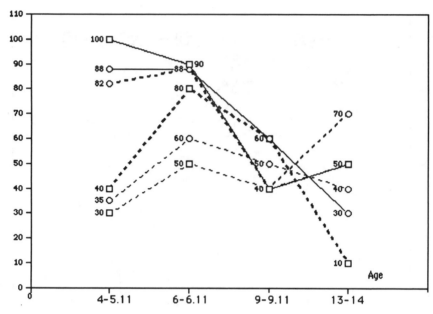

Russian ○,   British □
Generosity —,   politeness - -,   honesty - -

FIG. 56. Percentages of Russian and British children who believed that prelinguistic infants are capable of upholding the moral norms of generosity, politeness, and honesty.

bad. That doesn't mean that the person can understand this." *Experimenter:* "What else is needed?" "You have to make the person realise things; the person has to have a good character").

When asked Question 51 about children who understand moral norms but don't obey them, which moved the question "Is knowledge of moral norms sufficient for real moral behaviour?" from a theoretical plane to a plane of real-life observations, all but five subjects responded in the positive, with their answers often contradicting their earlier statements. When asked to explain the discrepancy in the child's behaviour (i.e. violation of the norms which are well known to the child; Question 52), most preschoolers and some of the schoolchildren were unable to do this; the others produced four types of explanation. Some of the children explained the discrepancy by the fact that these transgressors didn't understand the moral norms properly or forgot them. Others accounted for the discrepancy by the defects in the transgressors' personalities ("They do this because they are bad people"; "Because they are hooligans"; "Well, they have bad characters, they don't like telling the truth"; "Because they were born like that ... they just want to do this; you can tell them whatever you like, they will still do it"). The other

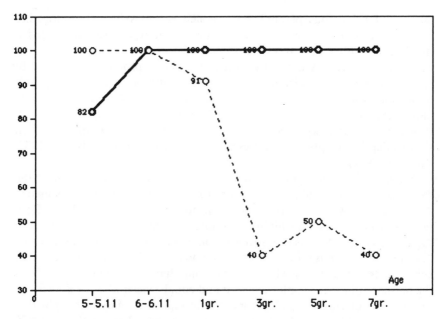

Children who believed that an infant would be capable of upholding moral norms in his or her actions if the infant knew about the norms (q. 50, - -o- -).
Children who acknowledged that there are people who violate moral norms despite the fact that they know about the norms (q. 51, —o—).

FIG. 57. Percentages of children producing answers in response to questions regarding the relationship between moral knowledge and moral behaviour.

two types of explanation were more psychologically profound and appealed to the insufficient development of moral motivation in the transgressors. Some of the children stated that the deviations were caused by the priority of pragmatic motivation over moral motivation ("Well, I think they need the things desperately, and this is stronger than the thought 'you mustn't't' "; "Well, perhaps, if a person needs something very much the person cannot restrain himself any longer"; "Their will isn't strong enough"); others simply referred to the lack of moral motivation in the transgressors ("Well, I think they don't like it—to behave well"; "Well, they don't want to restrain themselves"; "Well, firstly, because they ... were brought up poorly, and you can't change them").

The study in Britain yielded answers to Questions 50 and 51 that were very similar to those offered by the Russian children.

To summarise, the data revealed some clear-cut age tendencies in children's judgements about the role of psychological functions. The *first* was the tendency of younger subjects to ascribe to a newborn infant a number of precocious psychological capacities and skills. Thus, together with an acknowledgement that the newborn infant experiences sensations, a significant number of subjects also ascribed to the newborn the inherent capacity to associate sensation with the objects that produced them, and to appreciate the relative distances between itself and objects. Curiously, this naive "nativism", which runs counter to the traditional view of the sensory–motor experience based acquisition of space perception in infancy (i.e. Piaget, 1936; Vygotsky, 1987), agrees with recent studies on infancy which showed depth perception to be present in newborn infants (see Bower, 1972; Bremner, 1994).

A significant number of the children thought that information about the social function of an object is inherent to a newborn's mind and is merely "reclaimed" by the newborn at the very moment it views the object. Both preschoolers and schoolchildren ascribed to the prelinguistic infant a capacity to relate its sensations to itself; in other words, to view itself as the "centre" of the sensations. Most preschoolers and many schoolchildren acknowledged that the newborn infant would have some knowledge about the presence of other people around it and could "reclaim" such knowledge on the basis of sensations alone; more than that, the children thought that the infant would be capable of associating between other people and itself. Lastly, most of the preschoolers and first-graders attributed the capacity to understand human speech to the prelinguistic infant, some of whom even believed that an infant who can speak but lacks other type of experience will be able to uphold some moral norms.

The *second tendency* ("the primacy of vision") was the children's inclination to view vision as the major basis of an association between sensations and external objects. As our data revealed, all the children ascribed this capacity to sensations in the visual modality significantly more often than to the other modalities.

The *third tendency* was the gradual acknowledgment of the role of the infant's personal experience for the development of its psychological capacities. Counter to the previous tendency, this could conventionally be called "the primacy of experience". Thus, a considerable number of first-graders and older children revealed a clear appreciation of the link between personal experience the infant receives through interaction with external objects and the infant's capacity to associate sensations with the objects that caused them. The infant's personal experience was also referred to as a source of the infant's knowledge about social functions of objects and about the presence of other people in the world.

The *fourth tendency* was the gradual awareness by the children of the part that language plays in the psychological development of the child. A significant number of subjects (mainly schoolchildren) linked the infant's capacity to associate sensations with external objects to the infant's capacity to speak and name the objects. The infant's ability to speak significantly increased the number of subjects who believed the infant would be aware of other people in its presence.

Lastly, within the fourth tendency, cases could be distinguished in which the children revealed a certain overestimation of the role of speech. For instance, some of the children thought that the mere learning of an object's name would bring with it knowledge about the object's social function and even the practical skills of handling the object. The verbal knowledge of moral norms was viewed by many children as sufficient for the capacity to really observe the norms.

This range of views which children develop on the evolution of certain psychological functions sows the potential "seeds" of various psychological theories (such as those which stress "nativism" or "empiricism", linguistic interaction between a child and his or her social environment, a child's independent experimentation, etc.) in their minds. Some of these "seeds" may be "provisional" (that is, reflecting the most recent and unexpected results of scientific studies); others will still look like naive generalisations. But this variety of views shows that the area reflected in this dialogue is, perhaps, one of the domains in children's minds that is least affected by contemporary scientific views and education, a fact that is not surprising when we remember the variety of conflicting views on human development which exists in contemporary psychology and which, in Vygotsky's terms, maintains the permanent "crisis in psychology".

DIALOGUE 2: "FREEDOM"

The aims of this dialogue were to establish to what extent children are able to appreciate and express verbally: (1) the feeling of being in control of their own voluntary actions; (2) that the motives and thoughts that force a person to act voluntarily are not themselves deliberately produced by the person; (3) that a person is not responsible for his or her immoral thoughts but is responsible for the implementation of those thoughts, provided he or she does so deliberately; (4) that a feeling of moral remorse occurs if an immoral act is committed; (5) that the freedom of moral action is based upon a person's moral self-image and not upon external incentives.

The questions were as follows:

1. Please, hold your hand up. Tell me, was it you yourself who lifted your hand up?
2. Can it be the case that it only seems to you that it was you yourself who lifted your hand up, but in reality it was done by a little man who is sitting in your head and pulling strings which make you move your

hands and legs, which makes you do something and think something. Can it be the case that this little man is controlling you?

3. Can your brain be viewed as being such a little man?

4. Therefore, if you wish to lift your hand up, you do this, don't you? And if you don't wish to, you don't do this, right?

5. And what about these wishes of yours—when you wish to lift your hand up or to eat—where do they appear from?

6. What do you think, is it you yourself who makes your wishes appear or disappear or do they appear in you independently and without your active involvement?

7. Tell me, is it you yourself who are in control of your wishes and actions, or is it your wishes that control your actions and you merely do what your wishes order you to do?

8. For instance, if you bet with somebody that you will not eat for the whole day and you get hungry, can you make your hunger disappear or not?

9. And if you are thinking of something right now—for instance, you are thinking about an elephant—can you or can't you make yourself stop thinking about the elephant right now?

10. And if a nasty dog is chasing you and you are scared, is it possible for you not to make yourself scared?

11. So who controls whom: is it yourself who controls your wishes and feelings or is it your wishes and feelings that control your actions?

12. Let us imagine that you see a smaller child than you with a nice toy in his or her hands and you feel that you wish to take the toy away from the child. Is it your fault that you have such a wish? Why?

13. And if you snatched the toy away from the child, is it your fault that you snatched it away? Why?

14. And if you break a nice porcelain vase and you felt like deceiving your parents about it, is it your fault that you feel that way?

15. And if you tell a lie about who broke the vase, is it your fault that you tell the lie?

16. Imagine that, for instance, you feel like taking the nice toy from the smaller child, but you didn't do this. Why didn't you do this?

17. And if you knew that nobody would ever find out that you took the toy away from the child and nobody would punish you, would you take the toy away? Why?

18. Imagine that you walk along the street and find a nice watch that has been lost by somebody. Would you keep it for yourself or take it to the police? Why? Would you be sorry to lose the watch if you took it to the police?

19. And if a pack of your favourite sweets fell from the counter in your local shop, and nobody noticed it except for you, would you keep the sweets

for yourself or give them back to the shopkeeper? Why? Would you feel good or bad if you gave them back? Why?

Two main problems were addressed in the dialogue: the relationship between freedom and voluntary action, and the relationship between personal freedom and moral behaviour. Regarding the first problem, the results showed that most children of all ages viewed themselves as being the authors of their voluntary actions (Questions 1 and 2; see Fig. 58). They denied that there was a "little man" in their heads who was in control of their actions, providing two types of justification. Some of the children thought that freedom of action was a capacity inherent to every human being ("No, there isn't anybody who would control my actions—it is only dolls who are like that"; "No, because I am a real human being"; "I don't think somebody can

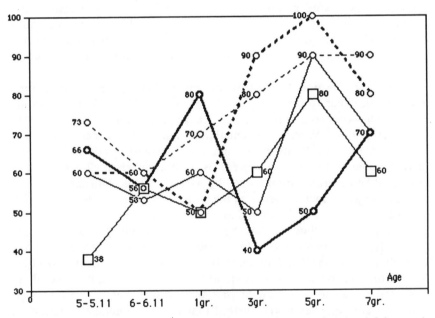

Children who believed that they were the authors of their voluntary actions (qq. 1 & 2, - - o - -). Children who believed that they were the authors of the motives of their voluntary actions (q. 6, —o—). Children who acknowledged that at least some of their wishes were beyond the area of their voluntary control (qq. 8–10, —□—). Children who thought that they were in total control over all their wishes (1) before the auxiliary questions were asked (q. 7, - - o - -), and (2) after the auxiliary questions were asked (q. 11, —o—).

FIG. 58. Percentages of children producing answers in response to questions regarding the relationships between an infant's actions, wishes, and capacity for voluntary behaviour.

control my actions, because this little man in my head—it can only be in fairy tales; it is in the nature of humans that a person can move his hands, legs, can walk and speak"). The children who produced arguments of this type acknowledged that the brain could be viewed as a "little man in the head" (Question 3), but they also commented that bodily movements and brain functioning are under the control of their thinking ("This is the human mind ... the mind does it"; "This is human thoughts ... they give the signals"; "It has long been proved that there is not a 'little man in the head', there is just the brain." *Experimenter:* "But your brain—can't we view it as a 'little man'?" "We can ... well, no, we can't, because it's me who is in control over my brain, I give the signals and my brain only transmits them"). Other children justified their judgements by referring to their feeling of being free in their actions ("No, nobody controls me, because I can feel that it is myself who did it"; "I can feel that it is myself who is lifting the arm and the arm is moving, and there is no 'little man' in my head, because there are thoughts in there"). Lastly, a third group of children produced trans-ductive and tautological types of justification ("No, because I am created like that, there is no little man in there"; "There cannot be a man inside a man").

Answering Question 4 about the origins of their wishes, most children linked them either to certain parts of their bodies ("They come from my head"; "They come out of my brain"; "They appear from your body") or to their perceptions ("When I see something I want it"; "I experience certain sensations, they affect my brain and then my wishes appear from out there"). Some of the children viewed wishes as an inherent characteristic of humans ("Well, wishes are provided by nature"; "This is instinct").

Most subjects saw themselves as the authors of their wishes (Question 6) ("I think that it is myself who makes my wishes, it is my inner 'I' who does it"); the remainder thought that their wishes appealed spontaneously and independently of themselves. No distinct age differences were observed. Regarding Questions 9 and 10 about the possibility of a person controlling (eliminating) his or her wishes voluntarily: Most schoolchildren and about half of the preschoolers thought that their wishes were subject to their voluntary control; they acknowledged that they were unable to terminate their feeling of hunger or fear by a mere act of thinking or to stop the process of compulsory thinking. The rest of the children thought that they could control their wishes.

In response to the question about whether it was themselves who were in control over their wishes or it was the other way round (Question 7), most children opted for the former; even after the series of auxiliary questions, the number of such answers did not decrease significantly (see Fig. 58). Some children (up to 40% in some age groups) were aware of the fact that wishes were beyond a subject's voluntary control ("My wishes appear on their own, but whether I satisfy them or not, this depends on me"; "My wishes are independent from my actions"). This result is in accordance with data reported by Inagaki and Hatano (1993), who found that many 4- and 5-year-olds were able to distinguish between bodily and mental properties, realising at the same time that the activities of the internal organs of a person are independent of that person's intentions.

Regarding Questions 12 and 14 (see Fig. 59), most preschoolers and first- and third-graders saw themselves as being responsible for the emergence of their immoral desires ("I would be responsible, because it is forbidden—to take things away that do not belong to you"; "I think I would be the one to

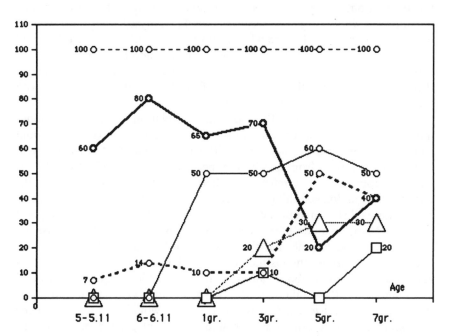

Children who thought that they were responsible for the emergence of immoral wishes in themselves (qq. 12 & 14, —o—).

Children who believed that they were responsible for the implementation of their immoral wishes (qq. 13 & 15, - -o- -).

Children who motivated their moral behaviour in an imaginative situation (q. 17) by (1) their feeling of compassion to a person in distress (- -o- -), (2) their desire to maintain a positive moral image of themselves (····△····), (3) other reasons (the rest of the children).

Children who motivated their altruistic behaviour in an imaginative situation (qq. 18 & 19) by (1) their feeling of compassion to a person in distress (—o—), (2) their desire to maintain a positive moral image of themselves (—□—), (3) other reasons (the rest of the children).

FIG. 59.   Percentages of children producing answers in response to questions regarding the relationships between feelings of personal responsibility, moral behaviour, and motivation.

blame, because it would mean that I was unable to educate myself well enough to be the honest person"). The remaining children saw themselves as not being responsible for the emergence of immoral wishes (increase 6 years to 11 years: $\chi^2 = 7.11$, $P < 0.01$). Most justified this by claiming that immoral wishes are independent of a person's conscious control "I wouldn't be the one to blame because wishes come and go on their own"; "No, I am not responsible for my bad feelings"; "No, I would not be responsible, because I just wish, I cannot do anything about it, but I would go away and not take the toy from a little child"). At the same time, all the children acknowledged that they would be responsible for the implementation of their immoral wishes (Questions 13 and 15). The children who could justify this pointed out that an action is a voluntary thing, in contrast to a wish or intention ("I would be guilty, because it would be myself who was unable to overcome my wish"; "It's me who would be responsible, because I should have restrained myself"; "I'd be guilty, because I didn't cut this wish out, I submitted myself to it"). Overall, the number of children who acknowledged their responsibility for their actions significantly exceeded the number who took responsibility for intentions alone ($z = 5.7$, $P < 0.01$).

In response to Question 17, about the motivation for a child's anonymous moral action, most fifth- and seventh-graders either said they would feel compassion for the smaller child ("It is not his fault that I have the wish to take the toy away from him"; "No, because I wouldn't like to make the child unhappy"), or they referred to their desire to maintain positive self-esteem ("If you do such things, and even if nobody found out, then ... this bad action will stay in your memory anyway. It will always be a sore point for you"; "No, I wouldn't take the toy away from a little child, because my conscience would tell me that this is no good"); other children produced tautological or irrelevant justifications. Similar judgements were given in response to questions about causes of altruistic actions (Questions 18 and 19): compassion ("I'd take it to the police station, because I would know that somebody had lost it and was crying"; "I would give it back to the storekeeper, because otherwise someone else might get the blame"), self-esteem ("I'd take it to the police, because my conscience would not allow me to keep it for myself"), and tautological reasons ("I'd give it back to the storekeeper, because it has to be done so") were typical justifications.

It can be seen, therefore, that many children as young as 5 and 6 develop a feeling of being in control of their voluntary actions and this feeling becomes significantly stronger with age. Most children were incapable of distinguishing between actions and the wishes that motivate those actions and viewed themselves as the authors of their wishes as well as of their actions (instead of confining their capacity of control to actions alone). Paradoxically, the strengthening of the sense of freedom that children develop regarding their ability to take control of their actions was accompanied by a growing awareness of the spontaneous nature of wishes; as a result of the confusion between actions and wishes, many children acknowledged that they were unable to deliberately produce or terminate some of their wishes, yet they thought that they could control them.

This illusion of being in control of their wishes persisted in most pre-schoolers and first- and third-graders, even when the voluntary action was put in a context of moral relationships, so that the children viewed themselves as being responsible for the emergency of immoral thoughts in themselves. However, this illusion disappeared in most fifth- and seventh-graders, most of whom revealed no difficulties in distinguishing between actions and wishes that motivate them, and they acknowledged that they were not responsible for the emergence of immoral wishes in themselves. Some of the children even managed to produce psychologically acceptable ideas about the nature of their moral motivation.

In the development of children's judgements about freedom, three major stages can be distinguished. In stage 1, the children readily agree that their voluntary actions are initiated by some external agent. In this stage, the sense of freedom and authorship that a child has over his or her own actions is unstable and can easily give way to the "mechanical toy" type of view of him or herself. Perhaps, this is a psychological regression to early childhood, when most of a child's actions are indeed directed from the outside, mainly by close adults.

In stage 2, the sense of freedom becomes stronger and more global, as it covers actions, wishes and moral behaviour. At this stage, the children feel themselves to be active subjects and don't see anything in them that they are unable to control. Characteristically, they view this capacity to be a mental action; because of this, they fall easy prey to the illusion of the self-sufficient and unconditional nature of their capacity to control all their actions and wishes.

In stage 3, this homogeneous and harmonic sense of freedom runs into trouble and the children begin to realise the involuntary and unpredictable nature of their wishes, particularly of those that are at odds with moral norms. Inside the homogeneous and "subjectively translucent" image that children have of themselves, there appear certain "hard" and "stiff" entities which seem to have come "from beyond" the child's mind and personality. The sense of personal freedom, which used to permeate all the child's actions and wishes, now only covers some of the child's actions. The child develops an awareness that some of his or her wishes are no longer a part of his or her "I"; he or she discovers that it is possible to have certain wishes without "having a wish to have them". Finally, children come to realise that they can (and must) resist such wishes, and this resistance also has certain specific wishes behind it (such as "to be in peace with one's conscience", "to avoid feelings of guilt", etc.).

These stages were not linked to any particular age. Thus, although the answers of most preschoolers could be covered by stage 2, a large number of children believed that their voluntary actions could be initiated and controlled externally (stage 1), and some denied that they were responsible for the emergence in themselves of immoral wishes (stage 3). Judgements related to all three stages were found among the answers of children of the same age and even within the answers of the same child. Nevertheless, certain age tendencies were apparent. The data show, for instance, that most senior preschoolers and primary schoolchildren (first- and third-graders) produced answers that would fit stage 2, whereas the fifth- and seventh-graders would fit into stage 3.

It may be assumed that the transition from stage 1 to stage 2 is an indicator of a child's departure from the emotional world developed in early childhood (where the overwhelming feeling is one of dependence on other people) and the development of a sense of autonomy against a general background of physical, social and psychological growth. At the same time, the increased social and moral requirements imposed on children of school age and the emergence of competing and conflicting wishes, leads to a growing awareness of the independent and uncontrollable nature of wishes and impulses, in contrast to actions which, to a varying extent, can be controlled voluntarily.

DIALOGUE 3: "FAUST"

This dialogue was inspired by the Johann Wolfgang Goethe's famous poem. Its aims were to determine to what extent children are capable of realising (1) the potentially infinite nature of human wishes and passions and their inherent incompleteness, and (2) the inherent impossibility for an individual of accomplishing all of his or her desires.

The questions asked were as follows:

1. Tell me, do you want something at the moment? What do you want?
2. Do you wish that your favourite sweets were always in abundance?
3. Do you want to become a famous author, a great scientist, or an outstanding artist when you grow up?
4. Would you like to have an opportunity to travel around the world and see all the countries and cities?
5. Would you like to be very handsome and good looking so that all the people would like you and admire you?
6. Would you like to be the most intelligent person in the world and know lots of things about space and nature, about people, animals, and plants?
7. Let us imagine that a wizard comes to you and says: "I am going to make all of your wishes come true and I will do everything you tell me

to do, but only until you say, 'All my wishes are satisfied and I don't want anything any more' ". As soon as you tell me that you will become my slave. I will put you in a room without doors and windows and you will be locked up there until you get old and die. Deal?" What would your answer be to the wizard? Would you accept his offer or not? Why?

8. [If the answer is "no"]: So if you accepted his offer, then a time would come when all your wishes would be satisfied and you wouldn't want any more. True?

9. [If the answer is "yes"]: Aren't you afraid that when all your wishes are answered and you have no more wishes, the wizard will put you in the room without windows and you will perish there? Why?

10. And if this wizard doesn't come to you, do you believe that all your wishes will sometimes come true anyway?

The results showed that most subjects rejected the idea of making a contract with the wizard. A typical reason for this was the fear of having to "pay the wizard back" when one's wishes were granted. ("No, I wouldn't, because I don't want to die"; "No, because I wouldn't like to sit in the dark room until I get old"; "No, I wouldn't make the agreement, because it is dangerous—to play games with a wizard, the wizard can do things in such a way that you would indeed die"; "No, because if the wizard could satisfy all my wishes, there would be no desires left, and the wizard would make me his slave") (see Fig. 60). A small number stated that a person should "provide for himself or herself" independently, but most children gave no justification at all.

Responses to Question 8 revealed that the majority of children in most age groups thought that their wishes had a certain natural limit ("The time will come when I'd have no more wishes, and it would happen much sooner than I'd like it to"); a significantly smaller number of children thought that their wishes had no limits ("No, human wishes can't stop, they are infinite"; "Perhaps, I will always have some unsatisfied wishes"). Lastly, most pre-schoolers and first-graders were sure that their wishes would be accomplished completely in due course in a natural way (Question 10; decrease 7 years to 11 years; $\chi^2 = 6.04$, $P < 0.02$).

We can conclude from these data that an awareness of the potentially infinite nature of human wishes was achieved by only a small number of children, and that the number of such children does not increase with age. The statements of many 5-year-olds about the infinite nature of their wishes (Question 8) were at odds with their refusal to make a contract with the wizard, which undermined the reliability of such statements.

The justifications given in response to Question 7 were very much alike across the age span. Those children who thought that their wishes were insatiable and who wished to make an agreement with the wizard demon-

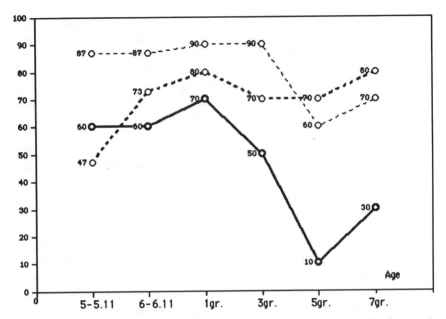

Children who said that they would not like to make a contract with the wizard (q. 7, - -○- -), with the rest of the children saying that they would.
Children who believed that in the end their wishes could be completely satisfied by the wizard (q. 8, - -○- -), with the rest of the children thinking that they could not.
Children who believed that in the end their wishes will be completely satisfied in a natural way (q. 10, —○—), with the rest of the children thinking that they will not.

FIG. 60. Percentages of children producing answers in response to questions regarding the finite versus infinite nature of their wishes.

strated they knew the continuous and infinite nature of human wishes; however, the number of these children was surprisingly small, despite the fact that certain areas of children's culture point directly to the fact that human wishes are fundamentally insatiable. Clearly, all of the children involved in this study knew Pushkin's popular poem "The tale of the fisherman and a fish" and other similar stories; however, only one child made a reference to tales of this kind in this study ("Well, there are no limits for human wishes ... There are even fairy tales about this: you do good things to a person, and the person wants more and more").

DIALOGUE 4: "UNCONSCIOUS"

The aims of this dialogue were to determine to what extent children are able to appreciate the presence of the following unconscious psychological mechanisms: (1) projection (Questions 1–4), (2) rationalisation (Questions

5–10), and (3) defence (Questions 11–14). In previous studies (Chandler, Paget, & Koch, 1978; Dollinger & McGuire, 1981), certain age trends were suggested for an understanding of defence. Thus, Chandler et al. (1978) told pre-operational, concrete operational, and formal operational children eight stories in which eight commonly described mechanisms of psychological defence were portrayed (such as turning against the self, denying, displacing, rationalisation, projecting, introjecting, repressing one's own feelings) and asked them to complete the stories. They found that pre-operational children failed to understand defensive transformations, concrete operational children could only understand defences involving inverse and reciprocal operations, and formal operational subjects were able to understand defences that involved second-order transformations ("operations upon operations").

Dollinger and McGuire (1981) presented children aged 4–14 years with seven stories devised to portray defensive strategies used by the story's characters. The stories depicted child characters who employed such defence mechanisms as repression, denial, displacement, projection, rationalisation, somatisation, and self-blame. The subjects were asked to explain why the characters in the story acted as they did. The older children revealed a better understanding of defence mechanisms, especially with regard to the rationalisation test, on which 10- to 14-year-olds performed twice as well as younger children, and the displacement task, on which a significant shift in understanding was observed at an earlier age (around 7 years). It was also found that children who understood defence mechanisms better performed better on Chandler's modified test of egocentrism (i.e. were less egocentric) than those with a poor understanding of defence.

While these studies revealed certain important features in the development of children's conceptions of defence, they were limited in several respects and further investigation was necessary. For instance, in Dollinger and McGuire's study such typical defence mechanisms as perceptual defence (i.e. not letting into one's mind objects and events which are in one's full view but contradict to one's concepts and attitudes) were not included and the rationalisation test did not involve questions about one major feature of rationalisation, its subconscious character (for instance, one can quite deliberately reinterpret events in one's favour, which does not involve rationalisation).

To fill this gap, in Dialogue 4 stress was placed on perceptual subconscious defences (projection and defence proper) and on the child's understanding of the fact that rationalisation involves a person's acting without that person being aware of the real determinants of the actions. Another aspect of this study was that the children not only discussed the actions of the characters in the story, but were also asked whether they themselves sometimes behave in the same "strange" way as the characters in the stories did.

The questions were as follows:

1. Tell me, please, what is this [a card taken from the Rorschach ink-blot test is shown]? What does it look like?
2. Imagine that one night when you were asleep, you got very hungry. What do you think you will see in your dream?
3. And if you were shown this picture [the same Rorschach card is shown] when you were very hungry and asked what this picture looked like, what would your answer be?
4. And if something scared you very much, and at that moment you were asked what this picture looked like, what would your answer be?
5. Imagine that one night when you are asleep a wizard (or, for the older children, a hypnotiser) comes to you and casts a spell (suggests to you) that in the morning when you go to school you will pick up three pebbles from the kerb and put them in your pocket. Now, morning comes, you get up and go to school as usual. What will you do on your way to school?
6. Why would you pick the pebbles up?
7. Will you know that it was the wizard (the hypnotist) who made you pick the pebbles up?
8. And if, while you were picking up the pebbles, somebody asked you what you were doing, what would you answer?
9. And if this wizard (the hypnotist) cast a spell (suggested to you) that you should refuse to eat your breakfast in the morning, would you refuse? Why?
10. And if you were asked in the morning about why you refused to eat your breakfast, what would you answer? Would you feel really hungry or not?
11. Listen, one day I asked a boy named Peter to do one simple task for me and asked another boy named Viktor to watch whether Peter was doing the task correctly. Viktor watched and reported all the mistakes that Peter had made. Then I asked the teacher to do the same task and Viktor had to watch whether she did it all right. The teacher made the same mistakes that Peter had made, but Viktor failed to notice the mistakes although he was looking very carefully. Why did Viktor notice the mistakes that Peter made and fail to notice the same mistakes made by the teacher?
12. If you were in Viktor's place, would you have noticed the mistakes that the teacher made?
13. Another day I asked a girl called Masha to watch how another girl from the same classroom did a task. Masha noticed all the mistakes that the other girl had made. After this I asked Masha to do the same task herself. Masha made the same mistakes that the girl had made but she didn't notice them and thought that she did everything all right. Tell me,

why did Masha notice all the mistakes that the other girl had made but failed to notice the same mistakes she made herself?

14. If you were in Masha's place, would you have noticed your mistakes?

Most children of all ages acknowledged the fact that hunger affects their dreams; they expected to see in their dreams various food products or themselves eating something (Fig. 61). The children who didn't realise or denied this either named objects irrelevant to eating or said that this wouldn't affect their dreams ("I would see something in my dream, but not necessarily food").

Comparison of the children's responses to Questions 1, 3, and 4 showed that more than 30% of preschoolers and most schoolchildren modified the names of an ambiguous object according to the need they were asked to imagine: if a neutral question (Question 1) evoked in the children images of "a skin", "a tree", "a cave", "a fresco", etc., then in response to Question 3 they named food objects ("ice cream", "candies", "salad", "meat", etc.) and

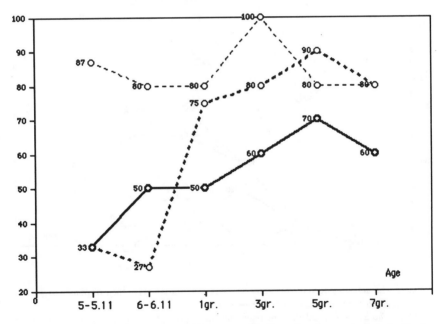

Children who thought that the feeling of hunger would affect what they see in their dreams (q. 2, - -o- -).
Children who believed that the feelings of hunger (q. 3, —o—) and fear (q. 4, - -o- -) would affect their perceptions.

FIG. 61. Percentages of children producing answers in response to questions regarding the impact that their needs have on their dreams and perceptions.

in response to Question 4 they named scary objects ("a snake", "a skull", "a monster", etc.); the rest of the children either repeated associations given in response to Question 1, or produced irrelevant associations (Fig. 61). Overall, the number of answers that revealed an understanding of the possible impact of hunger and fear upon apperception increased with age, significantly so for fear (6 years to 7 years: $\chi^2 = 7.72$, $P < 0.01$).

In response to Question 5, all the children acknowledged (some after a brief discussion with the experimenter) that they would have picked the pebbles up and saw the hypnotic state (or the magic spell) as the cause of this (Question 7) (Fig. 62). When answering Question 8, a large number of children produced judgements that revealed their understanding of the rationalisation mechanism ("I would tell the person that I would just like to play with the pebbles"; "I'd say I'd like to examine the pebbles, whether

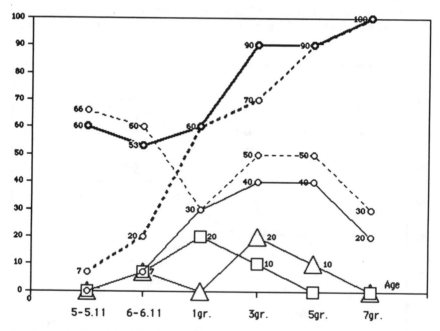

Children who acknowledged the phenomenon of rationalisation (1) in their responses to qq. 5–8 (- -o- -), (2) in their responses to q. 10 (—o—).
Children who acknowledged that the phenomenon of perceptive defence had occurred in the mind of a story character (1) towards a teacher (q. 11, - -o- -), and (2) towards him- or herself (q. 13, —o—).
Children who acknowledged the possibility for themselves of making perceptive defence errors (1) towards their teachers (q. 12, —□—), (2) towards their own behaviours (q. 14, —△—).

FIG. 62.   Percentages of children producing answers in response to questions regarding the mechanisms of rationalisation and perceptive defence.

they are nice or not"; "Well, I would think that I did this in order to show my friends that I was collecting various kinds of granite"). There was no clear age-related trend. The remaining children revealed no understanding of rationalisation ("I would tell the person that I didn't know why I was doing this"; "I'd say that I needed the pebbles"; "I'd say that I just wanted them"); even the special prompting of the experimenter didn't affect these children's answers (*Experimenter:* "But why would you want the pebbles, what for?" "Well, I'd simply pick them up ... how can a person explain an action if he doesn't know that he was hypnotised").

The number of children who had an understanding of the rationalisation mechanism when they were asked Question 10 increased significantly with age (6 years to 13 years: $\chi^2 = 5.06$, $P < 0.05$). Most schoolchildren confirmed that in reality they would feel hunger, thus revealing an awareness of the discrepancy between the state of their organism and the state of their mind ("There would be the feeling of hunger, because you want to eat, but you can't eat because the hypnotiser has told you that you shouldn't").

The most difficult questions proved to be those concerning perceptual defence mechanisms (Questions 11–14). Question 11 showed that with increasing age, significantly more children understand the mechanism (6 years to 9 years: $\chi^2 = 4.83$, $P < 0.05$) ("He didn't notice the teacher's mistakes, because he loved his kindergarten teacher very much"; "Because the teacher was a well-educated person, and because of that Viktor was not looking hard enough at what she was doing, but Peter was an ordinary boy and he could make mistakes"; "Because the teacher—she had graduated from the university, and Peter—he was only a schoolboy"; "Well, the teacher could not make errors"; "He knew that the teacher would do everything right"; "Perhaps there was a belief in the boy's mind that the teacher couldn't make mistakes, and Viktor ... despite the fact he was looking at her he kept thinking that she couldn't be wrong"). The rest of the children produced irrelevant justifications ("Because he was looking at the wrong side"; "Because the teacher obscured his view"; "Because he couldn't see well").

The number of children able to acknowledge that the perceptual defence mechanisms in a story character were also present in them (Question 13) was significantly smaller than the number who acknowledged perceptual defence with regard to the assessment of the teacher's actions by the character (Question 11) ($z = 5.09$, $P < 0.01$). The proportion increased slightly among schoolchildren ("Masha didn't notice her errors because she didn't want to get a poor mark"; "Well, everybody can notice mistakes in another person's actions, but regarding themselves people don't like to be critical"). Finally, almost all the children strongly denied that they would be uncritical to themselves (Question 14).

As can be seen from the above questions, one characteristic feature of this dialogue was its prompting structure, intended to examine whether the children were able to find the hints incorporated in the questions regarding some unconscious psychological mechanisms. It wasn't particular established pieces of knowledge or capacities of the children's minds that was tested in this dialogue, but rather the presence of "fertile ground" in the minds of the children that would allow them to grasp the prompts and achieve an understanding "during the very process of the questioning".

The data showed that the unconscious mechanism which proved to be most accessible for the children was the effect that our needs have on our dreams. The apperception and rationalisation mechanisms were considerably more difficult to come to terms with, with perceptual defence being the most difficult of all. This "hierarchy of accessibility" cannot be put down to semantic causes, such as differences in the wording of the questions. For example, the wording of Questions 2 and 3, which contained the allusion of the impact of the person's needs on the person's dreams and apperception, was identical; however, there were significantly more correct answers to Question 2 than to Question 3 ($z = 4.3$, $P < 0.01$). Conversely, questions that tested the children's understanding of the apperception and rationalisation mechanisms were asked in different ways but yielded similar answers. It would seem more likely that the "degree of difficulty" of the questions was responsible for how the psychological mechanisms were represented in the children's minds.

Clearly, the children probably had the opportunity to observe the effects that their needs have on their dreams more often than the effects their needs have on their perception. Opportunities to observe rationalisation and perceptual defence are also rare. What was surprising was not that many children failed to appreciate the mechanisms, but that a considerable number of them revealed a certain level of appreciation of the mechanisms, thus confirming earlier reports of young children's understanding of defence mechanisms (Dollinger & McGuire, 1981).

The fact that the number of children able to adequately explain the apperception, rationalisation, and perceptual defence mechanisms increased significantly with age can be accounted for either by the expanding nature of children's psychological experience or by their growing capacity to undertake "self-analysis", that is the capacity to "look inside one's mind". There is no doubt that in comparison to preschoolers, older children have a greater need to assess critically the erroneous actions of their peers and teachers, as well as their own mistakes; there is also an increase in the number of "perceptual defence" errors that can affect their judgements. It should also be borne in mind that the "understanding" of unconscious mechanisms that most children revealed was in no way complete. However, the children's capacity to capture the hints provided and express verbally some of the behavioural outcomes of the unconscious process shows that children have a much more sophisticated view of their mind than has been commonly assumed.

DIALOGUE 5: "INNER WORLD"

This dialogue aimed to determine to what extent children are able to appreciate and express verbally (1) certain attributes of their mind, and (2) the difference between the "inner world" of a human being and those of animals, plants, and inanimate objects. Although in psychological studies children are often asked questions about their dreams, emotions, and feelings, as well as about whether certain objects are alive or not, the questions here were formulated in such a way that the children were able to act as an external judge or observer rather than be in the position of a person who is looking "inside his or her mind". So, in this dialogue, an attempt was made to "peep into" each child's mind "from outside", as well as to encourage the child to put him- or herself in the position of subhuman creatures and objects.

The questions were as follows:

1. Let us imagine that we enter a dark, unknown room. We switch our torch on and its light beam illuminates various objects, including a table, a sofa, an old cupboard, etc. Now let us imagine that your mind and your soul are this dark room. We open the door, enter, switch the torch on. . . . What do you think we'll see?
2. Tell me, if you are hungry, what kind of feeling do you have?
3. And if you fell down and got hurt what kind of feeling do you have? And if you are asleep and see a dream, what kind of feelings to you experience? And if you are in the process of searching for a solution to a difficult task and you can't find one, what kind of feeling do you have? And if you committed something bad—for instance, you deceived your friend—what kind of feeling would you have?
4. Tell me now, if we take not the human mind but the mind of an animal— for instance, a dog's mind—do you think that it feels something if it is punched? What does it feel? And if the dog is chewing a tasty bone, what do you think it feels? And if the dog did something bad—for instance, ate a piece of meat that his master had prepared for himself—what do you think the dog would feel?
5. Now let us talk about the mind of a tree. If a tree has one of its branches cut off, does it feel anything? What do you think it feels? If there has been no rain for a long time and the tree is fading, what do you think it can feel?
6. If we hit a piece of stone with a hammer, would it feel anything? If the stone was put in a fire, would it feel anything?

In response to Question 1, most children described their inner mental world by analogy to the external world (Fig. 63). The children thought that they would see in their minds the room and the objects that were in front of them at the moment of the interrogation. Some of the children viewed the images they had in their minds as mere copies of the external world; others treated these mental images as transformed and changed reflections of what they saw in the outside world ("It would depend on my mood ... perhaps, we would see the same lounge... But if I had a different mood, then the image would be different"; "Well, perhaps we would see the chessboard... But if you are hungry, then it would seem to you that there is a vase with some fruits in it"; "Well, we would see some unknown objects, this sofa, for instance ... but it would be somehow deformed").

The majority of fifth- and seventh-graders viewed their inner world not as an analogy of the external world (whether it was an identical copy or not),

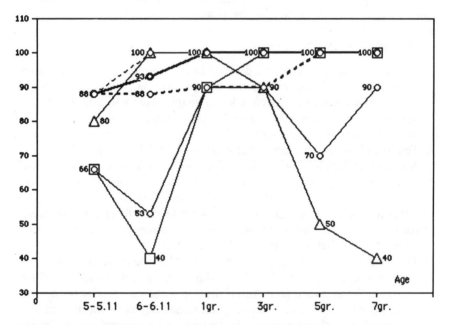

Children who thought that their inner world was a strict copy of the external display (q. 1, —△—).
Children who managed to name correctly their feelings and experiences in situations of (1) having the feeling of hunger (q. 2, - -○- -), (2) having the feeling of pain (q. 3, —○—), (3) having a scary dream (q. 3, —○—), (4) doing difficult work (q. 4, —□—), (5) violating a moral prohibition (q. 3, - -○- -).

FIG. 63.   Percentages of children producing answers in response to questions regarding their inner world.

but as something special ("Well, we would see something that is in my soul ... some kind of my moods"; "We would see what I am thinking at the moment"; "Well, there would not be this furniture there; rather, there would be some of my strong impressions there and my feelings, and something shapeless, I can't tell you exactly what ... what my will power is"; "We would see some good traits and bad traits of mine"; "Various feelings, my character, my attitudes towards everything").

However, direct questioning about a variety of feelings and experiences (Questions 2 and 3) revealed that most preschoolers and almost all schoolchildren were able to name the feeling accurately ("I feel hunger"; "I would feel pain"; "If I had a bad dream, I would feel scared"; "I would feel sorrow and disappointment"; "I'd anticipate that I'm going to be punished"); others, mostly preschoolers, named various events and objects rather than feelings ("Food, banana"; "I'd have blood soaking from my wound"; "I'd feel that a bear is chasing me").

Most preschoolers and all the schoolchildren ascribed the capacity to feel pain and satisfaction to dogs ("It would feel pain"; "It would have an appetite"; "It would taste the food"); the remainder replaced a description of feelings with a description of events ("A dog can bite you if you kick it") (Fig. 64). The number of children who attributed the feeling of shame to a dog slightly decreased with age; these children thought that the dog "would feel that it was not good to behave like that", "it would feel its guilt, but to a lesser extent than a human being". Basically, a significantly smaller number of children ascribed the capacity to experience shame to the dog than the capacity to experience satisfaction ($z = 5.7$, $P < 0.05$).

The majority of children in all age groups thought that plants could experience pain and thirst ("Yes, it hurts"; "It can feel the pain, because plants ... their every branch and every shoot is their heads, and their mouths, and their little hands and legs"; "It would feel that it is dying"; "It would feel that it needs water"). The rest of the children refused to attribute the capacity to feel to a tree ("The real tree ... it can feel nothing, it just fades." *Experimenter:* "And if its branch is being cut?" "It still can't feel anything, because it has no soul, no character").

Some preschoolers and first-graders thought that a stone could experience pain ("It would feel that it has been struck"; "It would feel pain"; "It would feel that it burns in the fire"). However, significantly fewer children ascribed the capacity to feel to stones than to trees ($z = 7.1$, $P < 0.01$), and most preschoolers and all children older than 7 denied that a stone could feel anything. This result is not in accord with Piaget (1929/1983), who reported that it is not until children reach 11–12 years of age that they are able to restrict life to animals and plants only. However, this may be accounted for by the way in which Piaget asked his questions about the origins of life (reproduced in subsequent studies; Carey, 1985; Laurendeau & Pinard,

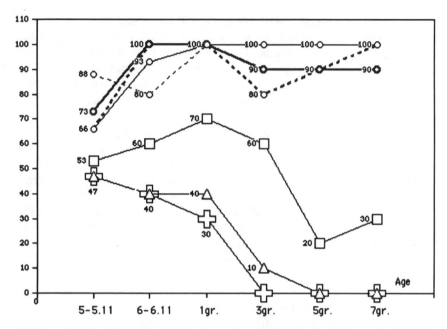

Children who believed that a dog (q. 4) can experience the feelings of pain (—o—), satisfaction (- -o- -), and shame (—□—).
Children who thought that a plant (q. 5) can experience the feelings of pain (—•—), and thirst (- -o- -).
Children who believed that a stone (q. 6) can experience the feelings of pain from a blow (—⟊—) and from the fire (—△—).

FIG. 64. Percentages of children producing answers in response to questions regarding whether animals, plants, and inanimate objects have feelings.

1962; Schwartz, 1980), which was to direct the child's attention to the external manifestations of life (such as feeding or spontaneous movements) rather than to the "internal dimension" of live creatures.

However, the results of the dialogue confirmed an established fact, that most children tend to identify their minds and souls with images of external reality, a phenomenon that Piaget called "realism of the child's thinking" (Piaget, 1929/1983). The children who revealed this phenomenon didn't use psychological concepts in their descriptions of their "minds", despite the fact that most of them were able to name their feelings accurately when asked directly about them in Questions 2 and 3.

The second phenomenon to be revealed in this dialogue was the anthropomorphic attribution of moral feelings to animals and the feeling of pain to trees and stones. This is another demonstration of the highly conventional character of the boundary which is drawn in contemporary

European cultures between objects that have "psychological dimension" and those that do not. It would appear that preschoolers have a rather poor notion of this boundary; however, they learn it very quickly when they start school. Thus, in the view of most preschoolers and first-graders, a stone— unlike a dog or a tree—doesn't have the capacity to feel pain. Furthermore, most fifth- and seventh-graders thought that the "inner world" of a dog doesn't include moral feelings. It was at this age that the number of children who viewed their minds as mere copies of the external world fell significantly.

Comparing the answers in this dialogue with those reported by Piaget (1929/1983), we can see that the children in the age range 5–7 years did indeed reveal a combination of two opposite points of view: on the one hand, they viewed their internal worlds as copies of the external world (what could be named "the externalisation of the mind") and, on the other, they tended to attribute the properties of the mind to inanimate and even non-living objects (the "anthropomorphisation of objects"). However, Piaget's description of these tendencies as two sides of the same coin (the failure of the children to distinguish between internal and external) seems unlikely; rather, these tendencies reflect two different trends working in the children's minds simultaneously. In so far as it concerns the externalisation of mind, it may indeed be the result of the confusion between external objects and internal images of the objects; this confusion in turn may be based on the confusion between more fundamental distinctions, such as between entities that have physical characteristics (location in space, divisibility, etc.) and those that do not, distinctions that are very difficult to come to terms with for preschoolers (Subbotsky, 1994). As for the second phenomenon (the attribution of psychological characteristics to plants and non-living objects), it may be based on a different type of confusion, namely one between objects that have psychological functions and those that do not. The boundary between physical and mental (or between mind and body, internal and external) isn't identical to that between objects which have minds (and, therefore, feelings, etc.) and those which do not. The acquisition of the first distinction by the child is closely linked with the enrichment of the child's psychological experience (self-analysis and self-observation), whereas the second distinction is much more dependent on cultural conventions (carefully analysed in cross-cultural studies, such as by Levy-Brühl, 1925) and is mainly imposed upon the child (and acquired by the child) through learning.

The differences in the underlying causes may, perhaps, account for the temporal gap that exists between the two phenomena. Indeed, although most 11- and 13-year-old children in this study were quite aware of the fact that their "inner world" was qualitatively different from external physical objects (that is, it was something "non-spatial" and non-physical), they still attributed the capacity to experience feeling to an inanimate object (a tree).

DIALOGUE 6: "ETERNAL LIFE"

The aims of this dialogue were to establish at what age and how children become aware of (1) the eternal need of a human individual to overcome the limits of his or her individual life, and (2) the dialectical relationship between the change that a human individual undergoes throughout life and the feeling of personal identity that is preserved despite the change.
     The questions asked were as follows:

1. Tell me, who lives longest, a human being or a butterfly?
2. Do you think that all living creatures die or are there some that live forever?
3. And what do people die from?
4. And what about you, would you like to live for a long time?
5. And if a wizard came to you and offered to make you immortal so that you would live forever and never die, would you agree or not? Why?
6. And what about other people, would they agree to become immortal? Would some of the people refuse?
7. If you agreed to become immortal, who would you like to be—a child as you are now, an adult person, or an old person? Why?
8. What would you do during this endless life?
9. And when you become an adult person, will this person be you or a person different from you?
10. And what will change in you when you become an adult person? What will stay the same?

     This dialogue revealed that most preschoolers and all schoolchildren were convinced that all living creatures (including man) were mortal; the preschoolers who thought differently either refused to name the creatures which they thought were immortal or named species ("a flower", "a butterfly", "grass") rather than individuals ("This is a butterfly. It always transforms into a chrysalis in the winter"). The answers to Question 3 (what people die from?) varied ("from illnesses", "from old age", "from accidents", etc.).
     Almost all the preschoolers and first-graders (and about half of the older children) expressed their desire to be immortal (decrease 7 years to 9 years: $\chi^2 = 4.03$, $P < 0.05$). Some children explained this desire with statements like "I want to live", "It's horrible—to die", "When you imagine that there will be a time when you will not exist, then the fear comes to you and you want a wizard to come and to make you live forever"; others justified it by their curiosity and desire to see the distant future ("It will be interesting to see what it will be like in a few thousand years"). However, a number of children didn't want immortality (Fig. 65), most of whom saw the negative consequences of being immortal ("It is now that I want very much to live,

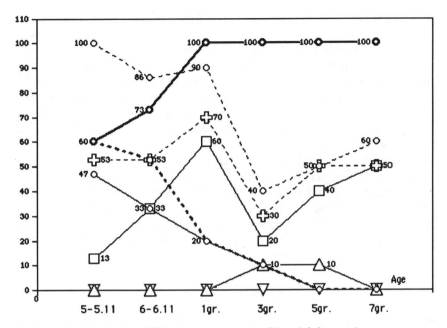

Children who thought that all living creatures are mortal (qq. 1 & 2, —o—).
Children who said that they would agree to become immortal (q. 5, --o--).
Children of the previous category who said that they would like to stay forever (q. 7) as a child
(—o—), an adult person (--⊕--), an elderly person (—▽—).
Children who said that they would like to devote their immortal lives to play activity
(--o--), learning and sporting activities (—□—), sciences and arts (—△—), with the rest of
the children having no definite opinion.

FIG. 65.   Percentages of children producing answers in response to questions regarding life,
death, and immortality.

but the moment will come when it will be indifferent to you... It's not that
you will be bored with life, but ... the life won't be interesting any more for
you") and the need to part with loved ones. Almost all children in all age
groups thought that other people would share their views on immortal life
(Question 6).

Most children who wanted to live forever thought being a young adult
would be preferable. Living immortal life as a young adult was seen to provide
many opportunities for all sorts of professional activities ("I'd like to be an
adult and a sailor by profession"; "I'd like to be an adult and to buy a car";
"I'd work in the factory like my father"; "I'd be a construction worker"), and
some stressed the social independence that adulthood brings with it. The
attractiveness of the image of a "permanent childhood" was significant
among preschoolers but faded among schoolchildren; the preschoolers viewed

their immortal future as a sort of "eternal kindergarten" ("I would play, eat, and sleep"; "I would buy a bike and cycle all the time", etc.). The image of an immortal old person appeared attractive to nobody.

Most children thought (Question 9) that when they become adults, they will retain their personal identity ("It would still be me, who else?"). Answers to Question 10 showed that most preschoolers and first-graders associated conservation of their physical characteristics with the retaining of their personal identity ("My eyes would stay the same"; "My brain would not change"; "My body and my heart would stay the same"; "I would have my hair unchanged") (Fig. 66). This view decreased with age at the expense of answers linking personal identity to psychological qualities ("My childhood memories would remain unchanged"; "My soul will be the same"; "My character will be the same"; "If a person is good in his childhood, then he would stay good"; "Something will stay unchanged ... I will still have the feeling that it is me") (increase 7 years to 13 years: $\chi^2 = 5.73$, $P < 0.02$).

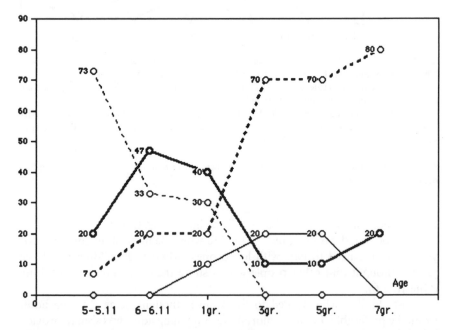

Children who thought that when they become adults they would still have the same physical features (—o—), names (—o—), psychological characteristics (- -o- -).
Children who failed to indicate what would remain the same in them when they become adults (- -o- -).

FIG. 66. Percentages of children producing answers in response to Question 10 regarding the properties that will change when they become adults.

There were few children who associated their personal identity with the permanence of their names.

Viewing these data as a whole, most preschoolers (apart from those who confused an individual and a species) were aware of the fact that all living creatures are mortal. All the children were also aware of the discrepancy that exists between their desire to be immortal and their knowledge that it is not possible; nevertheless, almost all preschoolers and first-graders thought that a desire for eternal life would be expressed by all people, except by the very ill and the aged. For most children, the desire for eternal life had a positive aspect: it was not the immortality in its own right that attracted the children, but rather the permanent opportunity to play, work, or to be engaged in some other sort of activity. The children viewed immortal life as a sort of an active exploration which could most successfully be achieved through becoming an adult person.

Another phenomenon (which was mainly a characteristic of the preschoolers) was the indirect link some children make between permanence of their personal "selves" and permanence of their physical features. Although the questions did not allude to the fact that one's features that remain unchanged with age are the keepers of personal identity, this was implied in the dialogue. Indeed, right after the children acknowledged that when they become adults they will be the same persons as they are now, they had to indicate what it actually was in them that would stay the same. As a result, all that is changeable, which normally leads to a person's death, was viewed by many children as the only permanent part of their personalities. It was true, however, that the children selected for this the most stable parts of the human body (hair, eyes, some internal organs like brain or heart). The fact that only a few children mentioned brain in this context seems to be in accord with the data according to which it was only elementary schoolchildren (but not preschoolers) who are able to appreciate the role of brain as a primary locus of psychological attributes and identity (Johnson, 1990).

Among 9- to 14-year-olds, there were some changes in their judgements about human existence. First, as children grow older, they began to appreciate some of the negative consequences that eternal life would bring about. Hence, a growing number of children refused to accept the offer of immortality, a refusal which, of course, should not be taken at face value: it is possible that the children who had lost their initial naivety of judgements were simply trying to devalue their secret desire for eternal life.

Second, the older children began to associate conservation of their personal identity in time not with constancy of their physical features, but with permanence of their psychological characteristics (i.e. with the mind, character, etc.). This would seem to be at odds with the answers reported by Johnson (1990), who found elementary schoolchildren to have a firm understanding of the brain as a bearer of psychological personal identity.

The contradiction can be explained, however, by the different wording of the questions used in Johnson's experiment and in this study. Whereas Johnson asked children directly about the role of the brain in personal identity (what would happen if a child's brain is transplanted in an animal or another person?), in this study the questions were formulated in a free choice manner (what will change in you when you become an adult person?), which encouraged the children to look for characteristics they thought to be linked with their personal identity.

DIALOGUE 7: "REALITY"

The aims of this dialogue were to examine whether children are able to understand (1) the limits that everyday reality places upon thinking and the activity of the individual (the impossibility of the immediate accomplishment of human wishes and the inaccessibility of another person's thoughts for direct observation), and (2) the positive role that these limitations play in making human existence possible.

The questions asked were as follows:

1. Tell me, if you wished hard for the microphone in my hand to turn into a sparrow, would it turn into a sparrow? Why?
2. And if you wished for a jar of sweets to appear in front of you, would it appear? Why?
3. And if you wanted to know everything that I am now thinking without actually asking me any questions, could you find out? Why?
4. And what about me. Can I learn what you are thinking right now? And in what way can a person learn about what another person is thinking?
5. Tell me, if you had a magic wand that could make all your wishes possible, what would you ask it to do for you?
6. Would you like to live in a world where all your wishes immediately became reality? Why?
7. Would you like to live in a world where the wishes of everyone immediately became reality? Why?
8. Would you like to live in a world where all your dreams immediately came true? Why?
9. [If the answer is positive]: Tell me, do you have only good wishes and no bad wishes or do you have bad ones too?
10. Tell me, are there only good people in the world or there are also bad ones?
11. So would you like to live in a world where all your wishes or those of other people immediately became reality?
12. And what about a world in which people are able to see each other's thoughts directly without even asking one another. Would you like to live in such a world? Why?

13. Do you sometimes have thoughts that you would not like to share with other people?
14. And what about other people, do they sometimes have thoughts that they would prefer to keep to themselves?
15. So would you like to live in a world in which people were able to see each other's thoughts?
16. Do you always have nice dreams or do you have frightening dreams as well?
17. So would you like to live in a world in which all your dreams immediately became reality?

The children's answers to Questions 1 and 2 showed that they were completely aware of the boundary that existed between their wishes and everyday reality. The children denied the possibility of their wishes immediately becoming reality: they either simply acknowledged that it was impossible ("No, it is impossible for an inanimate object to turn into an animate one") or pointed out that it was only possible in unusual realities like fairy tales or imagination ("No, it can only happen in your imagination, otherwise it cannot"; "No, I am not a wizard"). Some children stressed the spatiotemporal gap that exists between individual objects ("No, it can't happen, because the microphone is one thing, and a sparrow eats small beetles, and a microphone—it has no stomach, no memory").

A similar picture emerged for the children's answers to Questions 3 and 4: most children thought that direct access to other people's thoughts was impossible. Some of the children simply denied such a possibility, others referred to its as magic or telepathy which are impossible in real life ("No, people have no telepathic capacities"; "No, we are not wizards"), still others stressed the separate and enclosed character of the individual's mind ("No, I cannot do this, nobody can, because your life is one thing, and my life is another thing"; "No, you are you and me is me, I can't get into your brains"). The children believed that the only way to learn about another person's thoughts was to ask them or guess what those thoughts are on the basis of their behaviour. The small number of children who acknowledged the possibility of telepathy viewed it as a manifestation of extraordinary human capacities ("This can happen, yes ... but not everyone can do it, you have to practise a lot to be able to do this"; "You can learn about another person's thoughts. Not nowadays, no, but they could do it in Egypt").

Almost all the preschoolers and a large number of schoolchildren wouldn't have minded living in a world in which all their wishes immediately became reality. They explained this by their desire to achieve some practical goals ("Well, if you want to be asked a question by a teacher about something that you know well, you just think of it—and the teacher would ask you"; "I would like to live in such a world, because here you have to work hard in order to pass your tests, and in that world—you can just wish this, and everything would appear ready for you in your notebook"). However, many schoolchildren refused to live in such a world (increase 6 years to 9 years: $\chi = 14.87$, $P < 0.001$). One major reason was the children's fear that their negative wishes would also become reality ("No, I wouldn't like to live in such a world, because for instance I could think of something bad, and it would appear"; "No, because if I want something I would be unable to stop the wish and this wish could be a bad, wrong wish"; "No, because I sometimes think about something which I later regret"). Others were anxious about the overcrowded and bizarre nature of such a world ("No, because I think a lot of things, and if everything were to become real—it would be too tough in the world"; "No, because then I would have too many toys, there would be no room for them"). Whereas some were motivated by intention to achieve everything through their own personal efforts ("No, because I'd like to do everything myself"; "A person must achieve everything by his own efforts"; "There would be no pleasure in such a world, it's fun to do everything on your own"). After an auxiliary question (Question 9) was asked, the number of children who refused to live in such a world in response to Question 11 increased significantly (Fig. 67).

Most preschoolers and first-graders thought that they would like to live in a world where all their dreams immediately came true; most of the children were attracted by the unusual and fairy-tale nature of a world like this ("I'd like to, because if I had some fairy tale in my dream and if I liked it—it would become real"; "Yes, I'd like to live in such a world, because if I have a dream about a theatre, and a kingdom—I'd like to have this"). However, the overwhelming majority of schoolchildren refused to live in such a world (increase 7 years to 9 years: $\chi^2 = 8.05$, $P < 0.01$). One major reason for this was that bad dreams might also be turned into reality ("No, I wouldn't like to, because for instance you see killers in your dreams, and they would really start going around and killing people"; "No, because sometimes you have bad dreams"; "No, because your dreams are not in your control, and you can see something frightening and sinister in your dream"); another reason was the chaotic and disorganised character of such a world ("No, because in that world ... everything would be flying around in the air, the chairs and everything"). As in the previous case, the number of children refusing to live in a world where dreams came true increased significantly after the auxiliary question was asked (Fig. 67).

The children's answers to questions about the world in which the wishes of other people immediately became reality (Questions 7 and 11) mirrored almost precisely those given in response to Question 6. The number of children who refused to live in such a world increased with age (6 years to 9 years: $\chi^2 = 6.53$, $P < 0.02$); as previously, the major arguments against living in such a world were the existence of bad wishes and the chaos that

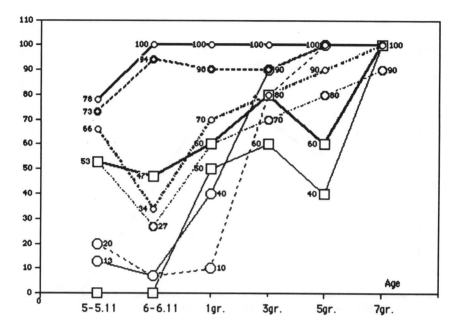

Children who said that they would not like living in the world in which all of their wishes (□) or all of other people's wishes (○) would immediately become reality, before (qq. 6 & 7, —) and after (q. 11, —) the children were asked auxiliary questions.
Children who said that they would not like living in the world in which all of their dreams would immediately come true, before (q. 8, - -○- -) and after (q. 17, - -o- -) the children were asked auxiliary questions.
Children who said that they would not like living in the world in which people could read thoughts of each other, before (q. 12, ---o---) and after (q. 15, ---o---) the children were asked auxiliary questions.

FIG. 67. Percentages of children producing answers in response to questions regarding living in a world where there were no restrictions on reality.

would reign in such a world. However, as can be seen from Fig. 67, this time the auxiliary question (Question 10) produced a significantly stronger deterrent effect than was the case with the world of accomplished personal wishes. This can be accounted for by the fact that the children acknowledged the appearance of bad wishes in other people more often than in themselves (see Fig. 68), with a difference between the positive answers to Questions 9 and 10 being significant ($z = 5.3$, $P < 0.05$).

About half of the preschoolers and all the schoolchildren refused to live in a world where people could see each other's thoughts; some did for moral reasons ("Well, it would be like peeping through a keyhole in the door"; "Well, every person has some thoughts which he or she wouldn't like to

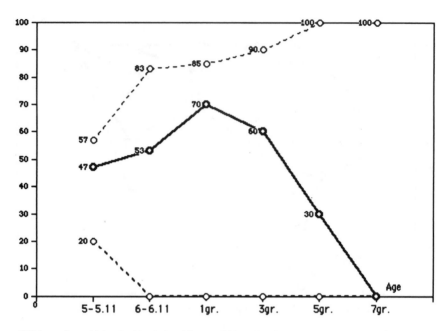

Children who said (q. 9) that their wishes could be (1) only good (—o—), (2) both good and bad (the rest of the children).
Children who believed (q. 10) that other people's intentions could be (1) only good (- -o- -), (2) both good and bad (the rest of the children).
Children who thought (q. 13) that they have (- -o- -) or have no (the rest of the children) thoughts that they would like to keep secret from other people.

FIG. 68. Percentages of children producing answers in response to questions regarding the moral content of their wishes and thoughts and other people's wishes and thoughts.

disclose"; "Maybe the other person doesn't want his thoughts to be known about"), others because they wanted to keep their own thoughts secret ("I have all sorts of thoughts, it is no good if everybody knows about them"), still others because they feared that they would not be able to maintain a stability to their thinking ("No, because for instance you are walking and thinking of something, and when you are passing another person you'll have his thoughts in your head and your own thoughts would vanish").

The children who were willing to live in a world of "transparent minds" justified this either by an interest in seeing what other people think or by hoping to benefit from such "mental contact" ("I'd like to, because if nothing comes to my mind and other people have plenty of thoughts, then I would learn about those thoughts and follow them"). Some children were also attracted by the easiness of communication in such a world. After the auxiliary questions (Questions 13 and 14), the number of children who wanted to live in a world of telepathy decreased significantly.

One general finding of this dialogue was that while all the children were fully aware of the limitations that everyday reality places on human actions, thoughts and wishes, it is not until around 7–9 years of age that they begin to acknowledge the positive role of such limitations. However, once they do acknowledge this, it is usually accompanied by fairly adequate and reasonable justifications. Thus, a significant number of children linked these limitations with the need "to keep things separate" and to avoid chaos. Another disadvantage of the absence of such limitations would be to lose control over the world of "accomplished subjectivity", which would become totally unpredictable. It may be assumed that this type of argumentation is a manifestation of the children's awareness of the fundamental metaphysical distinction between the realm of wishes and the realm of everyday reality, with the former being rather unpredictable and uncontrollable and the latter having an orderly and rationalistically organised structure.

Of the inadequate and irrelevant justifications produced by the children, most were of a "moralising" nature (for instance, rejecting the world of "accomplished wishes" on the grounds that "a person must achieve everything by his own efforts", or rejecting the world of "telepathic communication" because it would be unethical to look into other people's secrets). Nevertheless, even this kind of justification may be an indicator of some vague idea about the positive role of the limitation on everyday reality which the children were as yet unable to be more lucid about.

In sum, there is a certain temporal gap between the age at which children develop an awareness of the limitations on everyday reality (about age 5) and the age at which these limitations become to be viewed as necessary (about age 7). What sorts of factors are responsible for this gap?

As is the case with most achievements in verbal reasoning, two main factors contribute to an awareness of the necessary character of the restrictions that everyday reality places on human subjectivity. The first is the development of the cognitive means of awareness and the verbal capacity to express those mental states that the child can observe in his or her own mind, and the other is the enrichment of the child's mental experience. Indeed, as children's experience of social interaction grows, they are increasingly confronted with situations in which they have to restrain their impulses; consequently, the children begin to view some of their wishes as being alien to their "I"—something that, although it is a part of their minds, is undesirable and has to be restrained. To a certain extent, this experience can be enhanced by listening to others and reading books and stories in which the necessity of self-restriction is stressed (as it is, for instance, in a story by the Russian author Valentin Kataev, *Tzvetik—semitzvetik*). On the other hand, children learn various cultural symbolic means invented to highlight the areas to which these restrictions are applied (e.g. the demand "to achieve your goals on your own", "not to give your negative moods and intentions away", "to respect other people's privacy", etc.). It is only when children's experience and the cognitive means come together that the positive effect of the limitations on everyday reality become obvious for the child. The results of this dialogue indicate that this does not necessarily happen until the child reaches the age of 7–9 years.

CONCLUDING REMARKS: CHILDREN'S REASONINGS ABOUT THE METAPHYSICS OF HUMAN BEINGS

Looking at the overall results, it can be seen that children in the age range studied here provide very diverse and sometimes very profound judgements about various aspects of human reality, some of which are very close to the models accepted in rationalistically oriented social sciences, whereas others deviate strongly from them. Thus, on the one hand, children of all ages rightly ascribe a capacity for perception and differentiation between the senses of various modalities to the newborn infant, as well as a capacity to assess relative distances (which is in accord with contemporary infant studies; see Bower, 1972; Bremner, 1994). Similarly, most children consider themselves to be the authors of their own voluntary actions, acknowledge that they are responsible for carrying out their immoral thoughts, and are able to appreciate some of the mechanisms of the unconscious (such as the influence of needs on human dreams and human perception, the possibility for unconscious wishes to be transformed by human consciousness in order to fit the logic of real life). Many of the children were able to describe accurately the criteria that distinguish everyday reality from unusual realities.

On the other hand, a typical feature of most Russian and British children is the tendency to attribute psychological capacities to the newborn infant which, even according to the most optimistic of scientific views, appear much later in the child's life, such as a child's capacity to view its sensations as personal, to identify its body shape with the bodies of other people. All the Russian and British children considered verbal knowledge of moral norms to be a sufficient condition for the real upholding of those norms. Most of our subjects viewed themselves as personally responsible not only for their practical actions but also for their desires and motivations; they also viewed human beings as having a relatively short list of wishes and needs. Most children ascribed to plants needs and experiences that are pertinent to human beings only.

As was the case in the study of metaphysical judgements about the world, the replication study showed that, with regard to the judgements about human psychology, British children manifested similar phenomena to those shown by Russian children. For example, they attributed precocious capacities to a prelinguistic newborn infant, and thought that knowledge of moral norms was enough to enable a child to implement those norms.

However, in general, the British children were more cautious than the Russian children in attributing these precocious capacities (such as inherent knowledge about the objects that initiate sensations, or the skills necessary for using those objects in accordance with their social functions) to the infant. This may be an effect of the earlier age at which children begin school education in Britain compared to Russia, as well as a consequence of cultural differences in the children's development. Even if it is school education that accelerates the "psychological mindedness" of British children, then there is still the question of what it is in British schooling that produces this more sceptical view of the capacities of a prelinguistic infant, and of the limited improvement that acquisition of language brings about.

The most noticeable changes in children's judgements occur during the primary school years (first- and third-graders). It is at this age that most subjects begin to deny that a newborn has an inherent knowledge of an object's name (they do, however, attribute such knowledge to a child who has been taught language); they no longer identify knowledge about an object's name with knowledge about its function and with the capacity to handle that object appropriately. Already at this age, children do not ascribe to a newborn infant inherent knowledge about other people's existence, or a capacity to understand human speech or implement moral norms. It is also at this age that most children are able to acknowledge "perceptual defence" mechanisms, and realise that non-living objects do not possess an "inner world", which can only be attributed to animate creatures. Children of this age also reveal an understanding that stability and identity of the personal "I" of the subject throughout time is guaranteed by the stability of psychological qualities (and not, for instance, by the permanence of the subject's appearance or other physical qualities). Another important acquisition at this age is the realisation of the character and limitations of everyday reality, which distinguishes it from unusual realities like dreams or imagination.

At about the age of 11–13 years, most children show an understanding of other ideas about a human being which are pertinent to rationalism, such as the idea that immoral impulses and wishes can appear spontaneously in a person, who is not therefore responsible for them unless he or she implements them in his or her real behaviour. Children of this age no longer attribute moral feeling to animals, and many of them reveal their negative attitude towards immortal life, basing this on a realisation of the negative aspects that such an existence would bring with it for both the individual and society.

Thus, the results reveal that children's judgements about human reality within the age range studied undergo significant change. These changes are of two types. First, they include extension of the "actual knowledge" and information about the structure and genesis of human reality (for instance, the role of sensations, of speech, of the causes of violations of moral norms, etc.). Second, children's general capacity to understand the complex nature of human reality also develops, which creates in children a special zone of "potential knowledge". The latter was especially obvious in the children's increasing capacity to pick up "hints" given by the experimenter's questions and to realise certain ideas in the very process of conversation.

As is the case with respect to children's judgements about metaphysical problems of external reality, the development of children's judgements about metaphysical aspects of human reality is in the main not a result of deliberate learning and teaching. Rather, it comes from the spontaneous working of children's minds based on independent reading, watching TV and movies, everyday conversations, and observations of one's own and other people's behaviour. Children's judgements about human reality are also tightly linked to their ideas about the metaphysical structure of the external world: it is the authentic experience of the reality of their own minds that provides children with the idea of making distinctions between psychological images and physical objects, between the relative freedom of personal actions and the strict nature of physical events, between the chaotic structure of events in dreams and the orderly sequence of events in everyday life.

NOTE

1. This replication was carried out by Sara Griffiths as part of her BSc research project (see Griffiths, 1995).

4
The Development of Metaphysical Knowledge in Children: A General View

One feature of the human mind is its everlasting need to explain the world, to reduce complex and unclear knowledge to a few simple and clear notions, to elucidate the world's enigmas through concepts already available and at our disposal.

Philosophers of antiquity were the first to attempt to represent the world's diversity through a combination of the four elements—earth, water, air, and fire—or through a composition of small uniform balls called "atoms". In contemporary physics, theories of the structure of matter became more complex but their task basically remained the same: to explain what "protoelements" underlie the diverse world of elementary particles and whether we can view all known physical phenomena as variations on a limited number of "laws of nature". In other sciences, both natural and social, the quest for an explanation of the increasing number of new phenomena was no less intense than in physics.

But the external world—the world of nature and society—does not embrace everything that is to be explained. There is another world—the world of mental psychological phenomena, the world of human thoughts, fantasies and dreams—full of enigmatic and mysterious phenomena. And these are even more difficult to explain than natural phenomena. Indeed, natural phenomena exist for everybody and can be cognised by the joint efforts of people. In contrast, subjective phenomena are hidden in the inner world of an individual. They are displayed on the "screen" that only the individual can observe and that is inaccessible to other people. It is not

always the case that a person can evoke psychological phenomena purposefully. Sometimes a person's thoughts, images, or feelings slip away,
suddenly reappearing at the most unexpected moment and in the most
bizarre combination. Understanding the "laws" of this world is not an easy
task. And the "laws" themselves are very unlike the laws of nature.

And there are not just two worlds, an external and an internal one. There
is a "third world", a world of ideas (like the idea of necessary true knowledge, the idea of "cogito"), ideas which are neither clearly external (like
physical objects) nor absolutely internal (like dreams), but, being mental
entities, they exist independently of our minds (see Popper, 1975). These
worlds are tiny illuminated spots in the infinite depth of the unknown. But
on a scale of a separate individual human life, the "zone" of the already
cognised appears to be very large. The zone embraces knowledge and culture. This zone is what newborn children have yet to enter. From the first
days of children's lives, adults introduce them to this zone. The children can
hear the sounds of human speech, see the contours of things that surround
them, touch surrounding objects and human artifacts with their hands. In
other words, from the first day of their lives, children enter a special "river
of education" through which human experience is transmitted to them.

At the beginning, the river is narrow and shallow. It embraces only what
adults can teach children without the assistance of words. Gradually the
river becomes wider. Normally this is in kindergarten or in primary school,
where the children find themselves trapped in the "river of systematic
education". The latter reaches its culmination in secondary school and
institutes of higher education. Systematic teaching is one major route via
which children acquire culture and a mastery of understanding and explanation of the world. This route is usually in the direction "from elementary
to complex" and "from particular to general". At first, children master
writing letters and then master writing words and sentences. They first have
to acquire arithmetic and only after this do they pass on to algebra. In this
way, one step at a time, adults push children along the "river of education"
until they become adults themselves and reach the boundary beyond which
the scope of the cognised world comes to an end and where they need to find
their way ahead without anybody's help or assistance.

But there is yet another way to become cognisant of the world. This is
"from complex to elementary knowledge" and "from fundamental to particular". The problem is that the world is impatient. It cannot wait as
children, guided by adults along the "river of education", gradually become
cognisant. Instead, from their earliest days, the world attacks children's
minds with all its diversity and complexity, which overwhelms children's
capacity for explanation. Being bombarded by an abundance of complex
phenomena for which they are not yet able to offer any "scientific" interpretations, the children nevertheless have somehow to organise and explain

these phenomena. They have to explain them on the basis of that small portion of knowledge and experience that they have so far accumulated. Of course, not all natural and psychological phenomena become the objects of children's curiosity, and many of them the children simply ignore. But the number of such "unexplainable" phenomena do substantially exceed the number of events children are taught to explain in an "accurate" scientific way. While trying to overcome this mountain of new problems, children address themselves to adults. Perhaps, this is what causes children to continually ask "Why?". However, and not because of a fault on the part of adults, many of these "why's" are doomed not to be answered. Indeed, in order to explain to a 4-year-old "why the wind blows" or "why the grass is green", one has to depend upon knowledge that the child still lacks. And then the children are left to search for answers of their own. These answers are very unlike adults' interpretations and the time will come when the children treat these answers with laughter. But now the children need them. They need them in order to bring harmony to their chaotic world and reduce the "strain of not understanding".

Traditionally, such growth in spontaneous knowledge was reduced to the scope of physics. Although Piaget early on touched upon some metaphysical issues in his interviews with children (e.g. the origins of dreams), he did not follow these up in his later work. The growth in a child's spontaneous knowledge, as well as the development of purposefully taught capacities, has been viewed as a progressive "building up" of a "tower of knowledge", with elementary skills (e.g. the manipulations of sensorimotor objects) coming first, followed in due course by more complex skills (e.g. concept of conservation).

The progressive nature of cognitive development, which is usually linked to the development of psychological functions (thinking, perception, memory), does not, however, cover the complete development of mind. As was assumed in the studies presented in this book, any cognitive development has to have a starting point, a foundation upon which to "make sense" of the child's experiences and help the child to organise those experiences. I have argued that metaphysical intuitions are just what this foundation consists of. It is only on the basis of fundamental metaphysical distinctions (like that between mental and physical, sensory images and real objects, true and false knowledge, dreams and reality, free and "causal" actions, etc.) that the notions of experience and experimental (empirical) proof become possible.

And where does this foundation come from? Does it already exist when the child is born, a sort of universal "anthropological precondition" of development, or does it depend on the child's age and is culturally conditioned? Such questions are very rarely asked. One possible reason for this lack of interest in the metaphysical foundation of cognitive development is that such a foundation is beyond the traditional experimental approach, and hence it is difficult (though not impossible) to study using experimental methodologies. On the one hand, as was argued in the Introduction, interviews that allow for the application of sophisticated statistical procedures have to reduce answers to metaphysical problems to a simple "yes" or "no", which misses the very point of metaphysics—the process of metaphysical thinking. On the other hand, behavioural methods, which are usually highly effective in experiments on cognitive and personality development, are equally unsuitable, because, in contrast to social or moral concepts, metaphysical intuitions are of such a general nature that they cannot have unequivocal behavioural indices.

Another reason for this lack of interest in the metaphysical foundation of development is the view that whether we study it or not, it cannot change our knowledge about the development of any particular mental function and is always here, just like the air that we breathe; therefore, it cannot possibly be of any interest in applied educational studies. As a result, I was unable to find any systematic psychological study of the development of children's metaphysical proficiencies.

It was assumed here that the development of metaphysical knowledge in children can be approached by psychological means and that knowledge about this development can be of theoretical as well as practical importance. With regard to its theoretical significance, knowledge about the metaphysical foundations of cognitive development can shed new light on this development. Consider, for instance, the development of object permanence beliefs in children. Studied outside of its metaphysical context, the development of object permanence is usually viewed as an isolated series of transformations of an initial non-permanent "tableaux" (Piaget, 1929/1983) or certain inborn intuitions about the external world (Bower, 1972; Bremner, 1994) into increasingly stable and permanent objects. However, this kind of understanding throws up certain unintelligible ·paradoxes, for example how the idea of permanence can possibly arise in a world which is ruled by non-permanence. This paradox is one of "creating something from nothing" and has no plausible solution, unless it is assumed that the object permanence concept is transmitted genetically.

In a sense, this controversy may be viewed as an example of what has recently been termed the "learning paradox"; that is, the impossibility of logically conceiving a constructivist view of learning, as the learning of cognitive structures requires as a prerequisite that an equally complex cognitive structure already exists in the learner (Fodor, 1980; Pascual-Leone, 1980). With regard to the acquisition of knowledge, there are several possible solutions to this paradox on offer, most of them highly debatable (see Bereiter, 1985; Smith, 1993).

However, as far as acquisition of the fundamental distinctions of the world (to which metaphysical distinctions undoubtedly belong) is concerned, a special solution to this paradox can be offered. As these distinctions have binary structure (e.g. permanence *vs* non-permanence, physical *vs* mental, causally determined *vs* freely determined events, necessary true knowledge *vs* empirically true knowledge), the learning paradox can be dismissed if a change in the traditional paradigm (model) of development is accepted; namely, if the "replacement" model is transformed into the "coexistence" model of development (see Subbotsky, 1990a, 1993a).

Indeed, looked at in its metaphysical framework, the development of object permanence can be presented as reflecting one aspect of a more complex process, which is the growing awareness of the distinction between mental and physical worlds, with the former being a site for predominantly non-permanent entities and the latter consisting mainly of permanent objects. In this view, non-permanence is not replaced by permanence in the child's developing theories of the world, rather they co-exist in the child's mind from the outset, having their roots in the metaphysical structure of the universe and not in the peculiarities of the "geometry of genes".

In terms of educational practice and applications, knowledge of how aware children of various ages are of metaphysical concepts can help in constructing educational programmes and strategies that could facilitate various aspects of cognitive development. Thus, the series of analytical studies undertaken here (see Dialogues 6 and 7 in Chapter 2) can be viewed as a model for this kind of educational programme, developed to facilitate children's and adults' understanding of some of the fundamental structures of rationality (i.e. the division between the psychological and physical means of object representation, and the realisation that a certain almighty creative force has to be acknowledged as acting in the world). More specifically, some dialogues developed for testing children's awareness about the metaphysical aspects of human beings can be altered for purposes of psychological education, which in this case would take the shape of some kind of "shared activity", in which a child is "helped" to discover certain truths about human perception, moral behaviour, dreams, etc., rather than being "taught psychology" in a traditional directive manner.[1] Data on how children of various ages reason about freedom of action, the relationships between actions and desires, responsibility for one's deliberate actions, morality, and similar metaphysical problems can be of help to those who are interested in children's testimony and other legal problems involving children. Finally, empirical data regarding the age-related development of metaphysical judgements in children can be a source of reference for specialists in philosophy, sociology, theology, logical education, for authors writing for children and, in fact, for anyone who is not indifferent to the cognitive development of children.

With regard to the methodological aspect, it has to be stressed once again that studies of metaphysical concepts in children rely heavily on the children's verbal judgements. This is because a child's real behaviour (which was at the heart of my previous studies; see Subbotsky, 1993a,b) can tell us about his or her feelings and motivations, but it is the child's *awareness* of what he or she already knows which is the target of studies of metaphysical knowledge.[2] No wonder, then, that the effectiveness of the dialogues presented in this book depended on the children's linguistic proficiency. However, the fact that some children have poor linguistic capacities does not necessarily mean that their metaphysical knowledge is equally poor or altogether absent. For example, to discover the chemical compounds in the air we breathe, an advanced means of chemical analysis is required; this does not imply, however, that before this means of analysis was developed the chemical compounds were not in the air. This also suggests that what we call the development of metaphysical knowledge in children is a "growth of awareness" rather than a "growth of complexity". This "growth of awareness" can, however, be quite complex and is dependent on various factors (e.g. linguistic proficiency, cultural background, age, etc.). The basic objective of the studies presented in this book was to obtain a general picture of this "growth of metaphysical awareness" and the role the above factors play.

More specifically, the aim of the two studies reported here was to gain a general understanding of how children aged 4–14 years judge some fundamental metaphysical problems. In so far as a number of these problems have a variety of solutions, the major difficulty in undertaking such a study was that of selection. With regard to metaphysical problems dealing with the world as a whole, the problems discussed by Descartes, whose works also serve as a scale for the evaluation of children's judgements, were chosen. With respect to metaphysical problems which concern an individual human being, the selection of problems was based on such authors as Condillac, Goethe, Vygotsky, and others, who have contributed to the way human beings are viewed and treated by the contemporary rationalist European (Western) tradition.

To provide cross-cultural validity to the study, its major dialogues were replicated in Britain. As the results show, there was a strong similarity in the development of metaphysical thinking among Russian and British children, and the results will be discussed here in relation to both cultural groups.

The first part of the study showed that: (1) children aged 5–9 years are able to understand most fundamental metaphysical problems and they are capable of finding solutions to them that are close to those given by Descartes; (2) some of the Cartesian solutions were offered by a significant number of subjects aged 4–5, but only a small number of school-age subjects produce them; (3) solutions to some problems could not be offered by subjects across the age range.

The first group of problems included an understanding of the identity between "existence" and "thinking" and the close link between "truth" and "existence". At the age of 7–8 years, typical definitions of a true statement (or true knowledge) linked it to existence: "Truth is something that really exists in the world"; "If somebody tells something and it really exists—this is the truth, and if somebody tells something and it doesn't exist—it is false".

The idea of the indivisible unity of "object and subject" was also obvious to most 5- and 6-year-olds:"If I exist, the world must exist as well"; "If I can see the pen, then the pen must exist really and truly, it is not just what seems to me". One more solution which was close to the one suggested by Descartes was the distinction between dreams and reality. Most children as young as 6 described dreams as a special reality in which logical and causal connections between things were "relaxed" and there was no contiguity in the stream of thinking or acting.

Finally, the most important structure acquired by children within this age range is the distinction between body and mind, physical and mental phenomena. At the beginning (5- and 6-year-olds), body and mind are not separated one from the other; most physical properties, such as weight, spatial location, accessibility to senses, divisibility, etc., are attributed by the children both to their bodies and to their psychological entities (to their "I" and "thoughts"). By the age of 7, psychic entities lose their physical qualities and become completely autonomous of the body, so that, according to the children, even illness is unable to impair them ("It is my body that hurts, my thoughts cannot hurt, they only can think about the pain").

The second group of Cartesian solutions were the most interesting since, paradoxically, they were produced only by the younger subjects. For instance, 20–30% of 5- to 7-year-olds consider psychological entities (such as "I" and "thoughts") to be immortal. When asked what would happen to the "I" and "thoughts" of a person who died, the children thought that they would not die because "they are just letters", "they are just words and they don't exist". Instead, according to the children, the person's "I" will "turn into air", "will fly out and go into another man's head", etc. This type of reasoning is very close to that given by Descartes as well as to the broad idea of reincarnation of the soul. However, the idea became unpopular among children aged 9 and over, most of whom were strongly convinced that a person's "I" and "thoughts" die at the same time as his or her body.

Another problem was the Cartesian version of the proof of the existence of a Supreme Being. About half of 5-year-olds acknowledged that an "almighty wizard" existed in reality (they saw it residing in "the other planet", "the woods", "the mountains"). However, most 6-year-olds and all the older children emphatically denied such a possibility. Despite the fact that most of them acknowledged that the "almighty wizard" could exist in their minds and that the wizard was so almighty that he could even come out of their heads and sit down beside them, they denied that it was possible for such a creature to really exist. More than that, in the discussion that followed the dialogue, most children repeatedly acknowledged that the "wizard" was almighty and able "to do everything" only in order to deny this very "almightiness" over and over again.

This resistance to the ontological argument was equally strong among Russian and British children and adult subjects. A special analytical study with adult subjects which aimed to determine the causes of this resistance showed that the denial was based on psychological rather than logical reasons. A further inquiry into the nature of these reasons revealed that it was the subjects' strong belief in object permanence (i.e. in the fact that a mental image cannot spontaneously transform itself into a real physical object) that made nearly all subjects reject the ontological argument. As soon as this belief was (if only situationally) shattered, a significant number of subjects became more receptive to the idea that the real existence of an almighty being must necessarily follow from the mere idea of such a being.

Lastly, the third group of Cartesian solutions remained inaccessible (or were completely ignored) by most children across the whole age range. This was displayed very clearly when the children were asked to allocate subjective qualities of objects (such as sense of "redness", "warmth", and "pain") either to the subject's brain (sense organs) or to the external objects themselves. Contrary to Descartes' view, almost all the children allocated "warmth" and "redness' to the external objects rather than to the human perceptual apparatus; with respect to pain, however, the answers were in accordance with those of Descartes.

More specifically, this confusion between the subjective and objective qualities of objects affected not only visual and temperature perceptions, but sensations of other modalities as well, and it was experienced by adult subjects to the same extent as children. The analytical study in which various interventional methods were used revealed a strong and persistent character to this confusion and showed that it can only be partially overcome by creating a conflict between the views of various people regarding the same objects.

The second Cartesian solution that most children were at odds with was the statement about the conventionality of objects' names. Until age 12, all the children claimed that names were permanent qualities of an object and could not be changed (which was also in accordance with the data of Piaget). Only at age 13 did some children agree that objects' names were conventional.

The main result of this part of study was therefore that children as young as 6 produce solutions to many fundamental metaphysical problems similar to those given by Descartes. The question is how these solutions can possibly have penetrated the children's minds. As far as the metaphysical questions discussed are beyond the scope of the school curriculum and routine verbal communication, it is reasonable to assume that they are the result of the spontaneous working of the children's minds. Of course, it is unlikely that the children invented such solutions independently; rather, it is more plausible to assume that they absorbed them from the cultural materials that are provided within their social environment.

Regarding the second type of metaphysical problems (those that dealt in the main with human reality), the picture that emerged was rather complicated and multidimensional in nature. Yet it was possible to distinguish certain patterns which reflect the basic changes that occur in children's social life and in their way of thinking as they grow older. We can see this most clearly when comparing the answers of preschoolers with those of third-graders; the answers produced by first-graders (7-year-olds) tend to occupy an intermediate position between the two.

Thus, most preschoolers revealed a certain "anthropomorphism" in their judgements about human psychology: they tended to ascribe to a newborn child (and even to inanimate and non-living objects) many characteristics that they themselves possess. Paradoxically, with respect to certain of these capacities (such as an inherent capacity for depth perception), these anthropomorphic views approach some of the latest discoveries in studies of infancy. The basic pattern of the children's answers, however, revealed their tendency to view human infants and even inanimate objects by analogy with themselves, which means that the parallels these views might have with the scientific discoveries are nothing but coincidental.

Those *dynamic factors* that underlie and promote the psychological development of a child (e.g. the child's practical activity with objects and human artifacts, education, learning, communication and interaction with people, the child's changing position in a social group with certain responsibilities and privileges attached to it and with appropriate motivations that it produces), which are permanent and which eventually bring about changes in the *static components* of human psychology (which are normally described as sensations, perceptions, language abilities, moral behaviours, etc., and can be measured by psychological means), are still concealed from the child's "mental eye". These dynamic factors don't figure in preschooler's explanations and justifications, and the end effects that these factors produce are viewed by the children as inherent human capacities.

Thus, in the children's views, sensations (visual sensations in particular) "usurp" the results of the practical activity and education (such as the holistic and "object-related" nature of perceptions, the capacity of a human individual to distinguish between "my" and "alien" in his or her mind, the individual's capacity to relate his or her perceptions to his or her person, etc.); the children think that a newborn infant who has no capacities but sensations can, nevertheless, be aware of the personal character of his or her sensations, knows that there are other people in the world and that they look like him or her, and is even able to understand human speech. Regarding the appreciation of the role of speech by this group of children, on the one hand they could not see any link between the development of the above-mentioned capacities in the infant and the development of the language, but on the other, they thought that an object's name contains knowledge about that object's function and even provides the infant with the skills to use the object; they also thought that the mere knowledge of moral norms enables an infant to conform to those norms. Speech and knowledge of an object's name are not, therefore, viewed by the children as necessary conditions for being able to understand what objects are; however, the names, if acquired, are enough to bring about the capacity to know about objects' functions and even to use the objects appropriately. Objects' names, as they are, represent for the children the effects of those factors which the children are as yet unable to appreciate—that is of education and practical activities with the objects.

With respect to other problems, the children of this age revealed certain common strategies. For instance, they were reluctant to acknowledge that some of their wishes are beyond their voluntary control (the illusion of being in total control of their emotions and wishes) and thought that they were responsible for the emergence of immoral wishes in them (Dialogue 2); they believed that their wishes could be completely satisfied in due course (Dialogue 3) and revealed a relatively poor appreciation of unconscious mechanisms, such as apperception of perceptual defence (Dialogue 4); they expressed their wish to have immortality, which many of them viewed as a sort of "eternal play" (Dialogue 6); they were also unaware of the negative consequences of living in a world of "accomplished wishes and dreams" (Dialogue 7).

The views of most school-age children differed substantially from those described above; their beliefs are much closer to those of educated adults in European cultures. First, the paradoxical combination of the under-estimation of certain functions of language in the human mind with the overestimation of its other functions, which was a characteristic feature of most preschoolers' judgements, fades away and eventually disappears. Second, most senior schoolchildren no longer think that mere sensations contain knowledge about the names of the objects that produce them; they also no longer think that the mere learning of an object's name brings with it either the knowledge about its social function or the skills which enable one to use it. The children also become aware that knowledge of moral norms by a child does not necessarily means that the child will conform to those norms in his or her everyday behaviour.

Certain age trends were noted among the children of school age. For instance, the views that older schoolchildren hold regarding certain meta-physical aspects of human reality correspond to the models held by contemporary rationalist social sciences to a considerably larger extent than those held by younger schoolchildren. Thus, most fifth- and seventh-graders understand that many human desires and wishes are spontaneous in nature and that it is only the implementation of wishes that is subject to voluntary control and personal responsibility (Dialogue 2). They realise that human desires cannot be satisfied completely in a natural way (Dialogue 3); they can better appreciate the role of certain unconscious mechanisms (such as the effect that individual's needs have on the individual's apperception; Dialogue 4); they no longer attribute psychological qualities to inanimate objects (Dialogue 5); they are able to understand better the negative consequences of immortal existence (Dialogue 6) and the existence in the world of accomplished wishes and dreams (Dialogue 7).

Besides differences in the views of younger and older children, some curious similarities were also revealed. For instance, a capacity to appreciate distance from objects was attributed to newborn infants by the overwhelming majority of children in all age groups; most of them also attributed to newborn prelinguistic infants the capacity for the personal relatedness of its sensations (Dialogue 1, part 1) and understood the role of speech in realising other people's existence (Dialogue 1, part 2). Approximately equal numbers of children of all ages thought that they were the authors of their wishes (Dialogue 2), believed that their wishes could be completely satisfied by a wizard (Dialogue 3), were able to appreciate the effect that their needs might have on the content of their dreams (Dialogue 4), attributed psychological qualities to plants (Dialogue 5), and refused to live in a world of "accomplished dreams" after being asked auxiliary questions (Dialogue 7).

It is clear, therefore, that in children's judgements of human reality, certain trends can be observed that had earlier been reported to be present in children's judgements of physical and natural events (Piaget, 1929/1983, 1930, 1962), namely: the transition from anthropomorphic views (which comprised "finalistic", "moralistic", and "artificial" judgements) to more "physicalist" views, from the predominant reliance of children in their judgements of an infant's capacities on the static and phenomenally "visible" parameters (such as the immediate perception of shapes and names of objects) to a better appreciation of the "invisible" dynamic processes (the infant's practical activities with objects, interaction with other people, learning). The most prominent changes were observed to occur in children aged around 7 years. It may be assumed that these changes reflect certain universal mechanisms in the development of children's thinking, which affect children's metaphysical judgements as well as their judgements about physical objects and events.

However, these universal changes affect only some of children's metaphysical judgements, with the rest remaining unaffected and independent of age. It is true that those judgements which are affected by the impact of these universal changes tend to be judgements that are viewed as "correct" by most adults in European cultures. However, as mentioned before, viewing these changes as "progressive" should be treated with caution. For instance, the view according to which a newborn infant can appreciate spatial distances, which was shared by many children independent of their age, was likely to have been accepted as totally wrong by many psychologists at the beginning of this century [see, for instance, Piaget's account on the sensory–motor based acquisition of space perception in infants (Piaget, 1936), or Vygotsky's arguments against the possibility of the "orthoscopic" perception in infants (Vygotsky, 1987)]; however, the results of many recent studies seem to favour this view (Bremner, 1994). Although this consonance between children's naive psychology and recent scientific findings is, no doubt, coincidental, it is possible for similar coincidences to be found with regard to other "childish" interpretations of human reality revealed in this study.

Another problem with respect to children's views on human reality is the problem of determination. Clearly, some of the judgements look to be the result of the children's spontaneous thinking, both because of an absence of any special psychological education in contemporary kindergartens and schools and because of the lack of knowledge and interest shown by most parents when "talking of human psychology" with their children. Consequently, all that is left for the children to rely on is their personal observations of their peers and siblings, plus their observations of their own experiences. There is no doubt, however, that children's judgements about human reality and human behaviour are somehow affected by the stereotypes of the contemporary European world outlook. In this study, the effect was clearly visible; for instance, in the children's views on the causes of moral transgressions: "the naughty character", "the lack of discipline", "the weakness of willpower", etc. All these typical popular explanations could well have been absorbed by the children from conversations they had had with adults, from books they had read, and other cultural impacts.

In summary, the development of children's judgements about the metaphysical aspects of human reality (as well as about metaphysical problems of reality in general) as shown in this study is a much more complex and rapid process than has usually been supposed. It unfolds as a series of developmental changes which reflect the general structure of the rationalist European world outlook; this process is, however, rather bizarre and far from being a straightforward linear progression or "growth of understanding". In fact, the process is so complex that it poses more questions than answers, questions that require further investigation.

NOTES

1. We have not discussed whether consciousness of a structure lags behind the construction and control of the structure or not (Brown, Bransford, Ferrara, & Campione, 1983; Piaget, 1954). We believed it sufficient for the present study to assume that whatever the answer to this question, metaphysical intuitions, due to their very general nature, can only be adequately manifested through a subject's reasoning (and through complex justifications for that reasoning) and cannot be studied via a subject's behaviour, which are able to express directly the individual's motives and intentions (Subbotsky, 1993b) but which are highly indefinite with regard to the individual's metaphysical intuitions.

2. Speculation regarding educational applications can only be preliminary, as the application of psychological methodologies to classroom practice is a very complicated procedure (see Shayer & Adey, 1994; DeVries & Kohlberg, 1987). Having spent more than a decade involved in such a task (Subbotsky, 1993b), I am fully aware of the difficulty of the "direct translation" of laboratory psychological experiments into long-term educational programmes. Yet it seems to me that verbal dialogues with children are closer to educational practice than traditional psychological tests are, as they involve a kind of "shared activity" between the experimenter and the subject, which is important for any educational intervention (Vygotsky, 1982).

Bibliography

Baron-Cohen, S., Leslie, A.M., & Frith, U. (1985). Does the autistic child have a "theory of mind"? *Cognition, 21*, 37–46.

Basett, R.L., Miller, S., Anstey, K., & Crafts, K. (1990). Picturing God: A non-verbal measure of the God concept for conservative Protestants. *Journal of Psychology and Christianity, 9*, 73–81.

Bereiter, C. (1985). Toward a solution of the learning paradox. *Review of Educational Research, 55*, 201–226.

Bland, S.R. (1994). *Children's judgements about "body" and "self": The roles of age and culture.* Unpublished manuscript, Department of Psychology, Lancaster University.

Bower, T.G.R. (1972). Object perception in infancy. *Perception, 1*, 15–30.

Brain, M.D., & Shanks, B.L. (1965). The conservation of shape property and proposal about the origin of conservation. *Canadian Journal of Psychology, 19*, 197–207.

Brainerd, C. (1973). Judgements and explanations as criteria for cognitive structures. *Psychological Bulletin, 79*, 172–179.

Bremner, G.J. (1994). *Infancy* (2nd ed.). Oxford: Blackwell.

Brown, A.L., Bransford, J.D., Ferrara, R.A., & Campione, J.C. (1983). Learning, remembering, and understanding. In P.H. Mussen (Ed.), *Handbook of child psychology* (Vol. III, 4th ed., pp. 71–166). New York: John Wiley.

Bullock, M. & Russell, J.A. (1984). Preschool children's interpretation of facial expressions of emotion. *International Journal of Behavioral Development, 7*, 193–214.

Byrnes, J.P., & Beilin, H. (1991). The cognitive basis of uncertainty. *Human Development, 34*, 189–203.

Carey, S. (1985). *Conceptual change in childhood.* Cambridge, MA: Bradford Books/MIT Press.

Carroll, J.J., & Steward, M.S. (1984). The role of cognitive development in children's understandings of their own feelings. *Child Development, 55*, 1486–1492.

Chandler, M.J., Paget, K.F., & Koch, D.A. (1978). The child's demystification of psychological defense mechanisms: A structural and developmental analysis. *Developmental Psychology, 14*, 197–205.

Childers, P., & Weiner, H. (1971). The concept of death in early childhood. *Child Development*, 42, 1299–1301.

Condillac, E.B. (1969). *Treatise on the sensations* (translated by G. Carr). London: Favil Press.

Descartes, R. (1950). *Selected works*. Moscow: Politizdat Publishing.

Descartes, R. (1988). *Selected philosophical writings*. Cambridge, UK: Cambridge University Press.

DeVries, R., & Kohlberg, L. (1987). *Programs of early education: The constructivist view*. London: Longman.

Dollinger, S.J., & McGuire, B. (1981). The development of psychological-mindedness: Children's understanding of defence mechanisms. *Journal of Clinical Child Psychology*, 10, 117–121.

Donaldson, M. (1983). Justifying conservation: Comment on Neilson et al. *Cognition*, 15, 293–295.

Donaldson, S.K., & Westerman, M.A. (1986). Development of children's understanding of ambivalence and causal theories of emotions. *Developmental Psychology*, 22, 655–662.

Duncan, T. (1987). *GCSE physics* (2nd ed.). London: John Murray.

Flavell, J.H. (1986). The development of children's knowledge about the appearance–reality distinction. *American Psychologist*, 41, 418–425.

Flavell, J.H., Everett, B.A., Croft, K., & Flavell, E. (1981). Young children's knowledge about visual perception: Further evidence for the level 1–level 3 distinction. *Developmental Psychology*, 17, 99–103.

Flavell, J.H., Green, F.L., & Farell, E.R. (1993). Children's understanding of the stream of consciousness. *Child Development*, 64, 387–398.

Flavell, J.H., Miller, P.H., & Miller, S.A. (1993). *Cognitive development*. Englewood Cliffs, NJ: Prentice-Hall.

Fodor, J.A. (1980). Fixation of belief and concept acquisition. In M. Piattelli-Palmerini (Ed.), *Language and learning: The debate between Jean Piaget and Noam Chomsky* (pp. 142–149). Cambridge, MA: Harvard University Press.

Geldard, A.F. (1972). *The human senses* (2nd ed.). New York: John Wiley.

Glass, G.V., & Stanley, J.C. (1970). *Statistical methods in education and psychology*. Englewood Cliffs, NJ: Prentice-Hall.

Goldman, R.J., & Goldman, J.D.G. (1982). How children perceive the origin of babies and the roles of mothers and fathers in procreation: A cross-national study. *Child Development*, 53, 491–504.

Griffiths, S. (1995). *A study into children's judgements on the human psyche: A cross-cultural comparison*. Unpublished manuscript, Lancaster University, Department of Psychology.

Harris, P.L. (1989). *Children and emotion*. Oxford, NY: Basil Blackwell.

Harris, P.L. (1990). The child's theory of mind and its cultural context. In G. Butterworth & P. Bryant (Eds.), *Causes of development: Interdisciplinary perspectives*. London: Harvester.

Husserl, E. (1977). *Cartesian meditations: An introduction to phenomenology*. The Hague: Martinus Nijoff.

Inagaki, K., & Hatano, G. (1993). Young children's understanding of the mind–body distinction. *Child Development*, 64, 1534–1549.

Johnson, C.N. (1990). If you had my brain, where would I be? Children's understanding of the brain and identity. *Child Development*, 61, 962–972.

Johnson, C.N., & Wellman, H.M. (1982). Children's developing conceptions of the mind and brain. *Child Development*, 53, 222–234.

Johnson-Laird, P.N. (1990). The development of reasoning ability. In G. Butterworth & P. Bryant (Eds.), *Causes of development: Interdisciplinary perspectives* (pp. 85–110). London: Harvester.

Kant, I. (1965). *Writings, in six volumes* (Vol. 3). Moscow: Mysl Publishers.

Kant, I. (1966). On the impossibility of an ontological proof of the existence of God. In A. Sesonske & N. Fleming (Eds.), *Meta-mediations: Studies in Descartes*. Belmont, CA: Wadsworth.

Kenny, A. (1968). *Descartes: A study of his philosophy*. New York: Random House.

King, A.L. (1962). *Thermophysics*. San Francisco, CA: Freeman.

Kister, M.C., & Patterson, C.J. (1980). Children's conceptions of the causes of illness: Understanding of contagion and use of imminent justice. *Child Development, 51*, 839–846.

Kon, I. (1978). *Otkrytije Ja [The discovery of the "I"]*. Moscow: Politizdat Publishers.

Koocher, G.P. (1973). Childhood, death and cognitive development. *Developmental Psychology, 9*, 369–375.

Koocher, G.P. (1974). Conversations with children about death: Ethical considerations in research. *Journal of Clinical Child Psychology, 3*, 19–21.

Laurendeau, M., & Pinard, A. (1962). *Causal thinking in the child*. Montreal: International University Press.

Lévy-Brühl, L. (1925). *Le mentalité Primitive*. Paris: Alcan.

Levin, I., Siegler, R.S., Druyan, S., & Gardosh, R. (1990). Everyday and curriculum-based physics concepts: When does short term training bring change where years of schooling have failed to do so? *British Journal of Developmental Psychology, 8*, 269–279.

Lewis, C., & Osborne, A. (1990). Three-year-olds' problems with false belief: Conceptual deficit or linguistic artefact? *Child Development, 61*, 1514–1519.

Light, P. (1986). Context, conservation and conversation. In P.M. Richards & P. Light (Eds.), *Children of social worlds: Development in social context* (pp. 170–190). Cambridge, UK: Polity Press.

Matthews, G.B. (1980). *Philosophy and the young child*. Cambridge, MA: Harvard University Press.

Matthews, G.B. (1984). *Dialogues with children*. Cambridge, MA: Harvard University Press.

Murray, F.B. (1990). The conversion of truth into necessity. In W.F. Overton (Ed.), *Reasoning, necessity, and logic: Developmental perspectives*. Hillsdale, NJ: Lawrence Erlbaum Associates Inc.

Nagy, M. (1948). The child's theories concerning death. *Journal of Genetic Psychology, 73*, 3–27.

Neilson, I., Dockrell, J., & McKechnie, J. (1983). Justifying conservation: A reply to McGarrigle and Donaldson. *Cognition, 15*, 277–291.

Nye, W.C., & Carson, J.S. (1984). The development of the concept of God in children. *Journal of Genetic Psychology, 145*, 137–142.

Pascual-Leone, J. (1980). Constructive problems for constructive theories: The current relevance of Piaget's work and a critique of information processing simulation psychology. In R.H. Kluwe & H. Spada (Eds.), *Developmental models of thinking* (pp. 263–296). New York: Academic Press.

Piaget, J. (1929/1983). *The child's conception of the world*. Totowa, NJ: Helix Books.

Piaget, J. (1930). *The child's conception of physical causality*. London: Kegan Paul.

Piaget, J. (1936). *La naissance de l'intelligence chez l'enfant*. Neuchâtel: Delachaux et Niestlé.

Piaget, J. (1952). *The child's conception of number*. London: Routledge & Kegan Paul.

Piaget, J. (1954). The problem of consciousness in child psychology: Developmental changes in awareness. In H. Abramson (Ed.), *Problems of consciousness*. New York: Macy.

Piaget, J. (1962). *Play, dreams, and imitation*. New York: W.W. Norton.

Piaget, J. (1986a). Essay on necessity. *Human Development, 29*, 301–314.

Piaget, J. (1986b). *The construction of reality in the child*. New York: Ballantine.

Pillow, B.H., & Flavell, J.H. (1986). Young children's knowledge about visual perception: Projective size and shape. *Child Development, 57*, 125–135.

Popper, K. (1975). *Objective knowledge: An evolutionary approach.* Oxford: Clarendon Press.

Ratcliff, N. (1995). *The development of children's philosophical reasoning with regard to their beliefs about metaphysical concepts (a replication of a Russian study in an English setting).* Unpublished manuscript, Lancaster University, Department of Psychology.

Rée, J. (1974). *Descartes.* London: Allen Lane.

Russell, A., & Russell, G. (1982). Mother, father and child beliefs about child development. *Journal of Psychology, 110,* 297–306.

Russell, J., & Mitchell, P. (1985). Things are not always as they seem: The appearance–reality distinction and conservation. *Educational Psychology, 5,* 227–238.

Safir, G. (1964). A study of relationships between the life and death in children. *Journal of Genetic Psychology, 105,* 283–295.

Schwartz, R.G. (1980). Presuppositions and children's metalinguistic judgements: Concepts of life and the awareness of animacy restrictions. *Child Development, 51,* 364–371.

Shayer, M., & Adey, P. (1981). *Towards a science of science teaching: Cognitive development and curriculum demand.* London: Heinemann Educational.

Smith, L. (1993). *Necessary knowledge: Piagetian perspectives on constructivism.* Hove, UK: Lawrence Erlbaum Associates Ltd.

Smith, N.K. (1966). *New studies in the philosophy of Descartes.* London: Macmillan.

Subbotsky, E.V. (1986a). A child's conception of the relationship between bodily and mental phenomena. *Soviet Psychology, 25,* 61–90 (First published in 1985 in *Vestnik Moskovskogo Universiteta,* Series 14, *Psychology, 2,* 38–50).

Subbotsky, E.V. (1986b). Some characteristics of children's conception of the human psyche. *Voprosy Psikhologii [Questions of Psychology], 5,* 45–53.

Subbotsky, E.V. (1986c). A child's judgements about existence. *Vestnik Moskovskogo Universiteta [Newsletter of Moscow University],* Series 14, *Psychology, 4,* 8–20.

Subbotsky, E.V. (1989a). Cartesian ideas in children's minds. *Phylosophskaja i Sotsiologitcheskaja Mysl [Philosophical and Social Thought], 1,* 43–49.

Subbotsky, E.V. (1989b). Ontogenesis of consciousness and rational foundations of the mind. *Vestnik Moskovskogo Universiteta [Newsletter of Moscow University],* Series 14, *Psychology, 1,* 63–76.

Subbotsky, E.V. (1990a). The preschoolers' conception of the permanence of an object (verbal and actual behavior). *Soviet Psychology, 28,* 42–67.

Subbotsky, E.V. (1990b). Phenomenal and rational perception of some object relations by preschoolers. *Soviet Psychology, 28,* 5–24.

Subbotsky, E.V. (1991). Existence as a psychological problem: Object permanence in adults and preschool children. *International Journal of Behavioral Development, 14,* 67–82.

Subbotsky, E.V. (1993a). *Foundations of the mind: Children's understanding of reality.* Cambridge, MA: Harvard University Press.

Subbotsky, E.V. (1993b). *The birth of personality: The development of independent and moral behaviour in preschool children.* London: Harvester Wheatsheaf.

Subbotsky, E.V. (1994). Early rationality and magical thinking in preschoolers: Space and time. *British Journal of Developmental Psychology, 12,* 97–108.

Subbotsky, E.V. (in press). Understanding the distinction between sensations and physical properties of objects by children and adults. *International Journal of Behavioral Development.*

Subbotsky, E.V., & Trommsdorff, G. (1994). Object permanence in adults: A cross-cultural perspective. *Psychologische Beiträge, 34,* 62–79.

Tailor, M., & Flavell, J.H. (1984). Seeing and believing: Children's understanding of the distinction between appearance and reality. *Child Development, 55,* 1710–1720.

Teilhard de Chardin, P. (1955). *Le phénoméne humain.* Paris: Éditions du Seuil.

Versfeld, M. (1940). *An essay on the metaphysics of Descartes.* London: Methuen.

Voss, S. (1993). *Essays on the philosophy and science of René Descartes.* Oxford, UK: Oxford University Press.

Vygotsky, L.S. (1981). The genesis of higher mental functions. In J. Wertsch (Ed.), *The concept of activity in Soviet psychology.* New York: Sharpe.

Vygotsky, L.S. (1982). *Myshleniye i retch [Thought and language].* Moscow: Pedagogica Publishers.

Vygotsky, L.S. (1987). Perception and its development in childhood. In W. Rieber & A.S. Carton (Eds.), *The collected works of L.S. Vygotsky* (Vol. 1, pp. 289–300). New York: Plenum Press.

Weininger, O. (1979). Young children's concepts of dying and death. *Psychological Reports, 44,* 395–407.

White, E., Elsom, B., & Prawat, T. (1978). Children's conceptions of death. *Child Development, 49,* 307–310.

White, P.A. (1995). *The understanding of causation and the production of action.* Hove, UK: Lawrence Erlbaum Associates Ltd.

Wilson, M.O. (1978). *Descartes.* London: Routledge & Kegan Paul.

Woolley, J.D., & Wellman, H.M. (1992). Children's conceptions of dreams. *Cognitive Development, 7,* 365–380.

Wyszecki, G., & Stiles, W.S. (1967). *Colour science: Concepts and methods, quantitative data and formulas.* New York: John Wiley.

Zuberi, A.K. (1988). A qualitative study of Muslim children's concept of God. *Pakistan Journal of Psychological Research, 3,* 1–22.

Author Index

Subject Index

almighty
  being, 87, 196
  creature, 83
  subject, 75, 82, 87, 88, 90, 94, 125
  wizard, 16, 76–81, 83, 84, 86–91, 93, 125, 127, 128, 195
animated objects, 5
anti-dogmatism, 2
anthropological
  characteristics, 2
  essences, 7
anthropomorphisation, 90, 91, 94
anthropomorphism, 197
appearance and reality, 66
appearance–reality
  distinction, 67, 68
  tasks, 66
apperception, 168, 170, 199

behaviour
  altruistic, 159
  voluntary, 19, 157
being
  and thinking, 2
  and truth, 2
beliefs
  about the world, 2
  religious, 2
body–mind
  distinction, 59, 61

parallelism, 2, 58, 59
  relationship, 3, 8, 45, 58, 127

coexistence model, 193
cogito, 11, 12, 16, 26, 40, 43, 44, 124, 190
cognitive
  development, 6, 7, 127, 191–3
  growth, 7
concept of truth, 68
conceptions of mind, 5
consciousness, 2, 5, 40, 63, 186, 201
  stream of, 103, 107
conservation, 9, 67, 122
  concept of, 4, 191
  of personal identity, 179
criterion of truth, 1, 66, 68
cultural
  conventions, 175
  differences, 128
  factors, 10, 61
  historical, 3
  influences, 7
culture
  Christian, 76
  European, 2, 128, 129, 200

defence
  mechanisms, 131, 165, 169, 170
  perceptive, 168
  perceptual, 169, 170, 187, 198

211